WEIR'S WORLD

Tom Weir

WEIR'S WORLD

An Autobiography of Sorts

CANONGATE

First published in Great Britain in 1994
by Canongate Books Ltd
This edition first published in 1995 by
Canongate Books Ltd
14 High Street, Edinburgh EH1 1TE

ISBN 0 86241 480 6

British Library Cataloguing-in-Publication Data
A catalogue record for this book is available on request
from the British Library.

Typeset by Hewer Text Composition Services, Edinburgh
Printed and bound in Great Britain by
Mackays of Chatham, Kent

To Rhona
who encouraged me to persist in
disentangling many a knot in the rope
of words in this 'autobiography of sorts'.

Acknowledgements

My thanks to editor John Beaton who saw it before it went to the publishers and who approved of the mixing of past and present which I felt might bewilder the reader. Memory checks involved much consultation with Alpine Club and Scottish Mountaineering Club journals and searching out books – my thanks to their editors and writers of articles. Also to my old comrade, Douglas Scott, for some splendid expedition photographs, and to Eric Drew who took the front and back cover pictures on hill days we have shared. Fellow expeditioner W.H. Murray was helpful, too, in conversations we had about the style of the book when he read the manuscript but, like climbing a steep and testing pitch on rock or ice, getting up depends on more than style – each to his own. Eddie Philips, a pupil of Rhona's, took the pictures of me in my study.

Here are some words of wisdom from Hilaire Belloc:

> From quiet homes and first beginning,
> Out to the undiscovered ends,
> There's nothing worth the wear of winning,
> But laughter and the love of friends.
>
> *Dedicatory Ode*

1

How Far to the Top?

> An experience, especially in youth, is quickly overlaid by
> others, and is not at the moment fully comprehended. But
> it is overlaid, not lost. Time hurries it from us, but also
> keeps it in store, and it can be recaptured later and
> amplified by memory, so that at leisure we can interpret
> its meaning and enjoy its savour.
>
> John Buchan, *Memory Hold the Door*

The truth of that paragraph was brought home to me as I sifted through old
papers, one of them a letter from a man I met when a lad of sixteen over
sixty years ago. I had lost touch with him after he emigrated to Canada but
from our first meeting we were to share many mountaineering adventures,
although he was twelve years my senior.

In my mind's eye I could see the pair of us the first time we met near the
top of Ben Ime, highest point in the Arrochar Alps; me hurrying with all
speed in case I would miss the Sunday excursion train that would take me
back to Glasgow, and he coming towards me on his way down from that
top, a lithe figure, knickerbockers round his ankles, battered trilby on his
head, a long walking stick swinging in his hand. I took him for a shepherd
and, when close, called out to him, 'How long will it take me to get to the
top?' adding, 'I've a train to catch and can't afford to miss it.' He laughed.
'Go. I'll wait for you here, and see you to the train. I work on the railway.'
His letter brought back other memories.

My dear Tommy,

Well, here I am as large as life and enjoying the delights of living in
Victoria, keep fit, and while not climbing anything more than the
odd pimple, I still maintain outdoor pursuits walking, fishing,
swimming and gardening.

While, as you can gather, I am very happy in this part of Canada,
my mind often goes back to by-gone days; my first glimpse of Loch
Maree, the wedding at Dornie, and meeting Farquhar Macrae at the
renovation of Eilean Donan Castle; our wee camps at Camusunary in
Skye, Loch Coulin and the magic of the Torridon tops, sheer bliss.

Do you remember Cameron of the store at Kinlochewe telling us

1

of fishing a loch when he heard three keepers approaching, conversing in the old tongue: 'Will we throw him into the loch and confiscate his rod?' At which Cameron turning round said, and addressing them also in Gaelic: 'I have heard of one Highlandman attacking three, but never three attacking one!' Then he told them he was one of the best-known authorities on the Highland language in Inverness-shire. After that all was well. They apologised and advised him the best fly to put on to get a fish.

I may be wrong Tommy, but I sometimes think I enjoyed Scotland more in the old days. Like yourself, I had the call at an early age; cycling to the Trossachs, paying the toll of one penny to use the Duke's Road, camping by Loch Achray, peace and quietness. Then to the northern Bens and Glens, solitude and warm hospitality. I do appreciate the inevitability of the fact of more and more people invading the countryside, but I am not sorry we had it in quieter times.

You and I have a lot to be thankful for, Tom. I have followed your career and congratulate you on attaining the life-style you so much enjoy. I see, by reading of your adventures in the *Scots Magazine*, you have married a kindred spirit. Please convey my best wishes to her, and say 'hello' to Matt for me.

Good luck and good health in the coming years,
Yours aye,
John McNair

Within fifteen minutes of leaving John McNair that day I was back beside him, and telling him a bit about myself; that I was an apprentice grocer in Springburn, working in Cowlairs Co-operative Society, and if I wasn't away for the weekend walking the hills I was out every Sunday. He was amused that I had mistaken him for a shepherd. 'I used to work in the engine sheds at Eastfield in Springburn. I'm from Maryhill, and from about your own age I used to be away at every opportunity. Then I got the chance of an engine cleaner's job at Arrochar, and I jumped at it. It's a great place to live, but now I go back to Maryhill when I feel like a change.'

He had me green with envy when he told me that sometimes part of his job was to walk the railway line north from Arrochar to Ardlui at the head of Loch Lomond, hammer on his shoulder to knock into place any chocks holding the rails that had become loose. Later he was to become a fireman and an engine driver. Before he emigrated to Canada he once let me take the controls of the West Highland train high above Loch Long. I found it rather frightening as the train rushed through cuttings and high viaducts, engine swaying and pistons pounding while John shovelled, holding the furnace door with one hand and tipping the coal in with the other.

In a follow-up letter he wrote: 'How vividly I remember our encounter on Ben Ime, and you showing me the watch you won at the boxing.' Not long after my chance encounter with John I had met the Matt to whom I passed on his 'hello'. We happened to be sharing the same compartment on the train, and bound for the same destination to climb Ben Lui. It was the May holiday weekend, snow cornices and gullies shining against blue sky. We teamed up, and found our enthusiasms for hills and wild-life identical.

Later, as I got to know the reticent Matt Forrester better, I realised how out of character it was for this shy man to invite a stranger to share his tent and couple of blankets. We climbed seven peaks in our first two memorable days when the Highlands were at their best, cuckoos calling, skylarks singing, sandpipers, curlews, redshanks calling, and on the hills ring ouzels, wheatears and meadowpits.

I discovered that the big red-headed man not only knew a lot more about the hills than I did, but outshone me in the cooking line, frying up the most delicious lamb chops and sausages to go with our eggs. Matt was a butcher, and I was to enjoy his provender on our numerous trips over thirty years.

Another thing we had in common was a passion for rock climbing. Four years older than I, it was he who took me to Glasgow's celebrated Mitchell Library where the bound journals of the Scottish Mountaineering Club could be consulted, and diagrams made in notebooks for classic climbs we intended to try. The world was opening up for the pair of us just as Hitler was preparing to close it down.

Matt's introduction to John was when the three of us camped at Loch Tulla's western end for a twelve-hour traverse of four high tops culminating on Ben Starav above Glen Etive. He was impressed by John's speed over the roughest ground. It was only later he divulged that he was a marathon runner and that one of his records still stood unbroken after many years. But what truly delighted Matt was John's rich singing voice, apt to burst out at any time: at breakfast, or on reaching a top, revelling in the view. He had sung in light opera with an amateur company, and his repertoire of Scots and Gaelic songs was considerable.

Almost exactly one year later the three of us were camped in the rain at Sligachan, below the Black Cuillin of Skye, and 'the misty isle' was certainly living up to its name as we climbed Sgurr nan Gillean and Blaven before a hard crossing by Loch Coruisk round the coast to put the tent down on the edge of a cliff, about a mile short of Glen Brittle, the only reasonably firm ground we could find.

Next day saw us in misty Coire Lagan, in the very heart of the horse-shoe of peaks described by the Alpinist Professor Norman Collie as the finest range of small mountains in the world. Our search was to find the start of the 800-foot route he had made to the narrow summit of the highest peak, in 1896, Sgurr Alasdair. He had described it as 'difficult', part of it so steep that climbers are out of sight of each other. One pitch had been singled out as 'looking hopelessly smooth'. It was named the 'Red Slab'.

Once we had found the narrow edge of the lowest rocks we made good speed up the airy buttress, until we assembled on a ledge facing a smooth wall that could only be the Red Slab. Matt started up boldly, but soon retreated, saying, 'If that's real rock climbing, then I am no rock climber.' He offered the pitch to me, but before I could take off on it, he called me back. 'No, I'll have another go,' he said. I'm sure he feared I might fall off and he would feel responsible. John said he would try, but Matt was adamant. This time he didn't come back. The rope snaked out of sight into the mist, hanging clear of the rocks. Then came the glad cry, 'Come on! It's great!'

It was marvellous. Only the first few feet gave the feeling of insecurity on small footholds for nailed boots, and tiny wrinkles for the hands, then came confidence-making grips for hands and feet in exactly the right places. How wonderful to step on to the rocky point of the highest peak, and follow the classic horse-shoe known as the round of Coire Lagan!

It was as if the Cuillin were eager to give of their mysterious best, wrapping the pinnacles in mist; then from a swirling grey world shadowy peaks would loom above us, solidifying, only to be lost again. Opening below us we might glimpse a black edge of coast and grey sea, lost, almost as soon as seen, as we pursued a tenuous course up precipitous chimneys, along ledges, before gaining the easier ridge and keeping to it, finishing with the Inaccessible Pinnacle.

We were a happy trio as we arranged our bedding for sleep after a hearty meal cooked by the worthy Matt. Blankets down, and much wriggling, to make three in a two-man tent as little of a squeeze as possible, sleep was immediate, but not for long, as a fearsome rip of thunder startled us to wakefulness. At the same time rain battered down, and within minutes water was gurgling through the tent.

Let Matt's diary describe it:

It was almost midnight when the storm struck us, a vivid flash of lightning was followed by peal after peal of thunder which reverberated through the corries. Again and again it struck, till the sound resembled the British Fleet in action. The Cuillin are fearsome hills in any light, but in the awful clamour and brightness of that night their formidable appearance was intensified a hundredfold. Every burn roared in spate, and soon things in the tent began to float – books, cups, groundsheet, in fact everything. Added to the discomfort was the fact that the tent was on top of a cliff. Indeed to emerge it was necessary to sidle round a guy rope or else plunge into the angry sea. We endured the discomfort for two hours. Then we decided to make the hazardous journey to the Youth Hostel. The small member of the party was nearly drowned when 'dreeping' over a fence. He

4

landed in a ditch up to the neck, but emerged no wetter than when he went in!

I'd forgotten that sudden immersion that nearly cost me my life, but remember the crush of washed-out campers trying to get a stretch-out on the common-room floor of what had been Glen Brittle schoolhouse. Like us, most had abandoned their tents and gear, and departed in mid-morning to review the damage and try to dry out. John didn't bother. With a cheerful yell he cast his sodden sleeping quilt into the ocean and departed almost at once to cross the pass and catch the bus at Sligachan, for it was the last day of his holiday.

We were sorry to see him go, as the peaks were throwing off their engulfing clouds and we set off for the section of ridge running north from the Inaccessible Pinnacle. We had the sun up there, and a gauze of mist playing hide and seek with it on the rocky ridge, making us whoop with delight when suddenly each of us had our shadow cast on the mist surrounded by a circle of quivering rainbow, a rare effect known as a 'glory'. In the days that followed we had many a soaking on the classic rock routes we had read about, and managed to climb. Matt's diary records: 'never have I felt so sorry to leave a place.'

Although Matt and John had never met until I introduced them, both had been frequenters of a famous wood fire within easy reach of Milngavie on the outskirts of Glasgow. It was a kind of university of knowledge on the great outdoors. Matt described it thus in one of his writings:

> The fire was situated at the north end of Craigallion Loch, in a hollow encircled by pinewoods, and backed by the frowning face of Slackdhu and Dumgoyne. It had all the grandeur of the Highlands, yet it was only ten miles from Glasgow. At all seasons it was a howff for walkers and climbers – we did not hike then. Coming along the track of a winter's evening the glow of light and the merry shouts of laughter brought joy to the heart.
>
> It was the growth of the walking movement that brought disaster and oblivion to Craigallion. With the enthusiasts came the camp followers – the litter louts and despoilers. The fire was banned; the land proprietor forbade it under penalty of law. For a while the notice board was disregarded; a few hard cases persisted with the fire, but its day was done. Now all that remains of this well-known howff is a few charred rocks, pitiful reminders of an old meeting place.
>
> Craigallion fire was a grand fire, a symbol of something great and fine.

Aged sixteen, on a racing bicycle, I had extended my explorations to the Trossachs and Loch Lomond. That winter I joined the Springburn

Amateur Boxing and Wrestling Club, hoping by these manly sports I would add an inch or two to my stature. I was at a genetic disadvantage from the start for my brother and sister, like my mother, were on the small side. But I did win a prize or two boxing in inter-club competitions – until I was knocked off my bicycle by a careless motor cyclist and woke up in Glasgow Royal Infirmary with a broken collar bone.

But although I couldn't take a punch on the shoulder until the bone set, I could manage a pair of drum-sticks, and indulge in a passion which began at the age of eleven when I was admitted into the Boys' Brigade, the Springburn 148 Company. Normally to get into the BB you had to be twelve. I got in early thanks to my brother Willie. Two years older than I, he had come home from the Friday night parade with a pair of drum-sticks, announcing he was going to be a drummer in the pipe band.

Willie, however, was not assiduous. He quickly got bored practising the beats, and when he threw down the sticks in exasperation, I would pick them up and show him how to do it, for I was well ahead of him in performance. The result of this was that he spread it around that his brother Tommy was a rare wee drummer, and so arose the desire to march proudly with the band, and in time I became the leading drummer.

By the time I was twelve I was awarded a rope-tensioned side drum of full military length, alas too big to hang clear of my knees when marching, so it bounced up and down when I was beating it out behind the pipers. My secret fear was that it would jump off its attachment hook one day. That dread was realised on a very important occasion when Springburn Hill was lined with watchers. Pipes skirling, we were descending to link up with other companies to celebrate the birth of the Boys' Brigade movement. Then it happened! The drum was bouncing on the road with the smallest drummer on parade running after it. I was mortified, especially as the laughter was louder in my ears than the bagpipes.

At twelve years of age you could get a job as a milk-boy in our nearest Co-operative dairy, starting at 6 am, pay three shillings a week. I followed my brother who warned me that as a new boy I would be put through the mill on my first morning. He was right. As I got to the darkened dairy before the milkmaids arrived I was grabbed, stuffed into a big wicker basket designed to hold morning rolls, and promised I would certainly get a roll.

Clamped in darkness I was dragged at a steep angle up a stair, then another stair. 'Now you'll get your roll!' they shouted as they launched me from the landing, the hamper turning over and over, with me inside, as it crashed to the first landing, then to the bottom, where, a bit dazed, I was dragged out. Now I had to 'run the gauntlet' between two rows of boys, each having a skelp at me with the hard skip of his skull-cap. In due course I had the pleasure of being hamper-tosser to a succession of new boys as the old ones were compulsorily retired when they reached school-leaving age at fourteen.

As a lad I found the noise and stir of Springburn exciting. Each morning an army of locomotive workmen, thousands strong, answered the shriek of the hooters, the noise of their heavy boots clattering on the pavements, all in a hurry and in a uniform of dungarees. Noisy tramcars, bells clanging, would be chuntering up or down steep Springburn Road where shops of every kind faced each other, many of them bearing the logo of Cowlairs Co-operative Society.

In 1929 when I got a start as a message boy in one of its twenty-six grocery branches, most of the families of the 10,000 men employed in the four largest locomotive works in Britain were share-holders, using dividends on purchases as their savings bank. Devoid of any sense of history I had little idea that this most successful of Glasgow Co-ops had started with one shop and one employee in 1881, at a time when signalmen were paid twenty-two shillings a week, and locomotive men were required to put in 144 hours a fortnight – conditions that led to their first great strike. The Co-op had been founded to eke out the scanty wages of the railway workers.

Until Springburn became the workshop for the Edinburgh and Glasgow Railway in February 1842, it had been a quiet hamlet of weavers and quarrymen. Its hills and woods had running streams, and a farm called Springvale became the site of the first railway workshop. A mere eighteen years later Springburn had risen to be a renowned locomotive-building centre at a time when new lines were being laid everywhere, and more powerful steam engines were being developed to meet bigger challenges.

By the year 1900, fourteen years before I was born, most of the 27,000 inhabitants of Springburn were directly or indirectly getting a living from the railway industry. Ours was a railway family. The father I lost before I was two years old was an electrical engineer. My mother's father had been an engine driver. As a widow she had worked as an engine fitter before becoming a wagon painter in Cowlairs Locomotive Works. My early memories are of her in working overalls splashed with red paintmarks. For us children our mother's mother ruled the roost and saw to our every need. For my sister Molly the loss of Grannie when she passed away was too terrible to bear, and resulted in a nervous break-down, described by her so well in *Best Foot Forward*, the second volume of her autobiography.

Her first volume, *Shoes Were for Sunday*, captures early years of childhood and family life which are blank to me, as a result of severe concussion in a fall which blacked out pretty well everything that went before. I do have a memory of being knocked down a stair by another boy. I was about nine years of age at the time, and it seems I lay in a coma for such a long time it was feared that I might not recover. The medical prognosis was that brain damage had been done, and my school-teacher warned that I would be a slow developer – a finding that proved all too true. Though I was delighted to hear years afterwards that I was 'just average'.

But 'Wee Weirie', as I was nicknamed, if not much use at school, wasn't doing too badly on the drums – plural now – because I had a wee job performing in a cinema orchestra, playing the accompanying music to the silent films of that time. The drummer's job was to add realism to what was happening on the screen by creating sound effects where appropriate. I won the job by talking to the lady who not only collected the admission tickets to enter the cinema, but also sat behind the drum-kit.

I was fascinated by her antics, and by hanging over the orchestral pit watching her we got talking. I told her I was a drummer, and would love to do what she was doing. She invited me one matinee to stay behind, and when the audience dispersed she sat down at the piano and I made my debut behind a full drum kit: big drum, side drum on stand, cymbals, tom-toms, cowbell, triangle and a whole lot of objects for special effects. To simulate rain there was a small barrel filled with dried peas. By turning the handle not too vigorously the effect was realistic. There was also a mouth-siren, and a slap-stick for custard-pie-throwing comedies. Timing was important: the siren had to whistle as the custard pie flew through the air, the slap-stick had to be timed exactly as the missile hit its target.

These were the dying gasps of the silent cinema, and the hand-out of two shillings and sixpence for each performance soon came to an end. The 'Talkies' had already arrived in London with Al Jolson's *The Singing Fool*. Canned music resulted in a drift north of out-of-work musicians, as cinema orchestras in England were being disbanded. By a happy accident a drummer from London came to live near us, having landed a job at the Casino in the Townhead. This cinema featured variety acts as well as films, and before long this friendly drummer invited me to sit in with him some evenings.

I did, and soon discovered that part of the appeal of my presence as his deputy was that he could withdraw to the nearest pub while I took over the drums. As one brought up to believe in the Band of Hope message, and who had signed the pledge to abstain from all alcoholic beverages, I was appalled. Many a sad tale, illustrated with hand-coloured lantern slides, I had watched and heard, aghast at the violence of husbands beating their wives and letting their children starve because of their addiction to strong drink. I have to say, though, that my friendly drummer seemed not in the least affected by his indulgence.

On leaving Hyde Park Primary for Petershill Public School I became a pal of Andy Gemmel who was learning the trumpet and wanted to be a jazz player. We talked a lot about dance bands, but as the summer holidays approached his mind became focused on all the things he was going to do when he got to his uncle's croft in the Highlands. He painted vivid word pictures of waterfalls and the big salmon that leapt from deep pools and fought their way upstream against the rush of white water. He spoke with awe of Ben Nevis and the snow in the gullies of the huge cliffs. Just below the house there was a burn where he fished for trout, when he was not helping to milk the cows, feed the calves or turn the peats for carrying to the house when the fuel was dry.

He would be doing these exciting things for six weeks, while all I could look forward to was ten days at the Boys' Brigade Camp in Girvan. Now and again after school I was invited to his house, and one day towards the end of term, quite unexpectedly, I was asked if I would like to go with him to the croft for the first week of the holidays. 'See what your mother says, tell her you'll be well looked after.'

From Andy I'd heard a lot about the wonders of the West Highland Railway, but even so, I was unprepared for the reality as Helensburgh was left behind and we were on a ledge carved out of the mountainside high above Loch Long, and looking across the water to a spine of rocky peaks that rose higher and higher until the Cobbler came into view, three rock pinnacles, one of them resembling a shoe-maker bending over his last.

Before I had a chance to see the resemblance, we had turned away from the salt water loch and were now facing Ben Lomond, a sharp point towering above the biggest surface area of fresh water in Scotland, quite unlike the broad summit seen from Springburn. Now we looked across to the wild Craigroyston shore, roadless and spanned only by paths threading the rocks all the way to Ardlui. Then with the loch behind us we were into Glen Falloch, where the engines began to labour climbing past a huge waterfall on our right, our speed slowing on the steady gradient to Crianlarich where we had a long halt for breakfast.

On again, and Andy took me along the corridor to the very back carriage so that we could watch the two steam engines belching smoke as they pulled the train round a big horse-shoe viaduct sweeping from one mountain to another with the glen between them far below. I learned, too, that it was engines designed and built in Springburn that made this journey possible.

Now there was another test ahead, the crossing of Rannoch Moor, a desert of peat and water where, in blizzards, trains had been temporarily lost. I saw how the railway picks its way over the water on viaducts with nine clear spans 684 feet long. I heard how in order to get a foundation for the railway, roots of trees uncovered from the peat had to be over-laid with thousands of tons of rocks and ashes to carry the line over this roadless triangle. Next, beyond Rannoch Station we rattled though Britain's only snow-shed, 200 yards of corrugated iron, roofed to protect the line from being drifted over.

Soon we were edging off the moor and running alongside Loch Treig, on a northward course into the gentler country of Glen Spean, on the last lap to Spean Bridge – our destination. It was hard to take in all the wonders of that day: Ben Nevis, its mighty cliffs patched with the snow-wreaths that Andy had told me about; the white-washed croft house of Sronaba, cows

9

and calves grazing above the burn, and a scent of peat from the chimney, new to me, as well as the Gaelic tongue spoken by the friendly Gemmel family. I had come to a home-from-home of laughter and fun.

Yes, on this unforgettable holiday I saw the big salmon leaping the roaring Mucomer Falls, but it was Ben Nevis that perpetually drew my eyes, watching the mists curling round the 2,000-foot-high cliffs seamed with snow gullies that made me long to set my feet up there. Little could I have foreseen that at the age of sixteen I would be on top of these cliffs in bewildering mist, and very much afraid.

I was up there with a man of twenty-eight, an unemployed plumber by the name of Richie Wallace. We had met on a crowded bus between Loch Lomond and Glasgow, returning home from an Easter weekend I'd spent with some of my boxing and wrestling club friends. By coincidence our paths had crossed again a few weekends later. Richie lived in Govan, was a member of the Ivy Cycling Club, had toured Scotland, England and Wales, but had only recently taken to back-packing over the hills.

I have described my hungry adventures with the irascible Richie in my first book *Highland Days*, so I won't go into much detail of the test of endurance he set me. It began on Loch Etive's western shore by paths which took us to Glen Coe and over the Devil's Staircase to Kinlochleven, then over the summits of Nevis and Aonach Mor to Rannoch Moor and home over the top of Ben Lui to Loch Lomond. I won't say more, but that expedition has given me an aversion to heavy pack carrying ever since.

Richie had a habit I was eager to copy. It was licking the blob of thick condensed milk adhering to the tin after he had poured some into the tea. One breakfast I determined to beat him to it and, after milking my own tea and his, licked the tin, at which he bristled and snapped at me for filthy habits. Nor did he take it too kindly when I observed mildly that I had picked up the habit from him! Politics entered my life with Richie. A member of the Communist Party, he preached death to all capitalists, including men who were great names in exploration and mountaineering and whose deeds I longed to emulate. He would have shot the lot in order to follow the example of the Russians in 1917. According to Richie, Labour wouldn't get us anywhere. Ramsay MacDonald, the Prime Minister, was committed to public ownership, but with a minority Government was powerless against the capitalists. The collapse of the American stock market in 1929 had dragged us down and the capitalist world was in chaos: in Britain alone, two and a half million were unemployed. We needed a revolution. He wanted me to join the Communist Party, but I shrank from his extreme views.

Ah well, despairing of work in Scotland, Richie moved to London and later, in the 30s, wrote to me from time to time. We lost touch on the outbreak of hostilities in 1939. It was after I had been demobbed, following six years in the army, that I heard what had happened to him. Back working in Scotland, he had become engaged to be married, but on the eve of his wedding had put his head in the gas oven – why we shall never know – a strange end for such an adventurer.

My life-long friend, Matt, was the very opposite of Richie. I cannot overstate his educational effect on me at my most impressionable age. We used to meet every Friday evening at Townhead Library, equidistant from both our homes. After choosing books and discussing them, we would take a wee walk and decide whether we would go off after work the following evening, or agree to make it merely a Sunday outing. Saturday was a long, hard, working day for both of us, with a rush at the end of it if we wanted to catch the last bus or train to the hills.

This is the 'In Memoriam' notice I wrote for the Journal of the Scottish Ornithologists' Club following his untimely death:

Matt Forrester was 58 when he died of a tumour on 24th March 1969 after seven weeks in Glasgow Royal Infirmary. His last bit of bird news, delivered to me with excitement a few days earlier, was of three Lesser Blackbacked gulls at his window there. He left a bundle of diaries and notebooks spanning an interest in birds going back to his boyhood in Dennistoun, when horses and sheep grazed on the green banks of Glasgow's famous Molendinar Burn, and he combined nest-finding with fishing for 'baggies' (minnows).

I remember how he told me with glee that he could get all the volumes of Thorburn's *British Birds* on one library ticket. I recall too his amazing zeal for early rising, whether to comb the tops of the Cairngorms for dotterel or see what was doing on some Hebridean island. A natural loner, he paid the S.O.C. a big compliment by joining it, for he hated organisations of any kind; yet he was prepared to lead club outings to Hamilton and the Endrick, whence came so many of his published records. He was also a frequent visitor to Aberlady Bay.

Matt was a butcher in Lenzie. He liked his work, even though it gave him only Sunday and one half day a week for getting out. He took a bit of knowing, but those who did, found him a kindly, humorous and well informed character, enthusiastic on any matter relating to the countryside. Even in the declining health of the last two years he never lost his zeal. My last trips with him were to Flanders Moss and Loch Tay, just before he went into hospital.

This is not the place to talk about him as a mountaineer, which was his passion until the war. We explored the Highlands together in summer and winter, always combining climbing and birding. The drive he put into hard routes was transferred to ornithology when he was demobbed, and future trips usually focussed on birds.

Craggy-faced and ginger-haired, he served in the Scots Guards during the war, fighting and getting wounded in Tunisia – with the compensation of sighting birds on migration over the desert and on the shores. Then came Anzio, and capture by the Germans, when only a few of the Battalion were left defending a position they had taken, holding on for relief which never came.

But the army did him a good turn; on his release from Germany it posted him to the Solway, where he devoted himself to intensive birding. It was the mainstay of his life ever afterwards. He was a bachelor, and come Sunday or holidays he was away to his favourite haunts. It was the countryside as much as the birds he loved. He hated being indoors, even for a day.

It was not until after his slow death that I came across, in some cuttings of his newspaper articles, one that had appeared in the *Daily Express* and was signed Guardsman M. Forrester. He had written it in response to an invitation to *Express* readers. A money prize was offered for the best description of the house, where, if they had the money and opportunity, they would choose to live. This entry of Matt's, 'Where the Five Bens Meet', won the prize.

For the life of me I couldn't see any resemblance, but I wasn't in the mood for arguing.

'As like the Five Sisters of Kintail as anything I've seen,' Kenny said, but these dry arid hills of Tunisia were in no way similar to the grand peaks of Sgurr Ouran and its satellites.

It all started by Kenny – a native of Wester Ross – describing his dream home in the Kintail of his boyhood.

A small house it was, nestling on the braeside above the meeting of Loch Alsh, Loch Long and Loch Duich. 'The Kyles of Tir nan Oig,' he called it.

A green oasis in a brown moorland. From the doorway, of a fine early morning, he could watch the sun kissing the high tops of Glen Sheil, and lighting up the narrow ribbon of the Mam Ratagan, the road to Glenelg and the Skye Ferry.

Loch Duich in a frenzy of action, stirred by the west wind, with the solans fishing, intent on providing for their hungry young on some distant skerry.

At night the magic of the after-glow striking the Cuillins and tinting the Red Hills of Broadford.

Yes, a dream home indeed. For Kenny rests on far off Jebel Bou Arada, and Kintail knows him no more.

One thing I am pretty certain of, is that the form of that story reflects what Matt had learned at an Art of Writing evening class he and I had attended for a term at Glasgow University. Nothing of mine appeared in any newspaper until I had been to that class. From then on Matt became my sternest critic, for which I bless him, for henceforth, I put the same energy into my writing as I had on the drums.

As well as going out on the hills regularly with Matt, I was also the drummer in a wee dance band I had formed with three of my grocer pals. It came about because of an older grocer who played a variety of instruments and was a leading light in Cowlairs Co-operative Concert Party. This humorous man, Tommy Neilson, also ran his own dance band and radiated happiness wherever he went. His conversation was off-beat, full of Americanisms from the world of hot jazz. He was a small man, slightly built, with a squint in one eye so pronounced it was hard to tell whether he was looking at you or something else.

He had heard I was a drummer, and wanted to hear me play, so along to his room-and-kitchen house I went. The drum kit was set up, Tommy played the concertina, and I beat it out with him, the pair of us having a rare old time. Tommy was collecting gramophone records of the New Parlophone series of that time: Red Nichols and his Five Pennies, Miff Mole and his Molars, Louis Armstrong and his Hot Five, Joe Venuti the jazz violinist, Bob Crosby and his Dixieland Band, and many another. We studied the rhythms and tried to emulate the new ideas behind their stimulating play. Soon I was going out with Tommy on engagements, helping him to carry his unwieldy kit, and being allowed to play with the band when Tommy did a bit of scat-singing and clowning after the style of his idols.

Before long I was hunting down one or two of my own pals who were interested in forming a band of our own. Dougie McLaren played the fiddle, clarinet and tenor saxophone, Jimmy Carnie played piano and piano accordian, Tommy Campbell was on trumpet; and we even had an apprentice crooner, so we bought a microphone to make more telling the intimate and sickly words of the dance numbers of the mid 1930s.

My sister, Molly, happened to be in the house the evening we unboxed the microphone, and to test the loud-speakers we asked her to take the mike into another room and do anything she liked, sing or impersonate any of the stars of that time, which she was good at. We soon had to turn down the volume as a piercing voice singing 'Sallee – Sallee – Pride of our Allee' was Gracie Fields to the last soft intonation of 'all the world to me'. That was only the beginning, as she took off Scottish comedians and well-known American film star voices.

It happened that at this time an impresario by the name of Carrol Levis was touring Britain and arranging auditions to unearth 'Discoveries' – performers with talent. As he would shortly be coming to Glasgow, Molly was urged to put her name forward as an impressionist. She did. And it was Carrol Levis who projected her to a career on stage, film and radio. Playing with Tommy Handley in ITMA during the war led her to *Life with the Lyons*, the canny Scots lass of the Ben and Bebe show. Television brought her further opportunities.

Her boy-friend, Sandy Hamilton, whom she married before the war, had been in the Boys' Brigade during the time I was in the 148 Company, and he was to have an effect on my future by introducing me to photography as distinct from snapshotting. He persuaded me to join Glasgow YMCA Camera Club to gain access to a well-equipped dark-room, where he taught me to develop films and enlarge the negatives into real pictures with impact. I could not have had a better teacher.

Sandy was to have an influence on Matt's life too, for in the shipping office where he worked was a fellow-clerk who had a business share in a butcher's shop in Lenzie. His partners were looking for a trustworthy man. Sandy suggested Matt, who jumped at a job in a country district within easy reach from Glasgow. He liked it there, and the customers liked him, as was evinced by the large number of them who turned out at his funeral. It was in Lenzie that Matt produced some of his best short newspaper articles, and seeing them in print thrilled him more than the modest payment he received.

At this period of the mid 1930s, the writings of two outdoor men interested us greatly. One wrote under the nom-de-plume of 'Tramp Royal', who was a simple-lifer, travelling light and exploring out-of-the-way places. The other writer signed himself 'P.C.'. He was more of a naturalist, with a gift for creating word pictures of wild-life and scenery. We hoped one day we would meet up with these men of mystery. Little did we know that a September weekend, that had started really badly for us, would lead us to one of them.

We had planned to reach Glasgow Central Station to catch the 9.15 pm train to Blair Atholl, knowing it would be a rush for Matt. I had just made the platform, when along came Matt, and together we bundled our stuff into the nearest carriage. There wasn't a railwayman in sight, and we had literally arrived with only a minute to spare. Grinning happily as we settled down in the empty carriage, we watched another train pull out from the adjacent platform.

Five minutes passed, ten minutes, then the lights in our carriage went out, and the train began to shunt backwards to stop in a siding. We leapt out when we saw a railwayman with a lamp, and learned that it was the Blair Atholl train we had watched going out, and that Perth would be as far as we could get by train that night from Glasgow.

So instead of getting off the train at midnight to back-pack up Glen Tilt, we were dossing in our sleeping bags in the waiting room in Perth Station, with no hope of getting to Blair Atholl before 11.30 am. Our plan had been to cross over the Tilt hills and the Cairngorms to Aviemore. The best we could do now was keep to the glens and try to reach Corrour bothy

14

below Devil's Point before dark, a full twenty-four miles that would have to be covered at a gallop. Matt's diary records:

> It was a shock to find that the small bothy already held thirteen occupants, all getting down to it for the night. The one squeezed closest to the door made room for us. It was a relief to wriggle out of our sleeping bags in the morning and step outside to ease our cramped limbs and enjoy our position under the Devil's Point that loomed above, and look north to the cleft of the Lairig Ghru at 2,700 ft from where we would descend to Speyside and at Aviemore get a train back to Glasgow.

The kindly chap who had made room for us to stretch out behind the door joined us for the winding climb between 4,000-foot peaks to the bouldery 'U' cleft of the Lairig Ghru summit – then it was down into a glorious fragment of Caledonian pine forest. Our companion, tall, very thin and emaciated looking, carried a big pack that looked too heavy for him, but he went well, and impressed us by his knowledge of the wild-life of the area. He was a Glasgow man, and when I enthused about the articles on wild-life that appeared from time to time, and asked if he had ever read them, he admitted that he was the P.C. who wrote them.

This led to Peter Currie visiting me in Springburn. My mother's reaction to seeing him for the first time was 'My God, Tommy, he's skin and bone.' But she quickly fell for his gentle smile, and hugged him when he left, an affectionate gesture unusual for her to make to a stranger. She was to see a lot of him as he became a regular visitor, reading a stream of my rejected articles and suggesting where they had failed.

At the time I met Peter he had recently started his first job, with an art dealer to whom well-known Scottish painters brought their canvases to be exhibited for sale. Until then, Peter's sole income had come from writing. Because of illness from birth, he had never attended school, but had been taught at home. Even so, he had gained at the usual age the entrance qualification for Glasgow University but continuing ill health had prevented him from grasping the opportunity. Literature, birds, animals, flowers and the countryside were his interests. But without friends to share his joys something was missing.

He came out one night on a dance-band engagement with me, just to see what went on, and told me afterwards he would love to learn to dance, even it if were only to meet with the opposite sex. 'Take lessons,' I said, gave him a few addresses, and urged him to give it a try. Courageously he took my advice, and after a few lessons had made friends with a sonsy lass, as plump as he was thin. Within weeks he had proposed, was accepted, got married, and in time the happy couple became parents of a lovely blonde baby girl. When war broke out Peter became an inspector in an aircraft factory. He was a grandfather when last I saw him and was feeding short stories to the American market.

My own life-style was to change too. I believe there is such a thing as 'divine discontent'. I was not unhappy, but felt time was passing and if I was ever to get away from the grocer's shop I would have to square up to how it might be done. I also faced the fact that I was getting less and less pleasure from playing in the band two or three nights a week. I had bought the drum kit on hire-purchase. It was long since paid up. I decided to sell it to an unemployed follower of the band. He didn't have the money, but paid me back from his earnings when he took over from me. Now I had more time to devote to writing and photography, and was enjoying my camping and climbing weekends all the more for it.

Peter had expressed his belief that I had it in me to make a go at freelancing. 'You have the health and the energy that I lack,' he said. What I feared was that I might not have the creative ability.

On my fourteenth birthday I had put my name down as a candidate for any job that might come up for a message boy in Cowlairs Co-operative Society's Grocery Department. I knew the wage was the highest you could get in Springburn as a delivery boy – thirteen shillings and three pence a week, guaranteed for two years. With luck, if you were smart, you might be kept on as an apprentice grocer.

Great was my joy when I was told to report to the grocery branch nearest our house. It was like being a milk-boy again, traipsing up and down tenement stairs but, instead of long-handled cans suspended from each hand, I now had a large square basket on my head full of grocery orders, each partitioned off from the other for delivery to different customers. As a milk-boy you rarely saw more of the person you were delivering to than an outstretched arm taking the milk and handing back the empty can. As a grocery delivery boy you checked off the items, usually inside the house, and in that way got to know the occupants.

Nor was it all delivering groceries. There were other chores: washing the shop-front windows with a long-handled brush and slinging pails of water over them until the glass sparkled. You sprinkled water on the sawdust floor, then brushed it away to expose the bare boards underneath – the water kept down the dust; then you had the pleasure of laying a fresh layer of clean sawdust by hand, broadcasting it like a man sowing grain. There was an art in laying it evenly like a carpet, which gave me creative pleasure. I also helped stock the shelves with tins and jars of this and that. Eventually I donned an apron and helped make up orders for delivery.

It was about this time I joined the Springburn Amateur Boxing and Wrestling Club, and took part in competitions with boys of my own weight from other clubs. Boxing was my forte. After winning a prize or two on Amateur nights in Premierland in Bridgeton, Glasgow, I might have persisted but for the accident which broke my collar bone, already described. In time, however, my mother failed to prevent me getting a replacement bike, and then there was no keeping me at home.

Bent over the dropped handlebars of my racing bike I was off to the Campsie Hills every summer evening, ten miles fast pushing to Lennoxtown where I would traverse a big face of rock, interrupted by grassy terraces, all the while watching the skirling jackdaws, the wheatears popping in and out among the boulders and the hovering kestrels, and, at the same time trying to find new ways up the vertical bits. I'd gone there for the birds originally, but the climbing soon became more important. To my surprise, when I took a couple of boys of my own age to sample the fun I found they were terrified. By accident I had discovered something I was good at. In Springburn Library I found the very book to whet my appetite further, *First Steps to Climbing* by George Abraham, pioneer of Lakeland rock climbing.

The job I was doing in the Co-op didn't tax me. I enjoyed it. I was approaching my sixteenth birthday when it was usual to be dismissed, unless you were judged to be suitable for a behind-the-counter grocery apprenticeship. Great was my mother's joy, and great my apprehension, when just a fortnight before my birthday I was instructed to report to the head office for an arithmetic test and oral examination to assess whether or not I would be kept on.

My mother was up to high doh when I came back from that test bearing the glad news that I had passed, and would start behind the counter in the New Year following my birthday on 29th December. 'Tommy, it's a job for life,' she exclaimed, her lively brown eyes lighting up and giving me a hug. But even as she was enthusing over my good luck, I was half-wishing I had been given the sack. 'Born a man and died a grocer,' I was thinking. On the other hand it was a job, and in the dark days of 1931 that was infinitely better than not having one. It was in the summer of that year I did my big Highland walk with Richie.

Actually, there was quite a lot to being a grocer before the age of supermarkets and universal packaging. Most goods came in bulk: sugar in two-hundredweight bags; flour in hundredweight bags; Danish butter came in casks; cheddar cheeses weighed about fifty pounds; thick black tobacco came in rolls; smoked hams and sides of bacon were delivered with the bones in. Peas, beans, rice, barley came in loose, as did pepper and other spices. Much of any day was spent weighing and measuring these and other items, to stock the shelves and fill the drawers.

I was fascinated by the speed and skill of the grocers who, whether measuring quantities into pound, two-pound, three-pound or four-pound bags, could get the required weight almost exactly so that, working in pairs, one measuring, the other weighing, they could then set about sealing the stiff brown-paper bags with a special fold that required a strong twist of the thumb. They were also expert at making little pokey-hats with light-weight paper, each holding an ounce or half an ounce of pepper or other spices.

First year apprentices also went to a day-release class to learn more about the trade. What galled me was to have to work until 7.30 pm on Saturdays, the grocery half day being Tuesdays. Still, I could put these mid-week breaks to good use, reaching as far as the Trossachs on the bike, or ranging the moors, enjoying the sights and sounds of curlews, peewits and snipe. I knew burns where oyster catchers and redshank nested, and ground higher up where I could find golden plover, ravens and buzzards.

Yet, although writing was the one thing I had been complimented on throughout school, I put not a word on paper about my doings on the hills until I went to Torridon with John McNair at the end of August 1932, and on getting home tried to describe our moonlight camps, and wonderful sunny days traversing Ben Eighe, Liathach, Beinn Alligin, Slioch, Sgorr Ruadh and Beinn Liath Mor. But I didn't have the words to paint the pictures that were in my mind: I could not translate to paper.

On 2nd January 1933, because New Year's Day was a Sunday, Matt and I had a Monday holiday, and we planned to rise early enough to walk the mile and more to catch the West Highland train that left Queen Street Station at 5.50 am; get off at Bridge of Orchy and add Beinn Dorain to our lengthening list of Munros. It needed the bright flame of enthusiasm to set forth from our respective houses on an abnormally stormy morning.

Most of the journey north, of course, was in the dark, and the hills that surrounded Bridge of Orchy had an ominous green tinge suffusing their snows. Our route lay right above the station by a glen with a big waterfall, which was a misnomer that morning because its water was being whirled high in the air like smoke, yet it never as much as crossed our minds that conditions were too extreme for climbing, even when we were forced to our knees and had to crawl the final rise to the dim igloo which was the summit cairn at 3,524 feet.

There was no shelter, so we immediately turned about and started the downward crawl, which was more awkward because of the way our rucksacks pushed over our heads and added to the difficulty of seeing through the whirling snow-spume. Once down a fair bit, Matt rose gingerly to his feet and so did I. A few steps and I was wrenched into the air and hurled against his back, and down went the two of us sliding out of control. The only physical damage was the breaking of two flasks of tea in Matt's bag, whose contents soaked his dry change of clothing.

Even as low as 1,000 feet above Bridge of Orchy we were being blown about like drunk men, but whereas high up we had been blasted by the shrapnel of icy pellets, down here it was wet snow that hurled itself at us. Orphans of the storm we made for a hutted camp of navvies then engaged in the building of the Black Mount section of the new Glencoe road. We gate-crashed in, and without having to ask were promptly offered dry clothes and a place by the redhot stove while our soaked clothes steamed dry. The navvies were kindly Irishmen who boiled a kettle of tea for us, and we enjoyed their company until it was time to face the tramp back to Bridge of Orchy in what was now wind and rain. By the time we got into the train we were as wet as we had been before going into the navvies' hut. All we could do was ring out our clothes and steam in the warmth of the carriage.

Next day we discovered that the big tramway clock in Bath Street, a landmark in the centre of Glasgow, had been blown down in one hundred-mile-an-hour gusts, and that two climbers were missing in the Cairngorms. They were Alastair MacKenzie and Duncan Ferrier, whose bodies were found six days later. They had set out from the Shelter Stone of Ben Macdhui, underclad and ill-equipped, and had died of exposure.

What about us? Were we wise pushing on to the summit of Beinn Dorain in such ferocious conditions? The answer can only be 'No'. On the other hand Matt and I were very fit by reason of being constantly on the hills every week, come rain or snow. Our clothing may have been simple, but it was well tested. We were ignorant, though, and dangerously unaware of how quickly the fittest can die of exposure when body heat is lost more rapidly than it can be replaced.

Starting work on 3rd January was no hardship after that gruelling survival day. In fact the time passed quickly enough in any grocery branch because the counter was so busy with share-holding customers. In the 30s few married women other than widows went out to work, so the shops tended to be busy in the mornings, and after school when the children did the shopping. Between times there were plenty of jobs to be done. Tuesday was early closing and the golf-course called many of the grocers, while off I would go on my bike, as far as the Trossachs.

I used to get my leg pulled for not taking any interest in girls. Actually there was one who made my heart beat faster. She was the sister of a pal, and she also got Tuesday off, so in a bold mood I suggested we take the bus to Campsie Glen. It was a disaster, for I was too shy to excuse myself and go behind a bush for a pee, so she didn't get the chance either. No wonder she darted home the moment she got off the bus. I was in bad need too.

One of the benefits of working in a Co-op with twenty-six grocery branches was that you were moved around quite a bit. The remotest shop was at Mavis Valley, reached from Bishopbriggs tram terminus by a walk along the Forth and Clyde Canal. It was a mining village without electricity or gas in any of its houses, so we sold a lot of paraffin for lamps and cooking.

The eeriest shop I worked in, though, was Craigbank, the cellar being the eerie bit, a virtual catacomb reached by a trapdoor on the shop-floor and a steep wooden stairway. Down there you were in a rocky cavern, with quarry-like walls of naked stone, cobwebbed in its many recesses where huge spiders lay in wait on grey webs to catch flies attracted to the hams which hung on hooks from the rafters supporting the shop-floor above. On a butcher's table in that dingy catacomb I learned how to extract the bones from hams, roll them, girdle them in string, and hang them up until they were put on the shelf. On rock ledges fifty-six-pound cheddar cheeses wrapped in cloths were stored.

The big-game however was rats, and they were whiskery and large. Every morning before the shop opened to customers the staff armed themselves for the kill. One by one, all the lower drawers on the serving side of the counter were pulled out. The big moment came when the last one was removed, and any lurking rat had to make a run for it. The score rate was pretty high. But one day when the shop was busy, and the baker had delivered a tray of cream cookies and other fancy cakes, there was an incident. The customers were eyeing the newly delivered goodies, when out jumped a rat from behind a pile of tins and, in a kangaroo leap across the pastries, ran the full length of the counter, jumped to the floor and made out through the open door of the shop.

Women were screaming as the grocer known as 'Wee Geordie' held up his hands to calm them down, saying: 'It's only the shop kitten; something must have given it a fright!' A torrent of withering scorn greeted his explanation. 'No, no,' he continued to appease. I must say he carried it off well, for he was something of a comedian, and soon had them laughing; yes, and buying cream cookies too.

On the home front my brother Willie, or Bill as he was more generally known to his pals, was well into his apprenticeship as a mechanical engineer with Singers Sewing Machine Company, while my sister Molly, Dux of Hyde Park School, was at college, thanks to having been awarded a scholarship. Our mother was still working, but at an easier job than wagon painting. On returning home after a few weeks away, Molly had written: 'I had forgotten how young my mother was. How bright and wavy her red hair; how clear her pink and white complexion; how small and slim her build.'

Molly was a born swot. Despite winning the Gold Medal as the year's top student at Skerry's College, plus a Bronze in another subject, her cherished desires were to become an actress and a writer. These longings were being shelved meantime as she continued to study three nights a week at business classes, discovering in shorthand speed-writing that she could reach 300 words per minute. Her first claim to fame was demonstrating this speed in public at the request of the college. With her earnings she was also paying for elocution lessons.

Of course she did become a writer, and in her third book *Toe on the Ladder* she inscribed on the flyleaf: 'For Tommy who first stood me in front of a mike.' She is referring to the impersonations she did to test our microphone, that led to her being 'discovered' by Carrol Levis. In that book she also mentions the success of the wee dance band I had formed, by writing: 'Tommy was now playing the drums several nights a week after his day's work in the Co-operative, playing each Saturday night, and up at the crack of dawn on Sunday mornings to enjoy a day on the hills he loved.'

Too many band engagements was the straw that broke the camel's back. I not only wanted whole weekends on the hills, but more time for writing and work in the photographic darkroom. So I gladly gave up the drums, and for the first time since leaving school opened books really seriously in order to learn something from them; books on birds, books on mountains, books on exploration and most important of all, books on the nature of Scotland.

I'm glad all the same that I was discovering Scotland the hard way, walking the hills and glens in the 1930s before the changes of land use that were to follow after the war: the building of hydro-electric dams and massive ploughing operations for forestry. At that time Gaelic was widely spoken in the west; crofters kept cows and grew winter feed for them. It was a rare house that didn't have hens, and you were welcome to camp almost anywhere.

Also, because roads were bad and campers were few, there was a tradition of hospitality towards wayfarers. Indeed, when I was on my own, I found it hard to persuade kindly crofters to take money for eggs or milk. Often enough they pressed pancakes and scones on me, and invited me in for meals. Fares on all forms of public transport were cheap. That holiday in Skye when we were washed out cost no more than £5 for a fortnight, inclusive of travel and food. The following year, John, Matt and I were back on the Cuillin. The weather was vile, cold and wet, and after John left at the end of the first week, Matt and I cleared off to Kintail. Ironically, within twenty-four hours the sun blazed from a cloudless sky and we were burned to a frazzle climbing grassy hills, wishing we were back in the rocky Cuillin.

Back home in Springburn, frustrated at having so little time for doing the things I most wanted to do, and certain that as a grocer I was a square peg in a round hole, I saw a notice in a newspaper that set me thinking. In big letters were the words:

LET ME BE YOUR FATHER. DO YOU HAVE AN AIM IN LIFE? IF SO WHAT ARE YOU DOING TO ACHIEVE IT? THE PELMAN SYSTEM OF MIND AND MEMORY TRAIN- ING COULD HELP YOU.

I wrote for the literature. It sounded logical. The system could only work for you if you worked for it. It made no false promises. Hitherto I'd met the word Pelmanism as a card game we used to play at home. Cards

21

were placed face upward, then turned down, and each player was asked to name what was on the face of the cards below. The winner was the one with the best visual memory. My sister was red hot at it.

The course of fifteen lessons was priced at eight guineas, and for that sum each student would have a personal tutor to give guidance and mark the monthly examination paper. Hire-purchase terms were offered, and it was by this method I paid for a course that did me far more good than I ever expected.

2

Write, Write, Writing

Ye shape yer sheen wi yer ain shauchelt feet.
You shape your shoes with your own shuffling feet.
                                        Scots Proverb.

These words encapsulate the third lesson of Pelmanism: 'Your Purpose in
Life and how to achieve it.' With it there was a caution, not to cut the rope
that supports you until your hold on the new rope is firm and secure. 'As
for the rope you are dispensing with – don't hurl it from you as though
you were entirely rid of it. Let it go easily so that it dangles within reach.
Leave the old job with the respect and good will of your former employer.'
Wise words.

I didn't obey them, however, when in a state of fury I ignored the boss
who was telling me off, removed my apron and white coat, put on my
jacket, and walked out leaving him talking. The fault was mine. I had been
fooling at the ham machine with some mischievous boys. I'd waved the big
ham knife at them as if to cut off a hand holding down the scale-pan, thus
preventing me from weighing the ham resting on the glass plate on my side
of the counter. Alas, the knife caught in the chains of the brass balance scales;
down they tumbled, and there was the crack of broken glass.

The boss was a tall greasy-faced man with a discontented mouth, that
made him look perpetually displeased. He came at me waving his arms,
telling me that the expensive glass plate I had just broken rendered the
scales useless until it could be replaced. My response was: 'If you have any
reprimand to make to me, the front shop among the customers is not the
place to do it.' He followed me into the back shop, and I walked out. The
boss came round to see my mother that night. I said I would go back, but
leave after pay-day at the end of the week, and would be applying for my
superannuation money.

It was July 1939. I had long ago completed my Pelman course, and felt I
was well on the way to my dream of a full-time free-lance career in
journalism. I had learned to touch-type with the help of my sister. In
Pitman's shorthand my fluency was about 120 words a minute – I had
passed an exam at that lowly speed. Lots of my photographs had been
published in newspapers and magazines, and fewer of my articles were

being rejected. I could not have picked a worse year, though, for dispensing with the rope that was my main support.

I had clarified my aim in life rather ambitiously. On the Pelman questionnaire that came with lesson three I had declared that I wanted to be a naturalist and writer on Scotland like Seton Gordon – aristocratic author of a score of books on the highlands and islands. Additionally I aimed at being an explorer of the Alpine ranges of Europe and the Himalaya like Frank Smythe, mountaineer and ski-tourer who supported himself by writing books illustrated with his own high quality photography. Both writers depended on freedom to roam in order to write books for publication that financed their life-styles.

By leaving the Co-op prematurely I had no plan of action, nor any fancy for seeing the summer go to waste, so off I went with camp gear to the Isle of Arran for a few climbing days to think things over. It was harvest time, farmers were looking for help in the fields, and in Shiskine I was offered a job at fifteen shillings a week and my keep. First though, I said I'd have to go home to collect some stuff, so off I went, packed a case with books, lifted my typewriter and writing materials, and returned to Tighnfraoch Farm, Shiskine. I had left my bicycle in Brodick so, dumping my luggage to follow on the bus, off I pushed over the String road and in ten miles was at the farm gate. Within minutes of arrival I was leading a horse and forking corn stooks onto a cart.

Not until we had stopped work did the grim-faced, hard-working farmer take me to the stable and up a wooden ladder to show me my accommodation above the horse stall. It was a small room with a table and chair, a narrow spring bed, an open cupboard for hanging clothes, and was pervaded by a mingling of horse and tobacco smells. 'Will this do you?' It was more a statement than a question. My mind registered 'no' but my head nodded 'yes'. I went down the stair with him to collect my newly arrived luggage, and he said I would get some blankets when I came to the house for supper.

The farmer's name was Johnny Bannantyne. 'I'll call you when your supper's ready,' he said. When he returned with blankets for my bed, my typewriter was on the table, with my small library of books, and other writing materials. Seeing these signs of culture, I suppose, changed his mind about the room being good enough for me for, when the meal was over, I was shown a nice wee attic at the top of the house, and in there I moved my luggage where it was to stay for three months.

Shiskine is renowned as being the garden of Arran by reason of its good soil, famous for growing different varieties of Arran potatoes; Arran Banner, Arran Chief and so on. It was also the last stronghold of native Gaelic speakers. Communal gathering of the crops was the custom, the working gangs moving from one farm to another until the fields were cleared, using potato diggers, horses and carts. The nick-name of my boss I learned was 'Johnny Ban, the hashie man', because he was always in a hurry. He could carry a two-hundredweight sack of grain up a wooden ladder to the loft, and he expected me to do the same. It was in the farm-steading on the wet Sunday morning of 3rd September I learned that the inevitable had happened – we were at war with Hitler's Germany.

With foreboding, Britain waited to be attacked, but nothing happened and this prolongation of inaction became known as the 'phoney war'. My routine on the farm was to be wakened by a call of 'Tom' booming up the stair at 6.30 am, when I rose and brought in the bull with the cows, had breakfast, then did as I was bid, digging potato pits, riddling the potatoes for size, or working in the stackyard, threshing or whatever. The Pelman course laid stress on aiming at excellence whatever you did, however uncongenial the task. I knew the farmer was pleased with my work, from what other farmers had told me. I was well fed and his wife was very kind to me.

But I drew the line when, as daylight hours shortened, he broached the subject of pay one day as we were working together. 'You know, I've never kept any man on after the harvest was secured. I'd keep you on, but I'd have to drop you to eight shillings a week.' I said nothing. He broke the silence by saying: 'There's still a lot to do.' In summer I had worked every hour of daylight; even now I was out in the moonlight.

Before I spoke I thought hard about my answer. 'Mr Bannantyne, the last thing I want is to be a burden on the farm. I've done my best, and I think it's time for me to go home. My mother is on her own, and actually I'd like to get on with some writing because I've had little time to do any here because of the long hours of work. I'm not complaining, so if you make up my wages, I'll leave at the end of this week.'

I'd taken no money from the farmer while I had worked for him. I'd contributed to the upkeep of our Glasgow house from the superannuation fund, deducted from my wages when I was a grocer. My mother was delighted to have me back home. The country was at war, yet here was I doing nothing but 'write, write, writing', as she put it. I was on a sticky wicket, because paper rationing was in force, and more pressing political events had quashed the free-lance market.

I tried to enlist in the Royal Air Force, but having registered in Arran was told I would be called up when required. So I answered an advert in a newspaper for salesmen interested in books. The book concerned was Newnes' *Pictorial Knowledge*, an encyclopedia in several volumes. Reporting to the office I was interviewed by Mr McSherry who explained the first rules of door-to-door selling: get inside by means of your own personality and don't try to sell unless husband and wife are in the house. Make an appointment and call back then get the first instalment, which is not returnable if they change their minds after you've gone.

He explained that I would be given sixteen cards, each with the name of a family with children at school. 'You visit the homes in late afternoon and make an appointment for the evening. If they ask if you are from the school, you reply, "Do you mean the local school? No, I represent a higher educational body." If they ask "Is it books?" You reply, "All knowledge comes from books." ' He further explained that I would have a demonstration volume. I should ask how the children were doing at school – their names would be on the cards. I was then instructed to talk about how help at home makes such a difference and how the parents could help their children through *Pictorial Knowledge*. It would cost less than a penny a day over their schooldays and was a mine of up-to-date information. Then was the moment to clinch the sale.

I said I'd try it. I didn't like the deception of decent people, yet I had to admit that the books were worth the money. Sometimes I could have made sales but when I saw the parents were honestly trying to see how they could afford them, I would steer them away from immediate action, suggesting it might be better for them to wait until their circumstances improved. Some however would not be put off. On the other hand I had more than one annoyed householder telling me they knew what I was trying to sell and closing the door on me.

It was an experience I was eager to put behind me, and merciful release came when in May my military call-up papers arrived, ordering me to report to the Ayrshire Yeomanry, Town Hall, Kilmarnock on a date which left me four days of liberty, and off I went by train to Aviemore to use them tramping through Rothiemurchus, leaving its pine woods behind me for the Lairig Ghru, and by the Pools of Dee at 2,700 feet to climb up the snowy edge of the March Burn to reach the arctic plateau and slope gradually across to the headwall above Loch Avon and drop steeply to its shore and find the Shelter Stone where I'd never been before. The only sounds were the waterfalls, emphasising the silence as I sat outside and got the primus stove purring, deeply content as I waited for my soup to warm.

Many years after the war, when I was Principal Guest at the Cairngorm Club dinner in Aberdeen, the President in giving his speech produced the *Shelter Stone Book* and read an entry dated 26th/27th May 1940, by a person by the name of Tommy Weir, 41 Adamswell Street, Glasgow North:

Never have the Cairngorms had greater appeal than in this farewell journey of mine. Rain and sun in the right proportions, and grand mist effects on the tops. Still another day of freedom before the army calls.

He raised a laugh when he asked: 'Could that be you?'

After making that entry I had crossed over the tops of A'Choinneach and Bynack More, continuing on to Ryvoan bothy expecting to have this

26

shelter above the Robbers' Pass to myself. But outside it sat a lady knitting. She explained she was waiting for her husband who was in a hide photographing birds, and that they were staying in Aviemore and their car was in Glen More.

So inside I went, and was busy getting the fire lit, when the door opened and a cheerful bespectacled face appeared. After our hellos I told him I had just come down from the high tops, and he told me he had been cooped up for the last few hours in a hide waiting for a merlin to return to its nest in the heather, but had failed to get anything.

I told him that I, too, was interested in birds and had tried some bird photography with variable success, but that one of my pictures had won first prize recently in *Zoo Magazine*'s photographic competition, a shot of a tree creeper on a fence post with a fat caterpillar in its curved bill. 'Yes, I remember the picture well, for I was the judge of that competition and chose it as winner.' I was thrilled indeed when he told me his name was Eric Hosking, and many years after the war we were to meet again.

While I was enjoying the Cairngorms the German blitzkrieg was driving the retreating allied forces towards the Channel. In that encircling movement the British army lost most of its heavy equipment, tanks and artillery. The historian A.J.P. Taylor described its aftermath thus: 'Dunkirk was a great deliverance and a great disaster.' The deliverance was due to 'Operation Dynamo' by the Admiralty, employing a veritable armada of destroyers, passenger yachts, pleasure craft, fishing boats, cockle boats, Thames barges and lifeboats, so that 338,000 troops were evacuated under enemy battery fire and air attacks. It was 3rd June before the operation was completed; a horrific endurance test for those involved.

Prime Minister Churchill paid tribute to the 40,000 French troops who fought to cover the evacuation, knowing they could not escape and would be taken prisoner by the Germans. His words were: 'Let us remember that but for the endurance of the Dunkirk rearguard the re-creation of an army in Britain for home defence and final victory would have been gravely prejudiced.'

Back home in Springburn for one night after these splendid days in the Cairngorms, I was off next morning to Kilmarnock to become a soldier in the Ayrshire Yeomanry. The call-up papers said I could expect forty-eight hours' leave after registering. That respite was for recovery from the effects of inoculations that would have made everybody who got the 'jags' a feverish liability in the town-hall which was our billet. Before getting the 'needle', however, the day was spent queuing to draw army kit, battle-dress, denims, boots, cap, capbadge, socks, underclothes, field dressing, webbing equipment, anklets and pay-book. With all this in a kit-bag I travelled back to Springburn.

My mother took it all very calmly, but I could not help wondering what was going through her mind as I left in my uniform in such a troubled period of the war. I was twenty-five years of age, less than three years younger than my father had been when he left her in 1914; a couple of years later she was a widow with three young children to look after. I remembered how she had hated even the sight of my brother Willie and me playing at soldiers with toy guns when we were little, and now here was I, kitted out for the thing she most feared – war.

As for Kilmarnock, it was hail and farewell, for we entrained next day, our destination Bulford Camp as recruits to the 4th Field Training Regiment, Royal Artillery. Arriving there at the same time were battle-weary men in shabby uniforms, escaped from hell on the Dunkirk beaches, survivors of the British Expeditionary Force which had lost 68,000 killed, wounded, or taken prisoner. Left behind, too, were over 2,000 artillery pieces as well as 60,000 vehicles and 500 tons of stores. As for the RAF and the Royal Navy, 474 aircraft were lost, and 243 ships had been sunk at Dunkirk, six of them British destroyers.

Our red brick barrack block was situated below Beacon Hill amid 90,000 acres of training area of Salisbury Plain. As raw recruits we were there to be licked into shape, quickly, in case Hitler's next move would be to launch an invasion of Britain, by sea, air and parachute troops. So we had a lot to learn, and a lot of lazy, bad habits to forget. On any parade you had to be assembled five minutes before time, and God help you if your bed space in the barrack room wasn't laid out as per diagram and ready for inspection.

Pay parade was Friday, and after standing for a solid hour as the officiating officer went through the alphabet, it was a relief when he reached 'W' and out I stepped, saluted, took three steps forward, put out my hand to take the five shillings due to me, stepped back, saluted again, and was promptly ordered to stand in another queue. Those in the queue were told why, when the parade ended. 'You shower will have to learn how to salute properly, and I'm going to drill you until you can do it!' When I asked the duty officer if it would be possible to be paid once a month he nearly burst a blood vessel. 'The pay parade is a parade whether you get paid or not. There's no such thing as a private arrangement. You're not in civvy street now!'

June, July were quiet months, but this lull ended early on 7th August. By that time Belgium, France and Holland had been defeated; Denmark and Norway were occupied by the Germans, and thrilling air battles began above us, with planes falling out of the sky and parachutes opening as survivors floated down. The daylight Battle of Britain had begun, as 1,800 German aircraft attacked communications, airfields and RAF bases. Hitler believed that the RAF would soon succumb and his troops would then launch Operation Sea Lion, a full-scale invasion of Britain.

British intelligence, however, knew the date set for the seaborne invasion, and a massive strike by the RAF on waiting barges and ammunition dumps caused another date to be set, 13th September, when a further eighty barges were battered out of commission. It drew from the Germans a ferocious air reprisal on Britain, gloriously defeated by RAF fighter command. Britain had gained time and was now preparing for a full-scale invasion by Germany in 1941. That was the threat that was to involve me, for at Christmas 1940 I arrived in Dover. When Churchill said 'We will fight on the beaches', I didn't know he included me!

I had brought this posting on myself, by volunteering for it. It happened this way. On completion of my training and awaiting posting to a service unit, I was singled out to deputise for the Battery Clerk because I could use a typewriter. It was better than doing fatigue duties, and freed me from some parades. The main task was to work out guard rosters, make out leave passes, rail warrants and produce Battery Orders which it was the duty of every soldier to read. Nobody liked being on guard duty, so it was important that everyone took their turn, including me.

So I watched a lot of comrades disappear and more recruits arrive while it looked as if I was going to go on forever. I didn't mind. I climbed Beacon Hill most fine evenings, an easy walk above the Barracks, from which to watch the sunset over the vastness of the seemingly endless plain whose most important monument is Stonehenge. I had it to myself the first time I went to see it, and a profound impression its two concentric circles enclosing two ellipses made, the tallest stone twenty-one feet high. Incredible that the stones for this astronomical calendar had come from as far as Wales, rafted up from the Bristol Channel, and dragged over log rollers. On a recreational vehicle I could sometimes get to Salisbury and enjoy the wonderful feeling of peace in the medieval gateways giving access to a cathedral whose like I had never seen before, its spire soaring to 400 feet, the tallest in Britain, added in 1334, fifty-four years after the cathedral's completion in 1280.

In letters home I stressed the enjoyment of these walks and the sights I was seeing, assuring my mother I was well fed, and that she should stop sending me food parcels as we were getting all sorts of rationed goods that she was unable to obtain. I didn't tell her of our entire unit being laid low with food poisoning and of being placed on a diet of bread and milk until the looseness in the bowels passed, leaving us all very weak. Even Beacon Hill was an effort the first time I went up when we were allowed out.

It was in the very last week of 1940 that a demand order for a trained gunner came in from the 5th Super Heavy Battery stationed outside Dover. Apart from the fact that it was a rotten time to post anybody, we didn't have anyone who filled the bill. To his question, 'Who have we got?' I said 'me'. He said nothing, so I wrote out the posting order and rail warrant and awaited results. Shortly after that, the bell communicating me with the major rang, and in I went as a matter of routine to take away for mailing any correspondence he had been signing. In his hand was the posting order, and as if he didn't know me, he read out my army number, rank and name as if it were a charge sheet. To my admission of 'Yes Sir,' he looked thoughtfully at me and asked, 'Do you really want to go to Dover? You will be shot at a lot there. You know that, I suppose. Could I ask why you want to go?'

As far as I can remember my reply went something like this: 'It's a question of duty, Sir. There is nobody else to post but me.'

He thanked me for the work I had done in his office, wished me well, and next morning I was on my way. But owing to heavy bomb damage to the railway line, and arriving in London in the middle of a rain of high explosive and fire bombs, I had to spend the night in a hospital where the military police directed me, and had to hang about until I was put aboard a slow train for Dover. It was dark when I alighted at Shepherdswell railway station and reported to the guardroom close by. A telephone call was made, and I was escorted to a civvy billet in the village. My hosts were an elderly lady and her daughter, who gave me a meal and showed me to a comfortable bedroom. I reckoned I had landed on my feet.

As for the gunners of the 5th Super Heavy Battery, I thought they were the scruffiest-looking soldiers I had ever seen. After the smart turnout required of a training regiment, they looked a real indisciplined shower. I soon found out why, for they were getting about one night in bed in every three, doing guard duties through the hours of darkness, armed with rifles and Molotov cocktails as defence weapons, and by day working on two huge artillery pieces, twelve-inch howitzers, capable of lobbing 750-pound shells distances of fifteen miles with destructive accuracy. These were First World War howitzers, and were railway-mounted to be hauled by steam locomotives, so the unit comprised Royal Engineers as well as artillerymen. When on the move the entire unit was accommodated in horse-box carriages fitted with sleeping berths, but no seats. Cooking was done on railway platforms or on railway sidings.

But Shepherdswell was our base as part of the defence of south-east Kent, and when I joined the survey party I was to get to know this superb corner of England very well, from Romney Marsh all the way round the coast to the Weald of Kent and Canterbury. There was a lot to do, fixing the positions of strategic buildings the enemy might try to occupy when the expected invasion took place. Once these had been fixed, target-record forms could be made out, showing the switch, range and angle of sight needed on the guns to enable them to hit a given target. Observation posts had to be kept supplied with food and water ready for immediate occupation, to bring down fire on moving convoys or on any other concentration of enemy troops.

In the Battery we took it hard when visiting big-wigs paid inspection visits, and bullshit became the order of the day: there was a halt to everything except scrubbing, polishing, white-washing, blancoing of kit

30

and pressing of trousers. Happy was the day, though, when Montgomery took over as Corps Commander. He had other ideas of protecting Britain against invasion. He ended the waiting game that was draining the strength of troops through lack of sleep. Not for him the bullshit. He demanded that hard training was more important than standing-to. He had seen that many more could have escaped from the Germans at Dunkirk if every soldier had known how to handle the controls of army vehicles from Brengun carriers to motorcycles.

He soon had everybody in the unit away on courses to ensure this ability. He also introduced efficiency tests on all small-arms weapons, insisted that officers and men went out on cross-country runs and had physical training, and laid down a principle that a fully laden man should be able to carry another full-laden man for 200 yards – something that might be required to save a comrade injured in battle.

Each of our Nissen sleeping huts had been inserted between rows of apple trees, a mass of blossom in spring. Camouflage could not have been improved upon, but one afternoon we were strafed by a low-flying fighter plane. Bullets sprayed holes in the corrugated iron of our hut but there was nobody inside at the time. One day when two of our own spotter planes were just above the camp they collided. I was looking up, along with others, at the time because they were flying so low. With a mighty bang and a ball of flame the sky was filled with fragments like falling leaves. It was our sad duty to locate limbs that had been torn from bodies.

With constant air-raids, no work would have been possible if we had taken shelter. But one moonlight night was memorable for having not one passage of enemy planes, and for us it was lucky, because fire broke out in our motor transport section and caused a mighty blaze. The date is stamped on my memory for it was the night when Clydebank, the most famous centre of shipbuilding in Scotland, and probably the world, was blitzed, with a repeat performance the following night. Bombs were dropped on the town from darkness until dawn throughout both blitzes, and by the morning of 14th March 1941, 20,000 people had been evacuated to schools, church halls and other buildings, or to billets in other parts of the country. Little damage was done to the shipyards, but much to everywhere in the town. By Sunday, 16th, shipbuilders were back at work.

For me this was an educational period, getting practical experience as a battery surveyor, and finding a camaraderie based not on social class but on dependability. I never soldiered with better officers and men than in the 5th Super Heavy Battery. 'Squaddies' may wear the same type of battle dress, but in any unit a man tends to find his own level, be he cook, sanitary orderly, gun layer, driver, signaller, surveyor, or whatever. The army was more democratic than I would ever have guessed. Allowances were made for personal idiosyncrasies, even when the Manual of Military Law was breached. For example, it was known that I was an ornithologist, always on the lookout for birds, and one who would rise early to hear the dawn chorus in springtime. But the nightingale – a bird I had never seen or heard in Scotland – sings best when darkness falls, so one evening after lights out, I slipped past the guardroom, climbed to a spinney and enjoyed the bird's full repertoire of long-drawn-out single notes, beginning quietly, rising to a crescendo, then to phrases of astonishing virtuosity. That night I had the chance to compare the musicianship of several singers before returning to the guardroom at 2 am.

I walked in boldly to see if there was any tea on the go, and met the Orderly Officer eye-to-eye who had just signed the Duty Book. He knew me well, but spoke as if he had never seen me before. 'What are you doing out of barracks at this hour?' he demanded sternly. I answered honestly: 'I was listening to nightingales; we don't get them in Scotland, and they don't sing until darkness falls.' He turned to the Guard Commander, a good friend of mine. 'I'll leave Weir in your hands, deal with him as you think fit.' Bombardier Terlet was in a quandary. He did nothing, and I heard no more.

More serious was a split-second decision I made when Sergeant Major Pink gave the order 'Fall out the dental parade.' I stepped out and joined the others knowing their destination would be Canterbury, and that a concert by the Philharmonia Orchestra was being held in the Cathedral Crypt that afternoon. I reckoned there was small chance of being found out, until I took my seat and realised I was within vision of one of our Battery officers who saw me before I saw him. Retribution came that night, as I was bedding down in the hut, when in came the Survey Sergeant. 'So you sneaked off on dental parade. You thought you would get away with it. Don't bullshit me. I could make it hot for you. You know who saw you at the concert. I could get you fourteen days detention in the Citadel in Dover for what you did! You're being let off this time!'

The Dover Citadel was a terrible threat, for my closest friend in the Battery, Norman Pace, was awarded fourteen days there for what had become a custom and was not regarded as a crime. It was to travel overnight from Dover although your leave-pass did not begin until the following morning. It happened, however, that because of German air-raids paralysing the relief agencies, a mandate banning night travel to London had been posted on the Battery notice board, and warnings given that punishment for disobeying this order would be severe.

Bombardier Pace and Gunner Albert Cant chose to disregard the instruction. At Shepherdswell railway station, because the London train was about to move off, they boarded without exchanging their rail warrants, which meant that in London they had to report to the rail transport office for tickets. Inside were two military policemen who examined their passes, and so they were caught. On rejoining the unit seven days later, both were charged with absence without leave. They were taken to the cells in Dover Castle, and there had a humiliating time, being marched up and down the hill in full marching order morning and night, and between times were given degrading tasks to do, such as burnishing filthy lavatory buckets. Food was deplorable, and to sleep on they had wooden beds and pillows to match.

When Pace returned, having lost two stripes as well as a bit of weight, he said to me with feeling that he would rather die than repeat the punishment. As for Albert Cant, he said it was, 'damn-all. I'd break their hearts before they break mine.' Albert was a happy-go-lucky Yorkshireman who was never downhearted. Pace, an excellent surveyor and sensitive artist in water colour was deeply wounded by his experience and never again put a foot wrong, which is the objective of such punishment.

In 1941 I acted out of character by volunteering to be considered as air crew when it was announced that there was a dire shortage of pilots and navigators due to the losses of 1940 and the stepping up of air attacks. When interviewed in London I was honest when I said I was applying not out of inclination to fly an aeroplane but had put my name forward out of a sense of duty. It seemed to satisfy the interviewing board, for within minutes I was in a small office by myself and working fast on an intelligence test. To each question you simply put a tick for yes, or a cross for no.

Many of my answers were pure guesses, but I got a pass, and within a short time was posted to No. 9 Initial Training Wing at Stratford-on-Avon on the understanding that either I passed out in six weeks or would be transferred back to my army unit. So from army khaki I went into RAF blue and wore a whiteflash on my cap to indicate air-crew under training.

It was a tough course, with little free time to enjoy the market town on the River Avon where Shakespeare was born, with much marching and drilling and physical training as well as swotting to cope with exercises on navigational problems. It was difficult for one with my limited education, but thanks to a Bachelor of Science by the name of Arthur Pearson, who shared my billet, I got a fair amount of coaching, but feared I would fail for I was never able to give my best in examinations.

Pearson was optimistic on my passing out, but I failed without ever seeing an aeroplane, and while successful candidates drew their flying kit in preparation for moving out to Rhodesia or Canada for air training, I was posted to Brighton for eventual return to the artillery.

I kept in touch with Pearson. After becoming a navigator he was on night flying practice in Britain when his plane coming into land crashed. He was thrown out of the astro dome clear of the flames which burned the crew to death. His own injured leg left him with a permanent limp, but he served his time in the RAF as a sergeant navigation instructor. After the war, in a tearoom in Glasgow, I met one of my cadet comrades who had risen to the rank of squadron leader and who gave me news of some of those we had known. 'You were well out of it, fate did you a good turn. Most were shot down.'

For me in the late autumn of 1941 it was return to the army, via Brighton and St John's Wood RAF holding units, first stop the Metropole Hotel to await posting, and of course, fatigue jobs for me and other failed cadets. Washing the stairs one day, and putting in an extra bit of vigour as a sergeant approached, he called us to desist. 'Can any of you write shorthand and transcribe what you've written on the typewriter?' he asked and got no reply.

I was bold enough to ask if it was a genuine question, and if so what was involved. 'It's to report a court-martial and record the proceedings.' I said I didn't know if my 120 words a minute would be equal to such a demanding job, but if they couldn't get anyone better I would do it. I did it, fearful I might not be able to read my shorthand afterwards, but there were no complaints about the finished work and I was employed thereafter in the office until my posting to London came.

My arrival there was timely, for within a day or two I was reading with interest a notice inviting potential dance musicians to put their names forward for audition, stating instrument and experience. So down went my number, rank and name, and a few days later I was one of a number of jazz men grouped round a piano. Music was handed out. I tapped out four beats to the bar at fox-trot tempo and we were away. They were lively players. A few more numbers at different tempos and we were told we would hear the outcome later.

Very shortly afterwards I was rehearsing with the band, and enjoying very much being behind the drums again, playing at a few public functions, until, like all things that seem too good to last, it came to an end when the army demanded me back. That band, with the recruitment later of some top London professionals, was to become well known as the famous 'Squadronaires'.

I must say I was very touched by the welcome from my old buddies in the 5th Super Heavy Battery. In fact I was instantly promoted to lance bombardier in the survey unit. Better still I had the luck to get leave at the same time as Matt, and off we went to Ben Nevis and the Mamores for a few days in the superb winter conditions of spring snow and sunshine. It was March 1942 and I found Matt much more talkative as a soldier than he had been as a civilian.

In the October following our climb, General Montgomery was fielding 1,029 tanks, 1,451 anti-tank, 908 field medium guns and 195,000 men against Rommel in the second North African battle at Alamein. It was in that fierce action which swept the Germans out of Egypt that Matt was wounded and, in January 1944, landed in Italy at Anzio with the Scots

Guards where they held a position until their ammunition ran out and was among the few survivors to be taken prisoner.

As for me, soldiering in England, and seeing the break-up of the 2nd Super Heavy Regiment, I was one of the remnants posted to the 168 Medium Regiment RA, encamped in a collection of long black huts in delightful parkland near Ipswich and with that unit I moved to Tilbury for embarkation. Such was the congestion at the port however, to get us out of the way we were given two weeks' embarkation leave – an unexpected bonus at the beginning of June when the Highlands are at their best. One night at home in Glasgow, and off I went on the Inverness train, bound for Lairg in Sutherland. There I continued north in the Durness mail-bus, disembarking under the rocky peak of Ben Loyal.

I had never been here before, but Matt had told me of an empty house situated between Ben Loyal and Ben Hope, on the edge of a small birch-clad lochan. The house was furnished, he had told me, but was used only in the lambing season, and to get in I need do no more than insert a knife-blade to undo the window snib. By the time I was doing that, the sun was setting in streamers of gold and for weird music I had the long-drawn-out wailings of a red throated diver – for me heavenly music.

I won't labour my three delightful days of solitude below the furthest north 3,000-foot peak on the Scottish mainland, from whose top I could look out to the farthest Hebrides and the northern isles of Orkney and Shetland. The rocky tops of Ben Loyal I took in on the same day as I climbed Ben Hope, then I made off next morning across trackless country for Strathmore, where I knew I would find a footpath leading over a high pass to Loch Stack.

On that long and hard traverse I had every kind of weather, from rain to hail, with thunder and lightning at its worst on top of the pass so I was drenched when I got to a house marked 'Airdchuillin' on the map and had the luck to meet face to face a tweedy figure with a salmon rod in his hand, just about to go out on the loch for a cast. I told him where I had come from, that I was on leave from the army, and wondered if there was any chance of being put up for the night.

He didn't say no, but there was a reservation. His daughter had gone to Inverness to bring his wife back from hospital, and as he was speaking a car came into view on his gravel road. I stood back as he helped his wife into the house, feeling very much in the way on such an occasion. I was invited inside. Mrs Scobie welcomed me warmly, her daughter showed me a lovely bedroom. Soon the son came in from the hill, and I count the days that followed as amongst the happiest of my life.

The father John was head stalker for the Duke of Westminster. Son Billy in his teens was shepherding the hills. His sister looked after the house, and in the evenings we played ping pong, or we got out the chess board. As for food, I'd never tasted better trout than those from the waters of Loch

Stack, caught and eaten the same day. The mountains here, peaks of the Reay Forest, are among the barest in Britain, Lewisian gneiss capped with Cambrian quartzite and the low ground, scalped to the bone and riddled with innumerable lochs, gives the impression that the glaciers have only recently melted. In the mornings I was awakened by the ringing cries of greenshank and looking out of the window could watch black throated divers. In the days I was here I climbed everything within range including the 1,000-foot face of Creag Dionard.

Very reluctantly I left this happy family for the long journey by road and rail to Glasgow to have one night with my mother before returning to Tilbury. It was mid-evening and my mother's face was full of concern as she blurted out the moment I was through the door, 'Thank God you're home. The police have hardly been off the door; they've been looking for you in Skye. You've to report to them immediately.'

So round I went to the police office, gave my name to the sergeant, who put a call through to the Adjutant of the 55th Anti-Tank Regiment, and handed the receiver to me. After a few blistering words of rebuke for not leaving an address where I could be contacted, he was mollified when I told him how it came about that I was unable to do so, dossing out among the hills and far from any human contacts.

Now he gave me my orders. 'You'll report to Gosforth Park, New-castle. The Rail Transport Officer in Glasgow will change your rail warrant. How soon can you get here?' I asked if tomorrow would be all right as it was now evening and I had just arrived home after a long journey. To that he replied, 'You are granted a forty-eight-hour extension, that is two days from now.' No wonder I came away smiling! Back in the unit the squaddies were calling me a 'jammy bugger', which I could hardly deny, for they had been recalled after only a few days at home.

Gosforth Park had a truly rural feeling about it, lovely trees, a large marshy pond good for birds, a grassy meadow for parade ground, and comfortable huts for transit soldiers like us. One morning as I was crossing the parade ground I heard my name rapped out by the commanding voice of the Sergeant Major, and immediately stiffened to attention like a well-trained pointer dog.

Granite-faced, and nearly six and a half feet tall, he looked me up and down, while I did a quick mental check on myself. 'Did I need a haircut; were my boots shining enough; had I forgotten to put on my anklets-web; was my cap too jauntily set?' Crisply he said: 'Do you see that building over there. That is to be our "Quiet Room" for the time we are here. You are to be in charge of it. Every morning you'll go and collect the newspapers that are on order. Bring them back to that room and read them.'

With difficulty I prevented myself from smiling. 'Is this some kind of sarcasm?' I was wondering. He continued, 'I want you to cut out from the daily papers the most interesting bits of war news, and pin them up on a big

36

map board of the battle fronts, so that the men see the state of the war and read the latest reports and stories. You will also be responsible for attaching any amendments to the military manuals in the bookcase. You are excused parades and you'll get a fatigue party every morning to keep the place neat and clean. Any questions?'

I was too overcome to ask any. It seemed too good to be true, but the cushy job lasted only three weeks, and as the 'Quiet Room Boy' I suffered a lot of good-natured leg-pulling. The call to Tilbury came suddenly, and this time we were whisked across the Channel for Belgium, from where I was posted to the 79th Field Regiment of the 52nd Lowland Division. This Scottish regiment had been trained for mountain warfare, but found themselves fighting below sea-level at Walchern Island at the Scheld Estuary which had been flooded in 1944 to halt the German advance.

My war was in Fred Karno's army compared to Matt's in the Scots Guards, whose training schedule would have killed me, I think, swimming rivers in Lochaber, night marching over the Galloway hills in full kit, practising unarmed combat and house to house fighting. Down in Shepherdswell he reckoned it was real cushy, but this was to change as the imminence of a full-scale invasion of Britain faded and the accent was on offence not on defence. Seldom was our unit complete, so many of us, including me, were sent away on courses. I remember the first one well, not so much because of what I learned about driving all the vehicles I would be likely to encounter on active service, but of what happened at Uxbridge where the course was held.

It was tea-time when I entered the barracks, and anxious not to miss it, I dumped my kit-bag and followed some cap-less soldiers who had the purposeful look of hungry men. Peeping in the door through which they went I saw ATS girls ladling out platefuls of food. I strode boldly in, got service with a smile and sat down at an empty table to enjoy the scoff. Soon I had company, my neighbour asking me conversationally if I was on the course. I gave a non-committal nod, glancing round as fresh arrivals entered the dining hall, and for the first time noticed they were all military policemen.

I was in bad company. How was I going to escape undetected, for they were all big impressive-looking men and I wasn't? Very gently I slid out of my seat as if I were going back to the serving table, turned smartly for the door expecting any moment to be denounced as an impostor. But as I got back to my kit-bag my anxiety gave way to laughter as off I went to locate the place where I should be.

In Britain, earlier that year of 1942, the United States 8th Air Force established air bases for their B.17 Flying Fortresses and B.24 Liberators, and immediately a series of daylight operations against targets in France and other parts of German-occupied Europe were mounted. As the 2nd Super Regiment was a defence force, and was now more or less unnecessary we were gradually dismembered, and buzz-bombs and V rockets were falling round us before the last of us were posted abroad, so I never ever saw the whites of the enemy's eyes although we were at the receiving end of all they could throw at Dover.

So it was not until 1945 I crossed the Channel after many false-alarms.

I was in Belgium only from June until August and grew fond of it, especially as I had enough time off to make a study of its bird life. My German diary begins with the words:

Today I entered Germany via Venlo and Wesel to a billet in Munster. Overcast skies and a smirr may have been responsible for an increased feeling of depression, though the warning 'Heaven can Wait. 15 m.p.h.' as we crossed the Rhine, raised a smile as we eased across a temporary bridge that looked down on scrap-iron of the original bridge half-sunk in the river.

At Wesel, unhappy looking POWs were trying to clear a road through the flattened city. Refugees were everywhere, bundles on their backs or on bicycles. Munster, when we came to what was left of it, after a 1,000 bomber raid, had the bad smell of rotting flesh. We stopped at a ruin to brew tea and have a snack. Out of the debris children appeared like rabbits from below ground, dozens of them, begging for food. They got some too. We were glad to move on and find our billet.

Right now as I write this I am seated in the sitting room of one of the few remaining houses in Munster. My room is hung with a crucifix of Christ on the Cross; a framed picture of a Luftwaffe pilot hung with black, has a certificate below it showing some sort of distinction for bravery. The woman occupying the house has eight of a family, and quite proudly took me upstairs to see her youngest of eight children, in bed. 'Eight is no goot,' she said sadly. I go on Guard duty at 2.30 am.

My entry for 27.11.45 records:

Two days ago we arrived at No. 9 Civil Internment Camp, Badlippspringe, a place of misery and human suffering; miles of barbed wire and monotonous huts, utterly devoid of beauty, scarred with litter and debris. Guard and escort duties is our lot, 48 hours on and half a day off, then the same again. It is a life of grim monotony and bitter cold in this desolate spot which gets every wind that blows.

The civil prisoners get two cups of coffee, an eighth of a two pound loaf, and one bowl of watery soup daily. The hard floor and two blankets is their bed. Each day there are a few deaths. I know all of them have done evil deeds but you can't help feeling pity for them. They are such clever people. From scraps of wood and metal they make beautiful toys and working models, and trade them with the guards for extra rations – forbidden, of course, but the business goes on.

With demobilisation in the pipeline, some of these ingenious toys these civilian prisoners made were good keepsakes for soldiers to take home with them. Some cushy jobs were being vacated too, and I was lucky enough to step in to a ration clerk's job in the Quartermaster Stores. It was not only a nice easy task but I had a billet in a room for two with the other clerk, and an old Wehrmacht prisoner as a servant. We called him Joseph after Goebbels, the arch Nazi.

Our job was to work out the daily ration strength, and submit figures for our own troops, Russians who were also on our strength, German prisoners of war engaged on fatigue duties, and civilian prisoners. Each of these had a different entitlement. When the amounts were added up and approved, our duty then was to drive to Munster, collect the stores and allocate them.

When the work was done I was free to explore the countryside within easy reach of the camp, where there was a river with kingfishers and grey herons, and woods with jays, crested tits and crossbills in them; further afield within easy Jeep range were fine heathland hills, with wide views to the Wesser Mountains. I'd also found a fellow climber with interests much the same as my own. He was a music-lover too, so we made the most of concerts and operas provided for the troops.

Then one day in January I was given the good news that I was on demob list and soon was entrained for Calais, destination Redford Barracks outside Edinburgh below the Pentlands. For the only time in my army service I had to strip to the buff for a lady doctor, who flashed me the quickest look of any medical officer who has ever inspected me. After that I collected a civilian uniform, pinstripe lounge suit and soft hat. Then bearing the new rigout in its cardboard box I went off home, feeling that if the army had done me no good, it had done me no harm.

3

Stepping Out

Ah. Fredome is a noble thing!
Fredome mayse man to haiff liking.

So wrote the fourteenth-century poet John Barbour in the *Bruce*.
Although February is not the best time to take a holiday I was off with
my demob pay with a young Royal Navy officer whose ship was being
refitted in Rosyth and who was free until he was recalled. So off we went
with camping kit, food and climbing gear by train to Beauly, and by Royal
Mail service to the head of Glen Strathfarrar to Monar Lodge where a deer
stalker by the name of Tommy Fleming lived surrounded by high snowy
peaks. My hope was that he would give us the use of his bothy.

He did. He also gave us the use of another bothy half-way up the length
of Loch Monar, where there are no roads, and our intention was to break
out over the hills to the Kyle of Lochalsh railway when our food ran out.
The weather could hardly have been stormier; gale-force winds, fierce
blizzards; and sometimes we had to crawl on our bellies when we were
unable to stand against the storm on the tops at over 3,000 feet. It was
tough on Charlie, fresh from the sea. For him, though, the hardest struggle
was sinking deeply at every step with a heavy pack on his back to get from
Loch Monar to Achnashellach railway station.

Then we went to Torridon, to Liathach and Beinn Alligin, back-packed
through to Shieldaig where we stocked up with food, and by good luck
were given a lift by a vehicle unloading stores, and dropped off at Kishorn
in Applecross on a gurly day of blowing snow. What we needed was a roof
over our heads, so I knocked on the door of a farmer who showed us a
rickety barn full of hay. We dropped our kit immediately and set off to do
battle with the rock and ice of Coire na Poite of Ben Bhan, now renowned
for hard winter climbing although little was known about that in 1946. It
was dark after we got down from a hard bit of climbing and an even more
difficult retreat, for we had failed to finish it.

Climbing was out of the question next day, and we had thought of
moving but did not which was a good job, for we were wakened in the
morning by a loud banging on the door of our bothy and a strong voice
asking if there was anyone up there by the name of Lieutenant Charles

40

Downie. It was the postman with a telegram ordering the sleepy Charlie to return to his ship immediately. 'Imagine them finding me here!' he exclaimed as he read it. But in the vicinity of Torridon and Shieldaig in February our presence would have been noted, the driver of the vehicle that gave us the lift would have been consulted, and phone-calls made, so it wasn't so mysterious.

Off went Charlie to Strathcarron to catch the train for Glasgow, while I caught the train from Strathcarron to Kyle of Lochalsh for the ferry to Skye, travelling by bus from there to Sligachan to finish at Glen Brittle House with the MacRaes whose lives are lived below the best peaks of the Cuillin.

In Skye, after snow and frost, the Cuillin ridge was in truly alpine condition, and after a day in Coire Lagan I embarked on a traverse in deteriorating weather from Sgurr Dearg to Sgurr a Mhaidaidh, without crampons and nicking steps easily all the way with the axe, the weathered snow was so perfect. It was a marvellous mountaineering day, even if the visibility was restricted; perhaps not quite so good as the one I'd had on Sgurr nan Gillean by the pinnacles a few days before. At the An Dorus gap offering a quick descent, I should have picked my way down. Instead of that I glissaded, that is let myself slide like a man on skis, lost control, went head over heels, and losing my axe slid down, sometimes head first, sometimes feet first, and realised I had damaged my shoulder when I came to rest.

From An Dorus it is quite a long way back to Glen Brittle. I felt weak, but hoped to enter the house unobserved and look normal when I came down.

Nancy MacRae, however, came through the door as I went in, took a look at me and said, 'You've hurt your shoulder and torn your jacket. Look at yourself in the hall mirror!' I did, and saw one shoulder was sagging, and that I looked very pale. Next morning Euan MacRae drove me to Broadford Hospital for an X-ray. The sagging was due to torn muscles, and that very good friend drove me all the way home to Glasgow to meet up with a very concerned mother.

The injury was useful, in that I now fished out all the notebooks I had filled during the years I was in the army, and rewrote them into the manuscript for an illustrated book about my wanderings in Scotland. By the time this was done I could use my typewriter to turn out twenty chapters and title them *Highland Days*. I then consulted the books of Seton Gordon, saw that his publisher was Cassell and Co Ltd, London, and off to them I sent my manuscript, hoping for the best, but fearing the worst.

What now? Time I got myself a job if only to appease my mother who couldn't understand this 'write, write, writing'. I went before an assessment panel at Jordanhill Training College for Teachers, was found suitable, but was informed that it would be a few months before I could be admitted. For something more immediate I went to the Army Rehabilitation Centre, and within days was directed to the Ordnance Survey, Dalkeith House, Edinburgh.

It was in Edinburgh that I faced a dilemma. During my army service in Kent I had become friendly with a Land Army girl in Canterbury, dark-haired, fresh-complexioned and with a lovely shy smile which showed beautiful teeth. She was the daughter of a farm labourer, and I had a kind of calf love for her. Nothing ever happened between us. We went for walks. Both of us were virgins when we parted. Our final meeting took place when she came all the way from Kent to see me in Edinburgh.

I had never talked about marriage with her. In Kent, once when I was due to go on leave she suggested coming to Scotland and spending it with me. I put her off, because I wanted to go climbing and not moon about with her. In Edinburgh I had to be truthful and be as blunt as I could about domesticity being not for me. I won't forget her stricken face. I have often wondered what became of this simple, trusting girl.

As for the Ordnance Survey, it was not unlike being in the army, in that you were always on the move working unsocial hours, mostly with men who had been regulars in the Royal Engineers, but were now civilians. Highly trained as topographers they were a pleasure to work with, always putting the job before themselves.

Within two weeks the OS posted me to a triangulation team in Glasgow engaged on hill territory well known to me, so I quickly earned a reputation of having a good eye for country. There is nothing like being in with the bricks! Also I liked climbing hills and was used to vertical ladders leading to rooftops of high buildings where Trig points may be situated. Even so in the kind of weather we get in Britain it was a patience-testing, cold and sometimes wet job, waiting for visibility. Our Chief was Tom Statham, who chose to begin work in the afternoon, so as to have all his observation points lit by beacons as darkness fell, and carry out his theodolite observations when refraction was lowest. Apart from the weight of the beacon lamp, each was lit by a twelve-volt battery. The theodolite itself weighed forty pounds. So once every lamp was in position Tom inclined to stick out any bad weather unless conditions became completely hopeless.

However a better job was coming my way, when I was posted to be one of a four-man triangulation reconnaissance team whose task was to decide where future triangulation pillars should be built in areas where the recce had been abandoned because of the outbreak of war in 1939. This took me all over Britain, from Suffolk and Norfolk, Leeds and Birmingham, to a summer and winter in the English Lake District. I lodged at Buttermere and discovered that these valleys have a secret life that the tourist knows little about.

It was while working on this difficult triangulation block that I received a weighty parcel one day, its sender Cassell & Company, London. There was only one thing it could be, *Highland Days*. My book was out at last, and I fondled the six free copies, pleased that in spite of economy standards the finished production was reasonable. The photographs were all by me, except one of the Tower Ridge of Ben Nevis by Douglas Scott; the clearly drawn maps accompanying the text were by his pal, Rob Anderson, climbers I had first met on the Campsies. Douglas was deeply interested in wild-life and photography. His influence on me was to have more bearing on my future than I would ever have supposed when I used his photograph in my book.

Although Douglas and I had lost touch during the war, it happened that both of us had been admitted to the Scottish Mountaineering Club before hostilities ended, and when we met up after demob, he was brimful of news about a trek in the Himalaya he had managed to snatch while soldiering in India with the Royal Corps of Signals. Travelling alone and camping in Garhwal he had come face to face with the sharp peaks of Kumaon which that great mountain explorer, Dr Tom Longstaff, has described as the most beautiful part of the whole Himalayan chain. In 1907 from a camp in the Rishi Gorge, Longstaff with two Italian mountain guides, Alexis Brocherel and his younger brother Henri, had penetrated the box-canyon of the Rishi Gorge, put a tent up at 17,450 feet on Trisul and in a single push of 6,000 feet reached its summit at 23,360 feet. Their climb set a world-record height climbed by man not to be exceeded until 1930.

That trio were the first human beings ever to look into the inner sanctuary of Nanda Devi, having just before that made a trek of 1,000 miles across the Himalaya. On this ambitious journey which began in 1905 the trio achieved another record on another 23,000-foot peak, Gurla Mandhata, when high on the mountain they were swept down 3,000 feet in an avalanche and in two minutes picked themselves up, minus hats and ice-axes and broken crampons but otherwise were only scratched and bruised.

It happened that in 1948 who should be Principal Guest at the Scottish Mountaineering Club dinner but the great man himself, Longstaff, a tiny elf with a Van Dyke reddish beard and sparkling eyes. He radiated such dynamism it was hard to believe that he had been born in 1875, had received the Founder's Medal of the Royal Geographical Society in 1928, and after forty-seven years in the Alpine Club was now its President. He could look back on twenty visits to the Alps, six to the Himalaya, one to the Caucasus, five to the Arctic and two to the Rockies. He had taken up medicine because he judged it would be the profession of the greatest use to him in a life of travel. At that moment I didn't know how useful he was going to be to us. What fascinated me was what he had to say about Scotland where he had decided to spend his last years. As I can't remember what he actually said, I shall quote from his autobiography on which he was engaged at that time and which was published in 1950. It ends with his view of Coigach in Wester Ross:

A true mountain country, aloof from lowlands, but within sight and sound of the sea. There is spaciousness here. Light and colour are always changing on hill and water. One is conscious of the continual movement in nature, in the sea, in running water and in the wind that drives the clouds before it in profusion across the sky. In winter, Atlantic gales and furious volleys of rain or sudden splintering hail keep the air alive and exciting . . .

Here our mountains are small, but they are steep sided, individual in colour, form and texture. They stand proudly in their own right. Clouds sweep over them. Snow turns them white. In fact as I see it they are true mountains. Half an hour's walk up the hill-side and we change the world about us in all its perspective. Seaward the Summer Isles are spread like a chart below. Away to the west across the Minch lies the long horizon of the Hebrides. On a clear day the peaks of the Cuillin can be picked out seventy miles to the south-west. The whole eastern skyline is of mainland mountains. They start with the rugged sandstone bosses of Torridon; then Slioch, over against Loch Maree; and above Gruinard Bay rise the spikes of An Teallach. The five tops of Coigach build a massy block in the south-east. Then comes Stac Polly with its cockscomb crest and strange lobster claws of rock; the crown of Cul Mor and the massive Atlantic watch-tower of Suilven. These peaks guard a wide sanctuary of moor and loch of which over 100 square miles is uninhabited. No man sleeps there. Beyond Edrachillis Bay rise the hills behind Scourie; and beyond those we can see nearly to Cape Wrath. And behold the sky, an hundred miles of it. So many things going on at once; clouds of every pattern with play of colour on sea and land; here bright sunlight, there a black storm. An enchanted land.

So I have come back there to live.

At that time I had no experience of mountains other than those of Britain, and I knew that if I was to achieve my ambition of being a mountain explorer I should go to the Alps, learn about glaciers and hazards of crevasses and ice-falls, subject myself to the rarefied air of the heights and learn to read avalanche dangers associated with permanent snow, affected by frost and sun. So in early July of 1948, off I flew to Geneva with two other climbers in the direction of Arolla. I didn't stay with them, because they had a lot of time on their hands. I had only a fortnight, but they introduced me to the chief mountain guide of Evolena, Pierre Maurys.

I wanted his advice, since with currency restrictions then in force, I had a mere £35 of an allowance. He smiled and nodded his head comfortingly when I told him that I wasn't trying to engage him, but wondered if he could direct me where best to go to find peaks suitable for me to climb on my own. The date was 11th July and none of the highest summits had been climbed that season because of unsettled weather and heavy snowfall.

I told him something about my background, and learned that he had been to the Lake District as guest of John Sugden, a member of the Fell and Rock Club, the object of his visit to gain some conversational practice in speaking English. The hotel in Les Hauderes where we talked was managed by his wife, and the pair were joint owners. As he ordered morning coffee, he excused himself to make a telephone call. When he came back he said, 'I have been talking to Madam Bierans in Chamonix. She is a Dutch lady who has engaged me for the whole season, but is playing golf until the weather gets better. I can go with you to the Dent Blanche if you wish, and climb with you as a friend. But first I must go to church, then at 2 o'clock we shall set off to the Caban Rossier. You stay here for family lunch. My wife will attend to the food we need for the climb.'

I could hardly believe my good fortune as we waved goodbye to his wife and two wee girls for the stony path zig-zagging ever upwards, past alpine meadows bright with flowers for grey moraines giving way to glacier ice where we were in shrouding mist and sinking into deeper and deeper snow. The plod seemed never-ending but at 8 pm we were at the caban, and soon bedded down 7,000 feet above our starting point.

At 4 am I heard the ring of Pierre's alarm watch. A meagre breakfast, and by 5.30 we were tying on the rope and embarking on the shadowed ridge, while all around us summits of peaks glowed in the red light of sunrise. Below us the glaciers had the soft sheen of satin. Technical climbing began almost immediately on iced rocks and frozen snow. Gaining height we were in a world of mountains, for level cloud filled all the deep valleys.

We could see now that the ridge ahead was in fierce condition, hung with snow cornices, the rock face hidden in new snow. It was a place from which a French party had retired the previous day because of avalanche danger. Pierre, who knew the face well, chose a rightward traverse, to the edge of the Grand Gendarme, whose pinnacle it was his intention to climb as being the safest way. Anchored to a good rock spike, I could take in the view behind me, the Matterhorn, Obergabelhorn, Zinal Rothorn, Weisshorn, Mishabel, the Oberland peaks and the Mont Blanc range.

I had read that of all the mountains in the world, none surpasses the high European Alps in form or variety, and that no other mountains can provide better training to the aspiring alpinist, or offer sterner tests in difficulty for the experienced. As yet I had no yardstick to judge the truth of this, for this was my very first encounter with glaciated peaks rising so high above deep valleys. Looking back, I realise how very lucky I was to be climbing with such a man as Pierre Maurys and to have the whole mountain to ourselves.

Most parties avoid the Grand Gendarme. Watching Pierre on its airy crest, his position would have satisfied the most earnest seeker of the sensational. Exposed above a great void, he had to remove a glove with his teeth at one point and, hanging on by one hand, tuck his ice-axe through the strap of his rucksack to leave his hands free to surmount the vertical crest of ice-veneered holds. He was smiling when I joined him and, pointing out the way ahead, said he was sure we would make the top.

Snow cornices and ice-plastered rocks, some rock climbing on clean stuff, more snow cornices, and at last, ahead of us, a fragile leaf of snow projecting into space – the summit. What a place for a photograph! But I needed my hands to protect Pierre in case of a slip, for the solid ridge was not easy to locate beneath the mass of snow.

We shook hands on top: 'I congratulate you on the ascent of Dent Blanche,' said Pierre, but it should have been the other way round. Pierre was the man to be congratulated after that bold lead. The half-hour spent on top was delightful. We had tea, beautiful stuff out of the flask, bread and raw bacon, and an orange, while all the time Pierre pointed out mountains, naming them until I could take in no more. One could only sit and let the awe of such a first Alpine experience sink into one's being.

So ended my first ascent of a 14,000-foot Alpine peak, and my discovery that climbing above 10,000 feet took more out of me than on my homeland hills. To my delight I found I was to go high again, when Pierre telephoned Madam Bierans that evening and she said she would be playing golf until the end of the week. Over a celebratory bottle of wine he said: 'Tomorrow we leave early, with food for an overnight stay in a hut. We leave our rucksacks below the Douves Blanc arête, go up by a route that I was the first to make, descend by an easy way back to our rucksacks, and go on to the caban.'

It didn't quite work out that way, as it was snowing and visibility was nil as we sat below what Pierre said was the arête. We sat for an hour swithering before Pierre decided to rope up and start what could be compared to a hard Scottish rock climb in bad wintry weather. I also had an introduction to artificial climbing and the use of combined tactics to overcome holdless sections in slippery chimneys. The hardest move involved lassoing an iron spike which Pierre had hammered in when he made the first ascent a few years before. Once the rope was over it, my job was not to hoist Pierre up, but keep him in balance on small holds at a high angle by maintaining tension as he moved up to the spike where he could climb free.

It was a very sustained route in steadily worsening conditions, and darkness was falling as we reached easy ground from where Pierre led me down and located our half-buried rucksacks, after a search. First thing was to get out a lantern and begin the long descent to Arolla, for there was no hope of finding the route to the hut in these conditions. It was midnight when we reached the valley and a hotel where we were welcomed with a hot meal and given beds for the night.

Arolla had no road to it in those days, only a track used by mules, and in the morning it was still snowing as we rustled along it back to Les Hauderes. The rustling was due to an arrangement of newspapers which Pierre had shaped into under-clothing to put on below our sodden garments.

Pierre, who was the Chief Guide in his area, did not confine his climbing to his own valley, but led ambitious clients anywhere in the Alps they wanted to climb. One of his favourite mountains was the Piz Badile in the Bregalia, where, in years to come, I had bad news of him. It was in the 60s, and I was in an Alpine hut in this range whose guardian was a mountain guide performing this duty while waiting for a broken leg to become strong again.

Talking with him as to what route he could recommend, I gave him a little of my background so that he could judge my competence. When I told him that Pierre Maurys had taken me up my two first Alpine climbs, and subsequently we had done some ski-ing together, I saw his face change at the mention of the guide. 'I have some bad news you can not have heard. Pierre was struck by lightning on the Innomata Ridge of Mont Blanc. His client, a Belgian, was missing and the rope had disappeared. It is believed he must have fallen trying to rope-down off the ridge. His body has not been found. Pierre was my very good friend and a guide of the top class who had done many many very hard climbs all over the Alps.' Pierre was fifty-eight, eight years older than me when he died in 1964. He was a man who lived for climbing.

As I write about the Swiss Alps there comes to me a vision of the Lake of Thun at Easter, the flash of apple blossom decking its shores and the pale silver of peaks poised an immense height above the train as it rushes along to Interlaken where you change trains for Grindelwald, to be ratcheted upwards through ravines and crocus-studded banks, then suddenly above you is the 7,000-foot immensity of the Wetterhorn, blocking the head of the valley. Even two nights without sleep, and the discomforts of third-class travel, could not diminish that impression of 1949 when I was on two weeks' leave from the Ordnance Survey.

Other members of our ski-mountaineering party were already in Grindelwald, and I soon located them and set to assembling fourteen days' food for four in preparation for an early departure the following morning to the Jungfraujoch. Our loads felt alarmingly heavy, but meantime we needed sleep. All too soon we were cramming skis and rucksacks aboard a train that climbs higher than any other in the world, via a vein hacked out of the interior of the Eiger, but with cut-outs for passengers to view the 6,000 feet of its infamous North Wall, scene of many tragedies.

How strange to emerge at last on a railway station like any normal one, except that this one has a magic exit at 11,400 feet, an ice tunnel that leads horizontally, but opens on nothing but uncompromising steep mountainside falling abruptly to the Aletsch Glacier, the largest ice-stream in Europe. It was our route down to a cross-roads of glaciers known as Concordia. But between us and its gentle gradient was the formidably steep drop from the tunnel which would require careful control in descent with heavy rucksacks. It was hard to know whether we should put skis on first, or shoulder the rucksacks before bending down to do so. That decided, we slid off in the snow-plough position, keeping the speed down by gentle turns on the uncompromising slope, then it was bliss to coast happily for seven effortless kilometres, until above us we saw our goal, the alpine hut perched on a rock, reached by steep ladders. Now we could lighten our loads by making a depot of half our food.

Rucksacks lightened, we turned our faces south-west towards another hut, the Hollandia, a 2,000-foot climb above us, and a hard push for bodies newly out from Britain, with ahead of us the bulging ice-falls and hanging seracs of the Aletschorn. It was a welcome moment when we topped the final rise and saw the cabin perched on the lip of a rock-ridge as the peaks flushed pink in the alpenglow.

Soup was uppermost in our minds as we entered the hut at 10,000 feet. It was packed with Easter weekend Swiss skiers, and all were up before dawn to climb a peak and descend on its frosty powder snow before the hot sun slowed it down. Skins fastened to the soles of our skis for climbing, we went for the Mittaghorn, by an ice-fall, to reach a crest of snow-powder so dry that it squeaked below our skis.

It was bliss up there, looking down to the soft blues of the Lauterbrunnen Valley, and letting the eyes range round the panorama of summits, Dent Blanche, Matterhorn, Weisshorn, Mont Blanc and its neighbours. Then off with the skins for the descent, a swoop on light powder, showering like diamonds at every swinging turn of the skis. All too soon we were at the hut, eyeing with pleasure the route we had taken down from the 3,890-metre peak. We had the same conditions next day for the Ebnafluh.

We got the Ebnafluh, but as the Easter skiers disappeared with whoops at the end of a superb three days, up shot the temperature and, roped together in case of hidden crevasses we might not see in such poor light, we made a careful descent to Concordia, and in the morning had a climb on a nearby rock buttress of the Kamm, returning to the hut early to get everything ready for a 4 am rise.

We were away by 5 am, the peaks clear-cut in a starry sky, an alpenglow suffusing the tops with pink as we climbed the great expanse of the glacier narrowing to our pass, the Grunhornluke. My diary records:

No morning since the world began can have been more perfect for the view that lay before us from its crest, snow sparkle underfoot; above us red rocks warm with colour, and the great face of our peak, the Finsteraarhorn, 14,022 ft, highest of the Bernese Alps, in rock, snow and ice, shadowed against a blue-green sky.

To reach it entailed a run down we had been looking forward to, a smooth descent on frozen snow with a surface of the lightest powder that made turning silent and effortless, and all too soon we were at the Finsteraar Hut, one of the remotest in the Oberland.

We wasted no time, dumping our gear. Skins on our skis, we climbed steadily upwards, and made for the Hugisattel to the North Ridge. One of our party did not feel able for the final rock and ice climb ahead. Three of us would not be dissuaded from what looked like a challenging route on a narrow crest exposed to a drop of 3,000 feet on one side. The climb was of the kind that Scottish mountaineers are familiar with in Glencoe and Ben Nevis. The decision to go on was mine, and step-cutting on frozen snow, and clearing rock holds of ice we made height quickly, conscious that clouds were beginning to drop on the mountain, and we were going to need all our time to get down before dark.

We made it, but kept the rope on for descent on skis to the hut, moving cautiously in a heavily crevassed area, and at 7 pm we entered the hut conscious of our good fortune in having had such a rich reward from first light to last. We had snatched it just in time, for snow fell all that night and all of next day and the following night. We had the hut to ourselves, until on the second day the door was thrown open and in came a Swiss guide with two of his clients. Then just before dark a party of four Swiss railwaymen arrived worried because they were due back at work next day, but the bad weather had forced them here when they failed to find the pass they were making for.

All we could do was sit out the bad weather, and it was still snowing when we left the freezing cold Finsteraar Hut for the climb back out, all linked to one rope, each taking a turn at trail breaking in exhaustingly deep snow. Not until we had pushed our way to the welcome of Concordia was there any respite from the gruelling hard work. We even had to push our way downhill so deeply did skis sink in the snow. But how good to get in to where we had food, and ransack it for a communal meal with chance companions who were now friends.

Next day we said our goodbyes, the railway party ski-ing down the glacier which would take them to the Rhône Valley, while ours went exhaustingly uphill to the Jungfraujoch which we had descended so

49

joyfully ten days before. With relief after an hour, we saw the black dots of people moving down towards us, and looked forward to reaching the trail they would have broken. They were a search party looking for the railwaymen, so were delighted to hear our news that they were safe and well.

In Grindelwald, back in the haunts of tourism, it was spring, and a joy in the morning to listen to the songs of wren, tree pipit, redstart and blackbird with a new thankfulness, while all around were the flowers of spring, violet, marsh marigold, crocus, stitchwort, cowslip and a host of others. The face of the Wetterhorn was in shadow, though its high glaciers were agleam, but my sympathies were with the grey rocks of the valley, the scattered chalets of beautifully carved wood, the tinkle of waterfalls, and all the other sounds and sights of mountainlands where people live out their lives. The fullness of life surged in me, and I knew I had the snow-world up there to thank.

My old friend Douglas Scott had been climbing in the Alps too, and when we met up again on one of my Ordnance Survey leaves he had a proposition to put to me. He began his electrifying suggestion this way: 'I think with our background at home and abroad, we're well qualified for an expedition to the Himalaya, travelling light, and living cheaply off the country the way Shipton and Tilman did when they forced a way into the Inner Sanctuary of the Nanda Devi basin by way of the Rishi Gorge in Garhwal. Why don't we organise something *now*, before we get too old?'

He was serious, and came up with the further suggestion that we make it a long trip, go in the spring and return in the autumn, form a partnership and combine photo-journalism and commercial photography to finance other projects. I thought it was a great idea, and said so, but that it would take me a year, maybe two years, to save enough money to finance my share of the trip and have enough to live on while we exploited the results of our travels. Such a trip was exactly in line with my Pelman aspirations, and it was decided that we set off in April 1950. I left it to him to book berths on a ship to Bombay, from where we would take a train to the foot-hills of the Himalaya.

That winter of 1949 I was employed in the Ordnance Survey in Chessington when a letter came to me from Douglas, telling me that three berths had been booked on the SS *Himalaya* for Bombay, the third for Tom MacKinnon, one of the most experienced alpinists in the Scottish Mountaineering Club.

I had hardly time to swallow this news before word came from Douglas that his friend W.H. Murray, author of the much acclaimed book *Mountaineering in Scotland*, wished to join us. This certainly raised the status of what was the first post-war British Himalayan expedition.

4

A Dream Comes True

Events then took a dramatic turn. Bill Murray certainly did not waste time. From him came a sheaf of papers marked Batallion Orders, and outlined what had to be done immediately. My responsibility was 'Food and Transport', lists to be submitted by 2nd March, 1950. They read:

> List all food to be bought in Scotland, estimate quantities for 100 days. Apply to the Ministry of Food for authority to buy butter, dried eggs and cheese. Apply to the Board of Trade for permission to ship rationed goods. Inquire from P & O loading date for SS *Himalaya*. Arrange transport to Tilbury Dock. Estimate number of food sacks required on the march, for grain. Weigh the total food and gear when bought and estimate coolie loads for the journey north from Ranikhet; then ask Mrs Fergusson of Essex House (with whom we arrange to stay for three days) to get an appropriate number of coolies to meet us at Ranikhet on 8th May, and to arrange a bus to meet us at Kathgodam railhead to lift us to Ranikhet by road.

Douglas had the creative role of poring over maps, working out an exploration plan, and listing the equipment needed to carry it out. Our leader, as co-ordinator, was busy writing letters, gathering information from members of the Alpine Club in London and the Himalayan Club in India. He also had to procure an Inner Line Pass without which our mountain plans in the troubled frontier bordering Tibet and western Nepal might come to nothing.

On the business side, since we were financing the expedition ourselves, and three of us were free-lances without jobs to go back to, we made an agreement that any profits made by writing, lecturing or broadcasting should be shared three ways. Bill, a professional writer, was contracted to supply articles to the *Glasgow Herald* during the progress of the expedition. I had a similar contract with the Glasgow *Evening Times*. These articles would be taken by runners to the nearest post-collection points. Our

51

agreement also covered an official book of the expedition to be written by Bill Murray.

As ours was the very first British post-war expedition and food and clothing was rationed we expected there would be much red tape to cut through. Not a bit of it. The interest and the good-will shown from all sides was heartening, suppliers doing their best for us, some refusing payment, and everyone we approached willing to help.

I left my survey job at the end of February and had all March for expedition preparation and packing. One disquieting thought that we could not ignore was that, as yet, the Indian Government had not come up with the required Inner Line Pass, without which Scott's imaginative plan for a 350-mile circuit that would take us close to the Tibet and west Nepal borders would come to nothing. Confident that we had done all we could do, we enjoyed a happy farewell dinner, with toasts wishing us success, from Scottish Mountaineering Clubmates, the venue being the dining room of the sailing ship *Carrick* moored close to the warehouse edging the Clyde where we had done our packing before sending off our cargo to Tilbury for loading on the SS *Himalaya*.

The blackest cloud that ever blotted my horizon came when on arrival at Tilbury to board the ship, I was given the dismaying news that our entire baggage despatched ten days earlier, as directed, had not arrived. A search of the ship's hold revealed it under a mountain of mail-bags. Until then I thought there was a lot to be said for slow-boat by cargo ship which was the Shipton-Tilman mode of travel when they travelled to Bombay to unravel the mysteries of the hitherto unpenetrated upper Rishi Gorge and reached the inner sanctuary of Nanda Devi – the Blessed Goddess.

Safely aboard, and two to a cabin, we could really get to know each other; two of us were tall, two of us small, so Big Tom was burly Tom MacKinnon. Bill was as tall as Tom, but lithe and spare like Douglas Scott who was nearer my height of five feet four inches. Bill had distinguished himself by his enterprise on the steepest and hardest rock and ice climbs pre-war, and his judgement of Douglas was that he was the neatest climber who had ever tied on to his climbing rope. I had climbed with Bill only once, and it was in winter on Ben Lui. I had never climbed with Tom, but had done a fair amount with Douglas. The four of us were in our mid 30s. In the fourteen days it would take to reach Bombay we hoped, by the aid of a language guide to Urdu, to learn enough to be able to communicate with the porters who would carry eighty-pound loads for us.

But there was so much of interest in the voyage, playing deck games, chatting to our fellow passengers, many of them emigrants to Australia in search of a new life, stops at Port Said; then the sail through the Suez Canal, that slower progress was made in Urdu than in a class-room. Bum-boats laden with merchandise streamed out to meet the boat at Port Said and their shouts and gesticulations to attract attention had a lot of humour.

'Hi, you, Mrs Simpson, you want a bag, leather, here it is, how much you give?'

Ashore, one pestering tout pulling at Scott's sleeve drew a sharp rebuke, which initiated the retort: 'Keep the head MacGregor, you're a Scotchman. You look like a spiv!' He drew a laugh from us and grinned hugely.

This was the way to learn about Middle East geography, with Suez behind us and seeing the high mountains of Sinai, enjoying the sight of flying fish skimming the waves and following down the Red Sea with Saudia Arabia to port and the Sudan giving way to Eritrea to starboard. Three days of torrid heat and the barren rocks of Aden welcomed us like a view of the Cuillin peaks of Skye at sunset. In moonlight we drifted into harbour.

Ashore, in the streets, we had never seen so many policemen in such short space, which was reassuring, because of the pestering hands of touts. We escaped by hiring a taxi which took us six miles out to Aden Crater, for a look at the famous water tanks.

Out of the taxi we were immediately taken over by a small Arab boy, who led us up a steep-sided gully, telling us that the giant tanks had been carved from the rocks by King Solomon and rediscovered by the British. Only the top tank held water, as little rain had fallen for seven years. The highlight though was when the guide lost his visitors who suddenly took to the steep rock face for a moonlight climb. Perhaps he wondered if we were trying to escape without paying.

Back at the bazaar hands grabbed at us on a long narrow street seething with bodies and sounds of eastern music from the stalls. In a pub where we went for a much needed drink, we met some Glasgow engineers, one of whom recognised Tom as his dispensing chemist. We were ready for bed when the ship pulled out of harbour, and next day, 600 miles out on the ocean we saw flights of bee-eaters on passage between Arabia and India. The North star was now low on the night horizon and the Southern Cross high. We were just one day from Bombay, reached on 4th May.

Two Himalayan Club members were there to meet us, and thanks to them, we cleared Customs with less trouble than we feared, and that evening were taken thirteen miles out of Bombay to a garden in a fairyland setting of tropical plants lit by lanterns. How welcome the Himalayan Club party made us feel, plying us with refreshments and giving us much helpful advice, and as we were being driven back to our hotel at 1 am, the SS *Himalaya*, ablaze with lights, was pulling out of harbour on its way to Sydney.

Next day more hospitality when a car and driver were put at our disposal by Mr A.R. Leyden who had been so helpful in getting us through Customs, and in whose garden we had been entertained. There was a lot to do before boarding the Frontier Mail train and settling down in a four-berth sleeper second-class carriage. Considering the pandemonium that breaks out at every railway station, we slept pretty well, wakening to find our bedding white with dust.

We looked out on a parched landscape, frizzled by heat, and were glad to purchase a huge block of ice on a melt trace which, placed on the floor of our dusty carriage, reduced the heat inside and kept bottles of ginger beer and tins of fruit cold in contact with the ice. As the landscape became greener numbers of birds increased, and Scott was able to point out to me drongos, minahs, egrets, storks, kingfishers, river cormorants, terns, vultures and many another.

At Muttra Junction on the second day, we had to change trains, and I was stupid enough to supervise the unloading of our luggage minus my hat, and follow the porters to where they deposited it for loading on to the train due to arrive five hours later. By that time in a temperature of 110 degrees I was wilting, my throat was sore and swallowing painful, and my sweat glands had packed up. Tom MacKinnon diagnosed heatstroke.

He got me a first-class berth, gave me medicine to gargle my throat with, but I don't want to remember the night of sickness that followed. At last we came to Kathgodam where, after a two-hour wait, a bus took us seventy miles from the plains to Ranikhet at 6,000 feet into cooler air, and at 6 pm we got to Essex House where we were booked to stay. I went to bed on arrival and a doctor was called. He diagnosed tonsillitis and with four tablets swallowed I was soon asleep. My temperature was 100 degrees.

Voices outside in the morning made me draw the curtains. On the lawn were Tom, Bill and Douglas looking with excitement at the snows of the Himalaya, and I was soon out in my pyjamas marvelling with them at the sight of mountains that looked even higher than our expectations – Douglas pointed out Trisul, Maktoli, Nanda Devi and Nanda Kot. A return to shivering and sweating drove me back to bed, and I was sorry to learn that Douglas too was feeling rather unwell.

For transporting our luggage, we reckoned we would need eighteen porters for the march to the Rishi Gorge, but not more than six to remain permanently with us once we had reached our base of operations. Mrs Fergusson knew the going rates for porters, which we would not try to reduce, but neither could we afford to go too high. Wage bargaining, we discovered, is an art, and when twenty-one Dhotials were lined up for us to select from, Bill assumed at a price agreed, and made his choice from the parade, he discovered the contractor was trying to do the impossible, take the breeks off a Highlandman by pushing up the price. After a short altercation, Bill told them to go away, and that we were not going to be held up to ransom.

In his mind he was sure they would return, and next day he was proved correct when the original agreement, of three rupees per man per day, plus one more for mountain work on snow, was accepted, the men to provide their own food. To buy this food an advance of twenty-five rupees per man was made, departure to be the following morning, 11th May. As for the Inner Line Pass, this matter had been cleared up too. It would be awaiting collection at Joshimath by the time we were in position to pick it up at the post office on the pilgrim route to the source of the Ganges.

The Dhotials were up and ready to go before we were ready. It was great to be marching, but for me it was an endurance test until 15th May, when the Dhotials had a rest day. Bill stayed with them in camp, while Tom, Douglas and I set off at 6.15 am to a dawn chorus of singing birds that reminded me of home, our objective the 13,000-foot summit of Jatropani. Climbing through jungle we cleared the trees at 11,000 feet enjoying tremendous views of the snow peaks framed by the mauve and red of blossoming rhododendrons, a sight that stimulated Weir and Scott, two sick men, to make the top if we could.

The peak was Scottish in character, its gullies snow-filled to near glen level, giving us a little rock scrambling to reach the final ridge which had us breathing hard. By contrast to our feeble efforts Big Tom was moving like a machine, but we made it, only just, while Tom forged on to another two tops on the ridge. It was four in the afternoon when we got back to camp and for the first time I felt hungry, and with enthusiasm tucked into a curry of potatoes, rice and liver of a goat with some of its flesh. The porters had bought the animal for twelve rupees while we were away. They had given Bill a present of a leg, cooked to perfection by Kuar Singh, and suddenly I felt back to normal good health and never looked back. Happy days were now ahead.

Actually Big Tom was the busiest of the sahibs in camp. We could relax but always some locals gathered to be treated for ills, real or imagined. While he was occupied dispensing pills, or painting a sore with iodine, or bandaging a wound, Douglas and I would be out with binoculars looking to see what birds were about the camp, tree creepers, minivets, woodpeckers, monal pheasants, and maybe a soaring lammergeir or griffon vulture, with wing-spans of eight or nine feet, the largest soaring birds in the Himalaya. Eagles are small by comparison.

On our ninth day we faced the last foothill barrier, a tiny gap at over 12,000 feet, the Kuari Pass. Douglas and I talked about getting away at 4 am for the sunrise and a mighty view of the new country ahead. But low clouds and battering rain foiled our plan, which was just as well, for Douglas was not going well on the 2,000-foot climb to the top, and was showing signs of unsteadiness on the steep 6,000-foot descent to the Dhauli Valley where at Tapoban village there is a Rest House we hoped to get into.

We found the Chowkidar – its keeper – but he would not admit us because important sahibs were expected. Our saviour was a Yogi in saffron robes who stormed at the keeper telling him that we were 'Guests of India', and must be admitted. The door was unlocked, and the Holy Man stayed for tea, regaling us with his creed of universal love and of one brotherhood of man. Scott badly needed rest. His temperature was 103 degrees. Tom plied him with medicine which cured his stomach pains, and in twenty-four hours he was up and about.

Our agreement with the Dhotials was that we would retain only six of them as permanent members of the expedition once the first phase of the expedition was over. At Tapoban it looked as if we were going to have a strike on our hands when it came to buying food for the climbing part of the trip. By dismissing all but six, they believed we were not honouring our contract.

We required an interpreter to explain our case, and one was forthcoming when the important sahibs who had booked the Rest House arrived. Mr Hartwell Singh was a friendly agricultural officer who had taken his degree at Edinburgh University, one of a party of four who were happy to occupy the schoolhouse and leave us in possession of their quarters.

Once they were installed and had supper we rounded up the Dhotials, and Mr Singh explained the illogicality of our taking a whole team of porters into the Rishi Gorge to sit there waiting while we climbed snowy mountains. We would choose six for the entire period of the expedition. These would be chosen before the major difficulties of the gorge. When he asked for volunteers wishing to remain with us for the four months, all put up their hands. The strike was over. They would help us into the Rishi.

Now we could give them an advance of pay, and make arrangements for the purchase of 300 pounds of food of the country, flour, lentils and rice, to supplement high altitude rations in the climbing area. My job was to work out what was required from our crates of stores, extract it, repack the crates and nail them up for leaving at Tapoban for collection on our return from the Rishi. It was hard work and I was glad of the help of Tom and Bill.

Our route moved north up the roaring Dhauli River and climbed on a path through terraced fields to Lata village described by Bill Murray as 'a mountain eyrie at 8,000 feet affording a vulture's prospect down the Dhauli.' A score and a half of families lived there, and in no time sick villagers were arriving, queuing for treatment for this and that ailment, the cheerful Tom never at a loss to offer something that sent them away happy.

We were off on the 24th at 6.30 am climbing 4,000 feet in three and a half hours to camp at 12,000 feet. We had walked 112 miles. Our immediate problem was to find a way down into the Rishi Gorge. Shipton and Tilman from this position, on what is known as the Lata Kharak, had experienced trouble finding a way into the Rishi Gorge. Flogging their way through deep snow they had gained two saddles in the ridge before they found one that looked possible. Bill Murray, as soon as the tents were up, decided to go up and see if he could find the correct col.

Able mountaineer as Bill is, he had us worried when at dusk there was

Above left: Tom as a young schoolboy aged 8.
Above right: Tom's parents. His father was killed in action aged 28 in 1916.
Below left: Springburn Road about 1955, just before the trams stopped.
Below right: Tom's sister Molly on holiday on Jura in about 1980.

Above left: Self-portrait, above Loch Maree, and *right:* the all-important bike
on a cycling-cum-climbing trip in the mid-30s.
Below left: Tom's best pal, Matt Forrester, cooks breakfast above Loch Lomond.
Below right: 'The happy Macrae family who gave me shelter when my
tent blew away in Carn More Crag'.

Above: Glen Lui, in the heart of the Cairngorms. The pines are a haunt of Scottish crossbills; on the tops ptarmigan are more numerous per hundred acres than in the Arctic. Dotterel, snow buntings, golden eagles and merlins nest here.
Below: Climbers on the top of Ben Nevis looking over the great cliffs which drop 2,000ft. In the middle distance climbers can be seen on Tower ridge.
Inset: Tom Weir in the late 40s, shortly after demob.

Above: From left to right: Douglas Scott, Tom McKinnon, W.H. Murray,
Tom Weir; on the first post-war British Himalayan expedition.
Seen here at base camp at Lampak near Tibet.
Below: Uja Tirche, at 20,350ft, the hardest peak climbed by the expedition.
The route followed the narrow ridge sweeping leftwards to the summit.

Above left: A father brings his child in the hope of a cure. It falls on Tom McKinnon to give counsel.
Above right: Tom McKinnon, top, and Tom Weir force the first problem of Uja Tirche on none too sound rock.
Below: Camp on the Tibet border near Milam, morning mists writhing round the Girthi Gorge, only traversed once before by Europeans.

Above: Thankful villagers of Milam drummed us out, the boy dancing to the rhythm.
Below: The sanctuary of Panch Chuli. Like a lady's frock of pleated silk the mountain falls in a dazzling curtain, foreground to the highest peak in the range, 22,650ft.

In the Raftsund in the Lofotens, Rulten towers above the settlement of Reknes. The mountains rise sheer above lonely houses.
Inset: 'Adam Watson and Douglas Scott with some local friends. We climbed, fished and met delightful people who baked bread for us.'

Above: Clouds boil around the shattered summit ridge of the Ouan Oukrim massif in the High Atlas of Morocco. On right, the peak of Clocheton.
Inset: In the High Atlas, from left: Douglas Scott, Tom Weir, Jim Green.
Below: Tacheddirt, a Berber village in the hills at 7,000ft, the peaks in the background reaching 13,000ft.

still no sign of him. He just beat the dark, arriving absolutely all-in, reporting that the going had been pretty hellish. Like Shipton, he had tried two false cols before he found the right one. He wrote: 'Up each I toiled several hundred feet in knee-deep snow, only to find myself on sharp rock-edges, from which cliffs dropped 6,000 feet to the Rishiganga. Then back I had to go, scramble over the rock-rib lower down, then try the next gully. The 7,000-feet ascent from Lata had been too much without a meal, and now I proceeded to pay the penalty.'

He needed all his remaining strength to reach camp, fits of shivering overtaking him as the night temperature dropped. He wrote: 'The situation was partially saved by the discovery, in the pocket of my bush-shirt, of a handful of sugar, in the form of sweets, which had been a parting gift from Miss Jenny McNeil of the old Tricouni Club of Glasgow. These got me back to the slopes of the kharak after a fourteen-hour day.' From the pot of stew kept hot for him, he could only manage a spoonful or two. He was running a temperature and it was bed he needed, warmth and sleep.

His recce was of enormous benefit though, but even with snow-gullies frozen hard it was strenuous as steps had to be cut with the axe to allow passage, and 2,000 feet of climbing took us five hours. Now we were on the wall dropping thousands of feet into the Rishi, and traversing horizontally across this drop, we provided a rope hand-rail for the porters to safeguard a slip which, if unchecked, would be fatal. Porters support their loads by a head band, not shoulder straps. One of our men, no doubt under stress, let the band slip from his head and away went a five-day supply of vital flour bouncing down into the lower canyon of the Rishi.

The strain was telling on our Dhotials; one was violently sick, the others showed signs of stress, but climbed with assurance on the difficult ground, with a welcome let-up when a grassy gully led to a spot with water trickling from a snow wreath where we could camp. Bill went well that day despite the effects of a lingering high temperature.

White frost furred the ground in the morning when we were forced up 2,000 feet to the Dharashi Pass climbing out of shadow into a flood of sunlight facing the most inspiring prospect any of us had ever beheld – Nanda Devi, draped in pale green ice, framed in the V of the Rishi. Bill described it poetically, 'A vast projectile bursting arrow-like from the bent bow of the Rishi Gorge.' Looking at the tremendous sweep of its south ridge, we doffed our balaclavas to the Anglo-American expedition of 1936, when Bill Tilman and N.E. Odell reached the summit of the blessed Goddess. How marvellous that Bill Tilman should have been rewarded with what was a height record for him, worthy reward for being with Shipton on the very first penetration of the Inner Sanctuary of Nanda Devi.

Scott and Mackinnon made off to climb a 16,000-foot peaklet for a view, while Bill and I dropped down 1,500 feet with the Dhotials and

57

were pulled up by gorge walls. Murray went forward to reconnoitre, but when an hour passed and there was no shout to come on I cautioned the men not to follow me. Footing was dangerous, shaly rock overlaid with earth in places, sometimes peeling off when pressure was put on it. Before I could stop them they were picking their way down after me. An offer of a rope was refused with smiles. I admired their neatness. However when we were forced upward again, I fixed a rope for them to steady themselves. Now we were forced through jungle to emerge on Murray having a siesta on a delightful alp.

Bill had identified this spot as Dibrugheta, described by Dr Longstaff who had been here in 1907 as the most beautiful place in the Himalaya. Ringed by pines we were in a grassy hollow alive with birds and bright with flowers. Rock peaks jutted round it on every side. Only one thing was missing to make it the perfect camping place – water. So we had to drop down a gully and camp in jungle, and there Scott and MacKinnon found us round a big camp fire. All of us, including the Dhotials, were fit except Bill who was still suffering a temperature but was picking up.

The next day was a hard one, thorny and rocky, that drew blood from the feet of the Dhotials and tore at their thin clothing. After much up and down work we dropped almost to the river, a haven of rest for the weary porters. Of animal life all we had seen as yet were a few musk deer, but birds were good, especially flocks of snow-pigeons, twisting white in the sun. On the water were blue-fronted redstarts, orange breasted and with fiery rumps.

The time had come now to pay off all but six of our faithful carriers, and the whole assembly formed round the tent, Bill sitting and handing each his well-earned cash. The ones we kept were Perimal, Goria, Sangia, Madbir, Pakir and Nurbir. The rejected could not conceal their disappointment. Kuar Singh our headman got a shock to be among the dismissed, but this country was too hard for one of his age. We complimented him profusely, and his profound 'salaam' showed he appreciated our words. Long after dark the men hung around the tent, anxious to prolong this happy occasion.

In the morning we shook hands with each man in turn, and thanked him for his outstanding work. The next job was to weigh our food in order to estimate our climbing time. It was so much less than I expected that I decided that from now on I would minimise this source of leakage by supervising the cooking. Now that we were close to the climbing area, we split the food, dumping eighty pounds worth in a cave for the return journey, and loading most of the rest on our six Dhotials.

Forty-three years earlier Longstaff had thrown a bridge across the Rishi to enter the Trisul Nulla which was our goal. He mentions boulders outcropping amidst the boiling water. It could be that we crossed about the same place, using hand-axes to cut down a pine tree and three birches and, after some complicated manoeuvres, got a foundation on which Scott on a safety rope crossed, followed by an unladen porter. Then the heavier pine was pushed across and the construction roped together. Now Big Tom crossed, and with rope hand-rails to assist balance fixed loads were ferried across.

A flash of lightning and a roll of thunder accompanied the last load across, and hardly were the tents down on the gravel than heavy rain ushered in storm. It was still raining when we packed up next morning and took a climbing route calling for the rope high above the river, before jungle forced us down to easy ground following the glacial stream which took us down to the foot of Betartoli Himal. The heavily laden porters were utterly weary. Where we put the tent down was our base camp.

We had something in reserve though to gladden three hearts at least. In selecting six Dhotials, we had bargained for three of them going high enough to need climbing boots, sleeping bags, windproof clothing, gloves and helmets. It was ex war-department stock, bought cheaply in the Glasgow Barras. Whoever went high would get the kit.

Our mountain, 20,840 feet, had never been attempted, but looked easier than the frighteningly steep spires of Changabang, Kalanka, Rishi Kot and other peaks of the 'Basin Rim'. Bill, despite not feeling too well, went on and found himself looking on the north-east face of our mountain, completely clad in snow and ice. It was agreed that all four of us should go high and satisfy ourselves as to the most likely route. Bill had thought of the east ridge from what he saw the previous day. But on getting to 14,000 feet the approach to the North Col by a rocky ridge looked a better proposition. That day we moved up to Camp 2, by a running stream ringed by peaks glowing pink in the sunset.

There was snow on the ground when we rose at 5 am and the Dhotials showed little enthusiasm. After toiling up loose stones for hundreds of feet we were able to traverse on snow to gain the rock ridge, demanding handhold as well as foothold, steep for laden men. Soon it became an arête and it was evident that the porters should return from here.

What lay ahead was dismaying. The comfortably narrow ridge suddenly plunged into space. Scott belayed while Bill climbed down a vertical section which landed him on a big block. He wrote:

I lay on the flat of my stomach and looked over the brink. Under my chin was a vertical wall of twenty-five feet, then leaning out like a tilted pencil, a huge finger of rock with a clear drop of 100 feet below. We might be able to climb down on a doubled rope, but if we did we could never climb up again.

Scott went down and confirmed, retreating to the two tents perched on platforms hacked out of the narrow snow-ridge.

59

It was a cold night, but we were reasonably warm in our double-down sleeping bags. But what a reward in the morning, Nanda Devi shooting skyward higher than any other peak of the Basin Rim, below us huge seracs above the ice-fall.

Sorrowfully we packed up, Douglas and Tom choosing to retrace the route of yesterday, Bill and I opting for a direct descent on what looked like snow but proved to be ice under a thin cover of loose snow. Crampons balling forced us to cut steps, gruelling work with heavy sacks. The most enjoyable bit was lower down, when we let the sacks slide and shot after them in a fast standing glissade. At camp we arrived within ten minutes of each other.

We now turned our attention to the 19,930-foot peak of Haunuman, one that Douglas and Tom had seen from their 16,000-foot peaklet on our way into the Rishi. They thought its south-east ridge looked feasible, and that two days might suffice on our way out from the gorge. So back we went to our bridge over the Rishi, and up to 16,000 feet in poor visibility of mist and falling snow. Cold prevented sleep that night.

Morning saw us grinding up a treacherous boulder-field between rock ribs, to face eventually a series of gullies edged by rock ribs, steep for 1,000 feet. At last we reached the misty crest and the ridge went well for another 1,500 feet, where we were stopped by a steep band of friable rock. After trying a few places, Douglas made a spirited lead climbing as though he were in Glencoe and not at 19,000 feet on unclimbed mountain wall.

We praised his bold lead, but had a shock coming to us when the ridge ended in a cut-off as on Bethartoli, the shifting mist adding to its precipitous plunge into space. We abandoned the climb, providentially as it turned out, for the poor weather became really nasty as we climbed downward, the traverses demanding a lot of care on slippery rocks. Snow was falling faster and mist thickening as we steered a compass course. Darkness was gathering and benightment seemed certain in nil visibility, when suddenly Douglas said he could smell wood smoke. We turned into the wind and found ourselves at camp. The Dhotials had kept a juniper fire going. We blessed them.

Hot water was on the boil. In no time we had soup and tea served to us in our sleeping bags, and marvelled at the turn of events that had led us to the tents when we might be shivering out there on the mountain waiting for dawn.

Retreating back to the Tapoban in the Dhaulinganga by the way we had come, our immediate concerns were to pick up the Inner Line Pass which should be waiting for us at Joshimath twelve miles away, and recruit local Bhotias for our northward march towards Tibet. Douglas and Tom made off for the Joshimath post office, and while Bill made a sortie for porters, I organised the baggage for the trek up the Dhauliganga.

This route to Tibet – a track above the Dhauli River rushing between 5,000-foot rock walls, a staircase sometimes built on stanchions – was thronged with Tibetans in homespuns and brick-coloured woollen boots with yakskin soles. Large bundles on their backs, they drove before them great flocks of sheep and goats, each animal fitted with saddle bags, containing salt and borax. They were descending to barter their Tibetan goods for Indian grain and rice.

Nomads were on the move too, dark-skinned and of low caste who offered us bantam eggs for sale. Well-dressed families in homespuns, travelling with their animals, were burdened with house-hold gear, moving higher up to homes they occupy during the trading season. Some carried baskets on their arms as well as on their backs.

Our immediate destination was Dunagiri at 11,800 feet, with stone walls and well-tilled fields, sweet-smelling scrub, wild roses and walnut trees, each group of houses having courtyards where wool was being spun and looms working. Children were rosy-cheeked and the women were comely.

There we had some enjoyable mountaineering. Above us was a rock peak of 17,830 feet. The first 3,000 feet was a slog, the second 3,000 was tricky enough to be interesting, with pinnacles, all fearfully loose, leading us on to the summit snow dome. Although we were denied the view of the higher mountains we were to explore, we were pleased with our speed up and down, showing that we were acclimatised.

Tom had been kept busy in camp doctoring the locals, the worst case being a young girl with a gangrenous foot, rotten with pus and toes shapeless. Next morning, he and Douglas were off at 2 am for a 16,600-foot rock peak, and while they were away I visited the village school full of lively children, squatting on mats, with slates and jars of liquid chalk.

Douglas and Tom were back with us eleven and a half hours later full of enthusiasm for a long rock arête which began low on the mountain and provided a granite edge almost to the top. Further, they had found a gully that gave them the father and mother of all glissades, taking them down 3,000 feet of steep snow on their bottoms. On hearing this news Murray and I arranged an early start, leaving in a smirr of rain and in darkness. The climb was all they said it was. We found the glissade too, and an exhilarating slide it was. At camp Tom reported a miraculous transformation in the foot of his patient, and her mother and the schoolmaster had been instructed in continuing the treatment.

Our plan now was to move ourselves and our excess luggage, loaded on five pack animals called jhibus or jopas (crosses between yak and cow) over a 13,650-foot pass. Moving ponderously these beasts wanted to go down, not up. They made it. But on the second day, on a higher pass at 14,790 feet our porters had to take some weight from their backs, or the animals might not have made it. Dropping down the other side we saw the village we were making for, Malari, startling in its ugliness in a parched landscape.

We needed native flour and tsampa, roasted barley, sufficient for five weeks to see us through the next part of our programme: climbing in the Lampak Mountains, then a traverse of the Girthi Gorges. We also needed porters, but the head man, thinking he had us on toast, broke the agreement we thought had been reached, demanding lighter loads and higher pay. We didn't want it to be said that any Bhotia ever put one over on Glasgow men so we shrugged him off, saying we were moving away to find other men.

This called his bluff. The wages offered were accepted, but in the end we left Malari with a queer convoy of nineteen porters, one cow, and a mixed quota of rice, lentils, flour and tsampa. In a 3,000-foot climb we saw a rich variety of birds, greenfinches, the vivid red and grey of a wall-creeper, gaudy as a butterfly, chukor partridges, scarlet rose finches, while higher up golden eagles circled over us. We camped on an alp of flowers.

In the morning we saw from this delightful spot a shining peak projecting above the clouds, identifying it on our map as Uja Tirche, 20,350 feet. It looked so near we could see a crest of pinnacles below twin arêtes, one above the other, the higher one ending at the pointed summit. We agreed we should go for it, and once the Malari men had left us we made up a three-day supply of high-altitude food and with the six Dhotials set off, climbing steeply in shifting mist to camp at 17,400 feet.

Tom disappeared into the clouds to see what he could see of the route we might follow in the morning. Douglas arrived with bad news: the Dhotials were feeling the altitude, one was sick, but they hadn't given up. By the time they arrived Tom was coming towards us with news. The pinnacles were craziest things imaginable. He had cairned a route to one he called the Sphinx, a monster with a cap on its head.

Then came the weary Dhotials, and we congratulated them for their good work, enabling us to get the tents up to about 17,400 feet. At 5.30 next morning we were off into the mist, Tom leading us to the Sphinx, and where his eye of faith had detected two chimneys splitting its vertical face, the upper one half filled with ice. Tom, roped to me, led off. The rock was atrocious, loose basalt but at least you could wedge yourself. The upper one felt more secure because of the ice, since up there the ice-axe could be brought into play fashioning holds for hands and feet and bridging across to the rock edge of the chimney.

What we could see of the way ahead involved us in much up and down work threading crumbling pinnacles of basalt, until bottle-green ice showed us we were at the hanging glacier edged by the ridge that should lead us upward to the summit. Retracing our steps a little we saw the rocks above were breached by a chimney. Climbing it, Tom decided we should mark it with a small cairn of stones as a route marker for descent.

When Bill and Douglas hove into view, we moved up, this time on crisp snow, ideal for crampons, alpine climbing so enjoyable that we were unaware of the effects of altitude until we came to an arête so steep that Tom, in order to see the best way forward in the mist, had to push his snow-goggles up. The only way was rightward, horizontally and up to a vertical snow-corniced edge. To safeguard us both, the best belay I could manage was about two inches of ice-axe blade angled to allow the rope to run over it. Once this was arranged, out he went on the traverse, stopping for a moment just as he approached the cornice, to tell me he was fairly enjoying himself.

Five minutes or so elapsed after he had disappeared over, the running rope telling me he was still moving, then there was a shout to 'come on'. It was a bold lead, and when I joined him I saw he had the same kind of minuscule belay as myself. Today, modern climbers would use ice-screws to protect such an awkward passage. When another of the same reared up ahead of us, we waited for the other pair so that we could move as a foursome for greater safety.

After that it was a kind of anti-climax simply to put one step in front of another in the mist until a thin blade reared ahead – the summit. A five-minute breather, and we were on the way down, discovering our crampons were balling up due to a softening of the snow, so we removed them. We had been going for about nine hours by this time and were going to need our time to get down in daylight. The first of the difficult traverses went well, but as the ice was fragile, we decided to descend below the lower arête to a rocky ridge where belaying would be more secure, though the traverse right across the ice-wall would be longer.

Tom was the first to launch out on the end of 200 feet of rope. Moving rightward meant that step-cutting had to be done with the left hand, the right clinging to a handhold in order to chip foot- and handholds.

It was exhausting work, each of us doing a stint. When it came to Tom's second turn to go out front, he decided he would use crampons for speed and greater safety. He did well, and was on his way back, using the steps he had cut when a foothold shattered, and down he went, sliding on his side until his weight came on the rope when he was yanked leftward and banged to a stop on the rocks. Had the rope broken he would have fallen thousands of feet. Before he could even register relief he was shouting. 'OK, come on now, next man out!' His only damage was a bruised shoulder. It was Bill's turn once more, and out on the wall, 150 feet from us, he would have a much more serious slide if he fell, but with superb icemanship he worked his way nearer and nearer the ridge, overcame the last step and let out a joyful shout as he fixed a belay.

While this little drama was taking place, the mists which had enveloped us all day were thinning and we looked over a vast cloud-sea with peaks of the Tibet border silhouetted against fire-tinted clouds. By the time we had joined Bill a three-quarter moon was silvering in a clear sky, and a frost crust making our footing more secure.

Would we manage to find our way through the pinnacles? Of this Big Tom wrote in his diary: 'It was a weird and wonderful experience traversing in and out of the pinnacles in moonlight and realising that the situation was completely in hand.' He it was who located the cairn, showing where we must traverse left from the chimney in order to reach the Sphinx. He it was who safeguarded us down its difficulties, coming down last man unsafeguarded. We passed the last problem nine hours from leaving the summit and reached the tent just eighteen hours after leaving it.

The Dhotials had kept a fire going in the high camp, and plied us with soup and tea, but all we really wanted was to get into our sleeping bags. What a reward there was for three of us next morning, awakening to the sun on the tents, and looking out on a whole horizon of shining snowpeaks, in contrast to undulating brown hills to the north, not unlike our own Scottish bens – but these were in Tibet – while immediately below us were savage Girthi Gorges which it was our intention to traverse and link to another great Tibetan trade route.

Alas, Big Tom did not share our joy, for he was snow-blind, the result of removing his snow-goggles in the mists of yesterday. He wrote in his diary:

Awoke very early in great pain with my eyes and found I could not open them. I got out of the tent and walked a few yards and had difficulty finding it. Douglas wanted to stay for photographs and kept me in food while the others went down to base, and sent up capsules of castor oil to relieve the pain. By evening my eyes opened more and more when protected by sun glasses. Steep and tiring descent.

That was Uja Tirche. Looking back on it I remember no other mountain day so full of surprises and sustained interest. Weariness fades before the enduring values, the joy of a hard-won summit, and the contentment of spirit in a new appreciation of being alive.

Tom was the botanist of the party, and at our two base camps in the next ten days revelled in the flowers he was seeing on the alpine meadows below the dramatic snow walls hemming us in. For stark contrast though, we were pinned down at 18,000 feet for two bad nights with wet snow shaking the tent fabric and forming puddles on the floor, but forced to retreat when there was no let-up in the monsoon weather. After that the riot of flowers at base seemed paradise as we enjoyed the singing birds, the sight of a falcon and high above the camp two of the largest vultures in the world, lammergeir and griffin.

We couldn't settle though until we had another go at South Lampak peak, 20,750 feet. We allotted ourselves four days, one night for Camp 2, another at Camp 1, the summit climb, and descent on the fourth day. We put the tents down on the platforms we had dug from the narrow ridge on our first attempt and the weather looked in our favour. But at 3.30 am when we looked out visibility was nil and we waited until six before we roped up, Murray leading until stopped by steep crumbling rock. Tom started up a couloir, but the high angle and the possibility of stonefall made him retreat. Security was non-existent. We had endured avalanches falling all night long, on both sides of our ridge on the first attempt, and as the weather was still dangerously unsettled we judged it wise to retreat.

The Dhotials had been a tower of strength in helping us to put up Camps 1 and 2. Of them Tom wrote:

Our accounts of their behaviour will surprise Himalayan travellers when we return. I think perhaps we were fortunate with our choice in the first place, secondly we have all gone out of our way to be friendly and helpful. When they became ill we have helped them with their loads or dispensed medicine in large quantities. On occasions we are firm, but always one happy family. In this way they carry to heights and over distances which have never been recorded by this race.

As per arrangement, the Bhotias from Malari arrived on 12th July with their pack-carrying goats to carry for us through the Girthi Gorges. They made a fine sight against the 7,000-foot ice-face of 23,000-foot Tirsuli, its crest three miles long. First, we had to leave Uja Tirche behind, by crossing its flank at 14,000 feet and it was alpine flowers all the way, scented and with all the colours of a garden. Over the pass and we faced a rock canyon with 7,000-foot walls. Yet there was a path of sorts, even if it involved rock scrambling, hands and foot work, above dangerous drops to the river 1,000 feet below.

That night we slept in a cave. When snow-gullies barred the route, steps across it had to be cut with the ice-axe, and the worry of sliding lifted from the brows of the porters. The goats knew well how to speed across. There was a lot of up and down traversing to avoid landslides and crags. Camp that night was by a glacial torrent, milky with silt. Tea made with it was thick, like soup, but it was harmless to the stomach.

Forced by the terrain to drop down to the river we came upon two primitive thatched houses, outside which were a couple of attractive women and a little girl. Their men folk were away, but from a stone pit deep in the ground they produced thirteen pounds of potatoes and gave them to us. Around the houses the land was cultivated, and irrigation channels had been dug. At two converging rock walls a bridge had been thrown across the river involving a steep climb down to it and almost as steep up dangerously loose rock and screes.

The crux of the route was the Unta Dura Pass at 17,600 feet with Tibet to the north-east and India to the south-west. Coming towards us as we joined this trade route were wild-looking Tibetans, wearing blue or brick-red robes, cloth boots on their feet, tall hats on their heads, some carrying swords, others ancient muskets.

Our men had moved well on the big ascent to the pass. They did even better on the descent, 5,000 feet down and thirteen miles from our camp of the morning. In rain next morning we entered Milam village in the Goriganga, a flat of fields, yellow with millet and fresh green, its houses of grey stone huddled together. It boasts the highest post office in India – open only in summer – and we expected our first mail from home for two months.

Without any volition of ours we found we were being directed to the house of the 'Doctor sahib', Len Moules, of the World-Wide Evangelisation Crusade. Thick-set and of medium height, he oozed vitality, and over cups of tea we learned that he had never been through the Girthi Gorges, nor knew of any Europeans who had forced the passage. The people living around him were traders, and right now were preparing a caravan taking grain and manufactured goods to Tibet, to trade for rugs, trinkets, salt or borax. On their return in October they would move down the valley to dispose of their goods at a big market held in November. Each trader had three houses, the lowest one occupied in winter. In April they moved higher with their animals, occupying their highest village here in Milam during the trading season.

We found Moules just in time, for he was about to leave Milam, so we got answers to some important questions respecting the feasibility of crossing high passes over 18,000 feet in the monsoon, against the flood conditions we might find if forced to go down and round the flanks of the mountains. Despite his uncertainty we opted for the high passes. Tom, whose three months' holiday had come to an end, decided he would go for Trail's Pass, crossing the glaciated saddle between Nanda Devi and Nanda Kot, travelling light without a tent but with a porter to share his forty-pound load.

While we were making ready and recruiting local Bhotias willing to cross the mountains, Tom made off with our best wishes in deteriorating conditions, rain and low clamped-down clouds, and I wrote in my diary: 'I'm inclined to believe he will be put off.' Just before we left to try crossing the Ralam Pass a soiled note delivered by a Bhotia told us that he had abandoned Trail's Pass for the long way round that he had hoped to avoid.

The Ralam Pass we were attempting is really a succession of three passes crossing this main Himalayan group at 18,470 feet and leads down to another Tibetan trade route, the Darmaganga. The mountains famous in Hindu mythology which we were interested in are known as the Panch Chuli – the five fires – the highest 22,650 feet. A climb of 5,000 feet took us over the first pass, then down 3,000 feet to Ralam village. Our visit was such an occasion that when the time came for us to leave a procession was formed, led by the young boys of the village.

In farewell each plucked flowers, and with a bunch in each hand did an eightsome reel-style dance, each one giving a solo in the centre. One imitated a monkey scratching for fleas, another made funny faces, others just threw themselves about. All this jollity was performed to the beating of drums. It gave a lift to our spirits for the big pull up, then a climb over glacier ice to a rock saddle leading down to the Yanchar Glacier. In six days we had peaks standing clear of cloud, the dazzle such that the men had to tease out wool and pull it down over their eyes to avoid snow-blindness. And we had the reverse, low clouds, rain and total invisibility. Into the bargain we had thunder and lightning. Falling stones called for vigilance.

We certainly were seeing the Bhotias at their best, true mountain men if hard wranglers when it came to paying them off down in the Darmaganga. Bill handled them well, stood firm on their contract agreement and refused them the extra payment they demanded. Not for nothing were they traders and not mere porters.

As for the superlative peaks of Panch Chuli, our highest camp was pitched at 19,000 feet. What lay ahead we could not tell until the enveloping clouds lifted. Our hearts sank when we saw what was ahead. The col which we hoped would be easy, rose sheer for nearly 1,000 feet, its base bearing the marks of avalanche. All that night avalanches fell, and stones falling continuously next day showed our judgement had been sound. The heat by day was excessive, yet at night we were colder than in any camp up to date. It was by no means dull waiting for dawn, much more like being in the thick of an air-raid.

Next morning we pushed down 7,000 feet to Camp 1, and the green meadows were welcoming indeed, as was the camp fire and the luxury of a large tent. I had had my fill of Panch Chuli, but Douglas Scott wanted to explore the other side, the glacier coming down from the south col. Bill joined him and they were satisfied that this route, though difficult, would be the way to the top.

Between times we had got to know the locals, by reason of our medicine chest, Bill Murray performing the role of Tom MacKinnon. His one notable failure was trying to pull the tooth of an old dame who pointed to her jaw. It was a loose tooth in the lower jaw, but every time Bill got the pincers on it bits of it came off but the roots stood firm. Bill said the hag was so tough that she never winced. It was he who lost his nerve, and gave the molar best.

Before embarking on the 150-mile march back to Ranikhet we were invited to an official celebration of our visit timed to begin at 8 am. In a downpour of rain we were ushered into a house, seated on a carpeted dais, and a wall of Bhotia faces pushed nearer and nearer us. All we could do was nod and smile or utter the word 'thik' (right). Then we were given cigarettes which made us choke and cough, with short-lived relief when alcohol made its appearance in the form of chang, tasting like vinegar.

From outside came drummers lined up to accompany us down to the village square. There we were seated on carpets while the drummers began a long tattoo. I decided it was time for this drummer to perform. So I collected the drums in a semi-circle and wielding a couple of big sticks beat out rhythms fast and furious. Given a spare drum I would have joined the band that marched us back to camp.

Mountains of clouds buried Panch Chuli when we left, descending on a good path and entering a scenery of wooded bluffs and ravines falling to millet fields. Cutting deeper, the glen became a ravine with rock pinnacles, the path winding through gleaming slabs and flowering shrubs. After the bleakness of the two other Tibetan trade routes we had travelled this one was lush. All the time we were losing height, the path crossing under waterfalls, climbing like a staircase in places, at other times spanning drops on wooden planks held to the rocks by stanchions.

Five days from base camp and we were able to buy mangos, ripe bananas and delicious Indian corn for roasting while we waited for torrential rain to subside and let us resume our journey. Sightings of red monkeys and grey langurs were frequent. Butterflies swarmed on the path, large swallow tail varieties, some with black forks and blue wings, some black and red. Birds were everywhere, kingfishers, bul-buls, shrikes, flycatchers, spotted fork-tails, pigmy owlet, crested hawk eagles and many another.

One evening, after exceptionally heavy rain, Panch Chuli came out of the clouds, the first time we had seen it since leaving base camp. Now it appeared as a point of snow utterly removed from the earth, dwarfing the foothills. A fortnight ago we had been camped under its crest, enduring heat, glare, rarefied air and loss of appetite, which together had been well nigh insufferable. Yet one view was sufficient to fill one with longing to go back, the discomforts forgotten, the revelation of the heights remembered.

5

A Brave Little Woman

There is a tide in the affairs of men,
Which taken at the flood leads on to fortune.
Shakespeare, *Julius Cæsar*

By the summer of 1951, after a disciplined twelve months of darkroom and
writing to fill the coffers, Scott and Weir had turned their thoughts to the
Lofoten Islands of arctic Norway and the mountains of Lyngen Fjord rising
north of Tromso, vividly described by their most devoted British explorer,
W. Ceicel Slingsby. The Lofotens he described as 120 miles of aiguilles of
gabbro and granite; the Lyngen peaks too were of gabbro with huge
glaciers streaming down, in some cases from a height of 6,000 feet. Travel
moreover was cheap by coastal boat and so was food. It sounded just right
for us.

Moreover we were in touch with a young zoology student by the name
of Adam Watson who during vacation the previous year had travelled to
the Russian border by fishing boats, allowing him the chance to bird-
watch in Swedish Lapland and Finnmark, before heading south to
Svolvær, capital of the Lofoten, travelling by trawler via the Faeroes
back to Aberdeen. A keen mountaineer, he was eager to join us.

At first our talk was all about fishing boats, but in fact he came up with a
better idea. Adam's father would be glad to put himself at our disposal: his
suggestion was that we should travel in his car to Newcastle, board the
luxury ship *Venus* for Bergen, and he would drive us up to Trondheim
where we could catch the coastal boat for Lofoten, and have a climb in the
Jotunheim and the Dovre Fjell on the way.

Sharing the cost, and camping, it was not only comfortable but cheap,
that is until we parted company at Trondheim and joined the throng as
steerage passengers on the daily boat that serves coastal villages all the way
to the North Cape. In this land of perpetual daylight in summer, travellers
go on and off at all times on the several nights it takes to reach there, loud
hoots on the siren being the signal for stops. We chose to sleep out on the
draughty upper deck rather than join the throng of passengers sleeping in
corridors, sitting on stairs, or wherever there was cover from the rain. We
were glad to leave the boat at Svolvær.

From now on life became idyllically simple, crofter-fisherfolk lent us their rowing boats and lines to catch fish for supper; they baked us bread, supplied us with eggs and potatoes at cheap cost, and sometimes treated us to delicious meals. We were privileged visitors in this northland because the islanders remembered with gratitude the British raids against German occupying troops from 1940 onwards, which were not only demoralising for the Germans but inspirational for the coastal folk, many of whose young men escaped with the attacking force and were taken back to Scotland, where they would return as freedom fighters in a shuttle service of innocent-looking fishing boats known as the Shetland Bus, raiding operations that were among the boldest of the war. The story is fully told in a book of that name by David Howarth.

We made a lot of good friends on that trip, among them freedom fighters who were mountaineers and who joined us on some climbs. That was in Lofoten. In Narvik, when I went into a shop to buy paraffin, I was promptly toasted in finspirit, for inner consumption, and the word as we tossed it down was 'Tirpiz', a neat way of saying 'Bottoms Up', that being the name of the battleship sunk by the navy in Narvik fjord in 1940 when HMS *Warspite* sailed in, blasting enemy positions and sinking several destroyers. The Germans were arresting people in the streets for smiling that day!

Lyngen and its gabbro mountains was beyond our expectations in the quality of its alpine scenery, and the trip inspired me to write a book about it, *Camps and Climbs in Arctic Norway* published by Cassell in 1953. The review of it in the *Alpine Journal* warmed my heart:

> This is a wholly delightful book. The author is one of these happy mountaineers who finds beauties and interests outside the actual work of climbing, one can easily imagine him clinging desperately, spread-eagled on some impossible granite slab yet keenly enjoying the colours of a clump of saxifrages in which his nose is temporarily buried. The book is full of interesting information on this Arctic land, of the fishing industry, its most important means of livelihood, and of the people, friendly and hospitable.
>
> The climbing throughout was of the highest order from the Dyrhausgstind, the only peak I share with the author, to the magnificent twenty-three-hour day on Jaeggevarre. All through the book the really splendid photographs are a delight, the author pays tribute to Slingsby, who seems to live in Norway still.

It warmed my heart because my first book, *Highland Days*, was such a damp squib compared to W.H. Murray's thrillingly descriptive and philosophical book *Mountaineering in Scotland*. Dr Tom Longstaff said it all when he wrote of it as being in a class by itself – and forty-three years on it is still regarded as a classic. Strangely, though, that first book of mine became more respected as it went out of print, and eventually readers wishing to possess it were paying as much as £20 for a work originally sold at twelve shillings and sixpence. This demand led to its being republished in 1984, a neat transposition of 1948 when it first appeared in the bookshops. It also went into paperback.

This second time round it had an introduction by a climbing contemporary, Professor Sir Robert Grieve who, as plain Bob Grieve, began his outdoor career about the same time as I did. He described its contents thus:

The information in this book is both dated and timeless. It is difficult to know whether a particular expedition or climb was done when he was seventeen or when he was thirty. The mountains and the weather have not changed. His love of the game is wholly stable. And time, to most of us in memory, is not a matter of duration measured by the ticking of a clock; it is a matter of intensity.

Tom writes vividly of what happened. He deals in a rush of words about something which happened to him; which he had fiercely dreamed of doing. I used the word 'fiercely' by careful choice. It is as I see him: his eyes and face, when he is intent on a rock face, lifting his binoculars to watch an eagle; or telling me something he is going to write. He is, above most men I've known, a man of strong intent and tenacity. But all these characteristics – not always those of peace – are devoted to the beauty of life of our countryside and its meaning to the human part of life.

Highland Days is fundamentally an innocent book. That was what I first thought when I read it forty years ago, and had known Tom for only a few years. We shared the same background, in the north of Glasgow, in sight of the Campsie Hills, true mountains to us, and our discovery of them on very long walks, mostly without money, were genuine explorations and escapes from the tenements where we lived.

By the time Tom had written this book my professional career had let me into certain kinds of public responsibilities and taught me how our environment evolved – including mountain country. When I talked to Tom about it, I found that he too had 'opened the books' as Jack London put it in his splendid book *Martin Eden*.

So I come back to why I used the word 'innocent'. *Highland Days* is really about Tom's own Garden of Eden, as it was in the beginning. His subsequent writings and broadcasts show his continuous growth of understanding of the need for what I once called 'the invisible web of administration' which one day our society may weave to protect the environment which nourishes us all. But behind any good

71

administration there must be heard the shout of joy from the Garden; and this book is exactly that.

I should tell you that the writer of these words, who is four years older than me, began walking the hills when his employer laid him off, with other apprentice draughtsmen, in order to keep married men in work at the peak of the depression in 1932. His high position today arises from his outstanding work as a Town and Country Planner, hence the nature of his words relating to the environment. Much of the Clyde Valley Regional Plan, 1946, was written by him when he was assistant to Sir Patrick Abercrombie.

That summer of 1951 when we were in Norway, Bill Murray was reconnoitring the Nepal face of Mount Everest with Eric Shipton, Michael Ward and Tom Bourdillon, and on that hitherto unexplored face they were shortly to be joined by two New Zealanders, one of them Edmund Hillary. Hillary was with Shipton when for the first time two climbers saw from 20,000 feet on Pumori a perfectly feasible route to the summit, if a way could be found through the wild labyrinth of the chasms and ice-pinnacles of what would be a very dangerous passage. And it was by the perils of this approach to the South Col, as the world knows, that Edmund Hillary and Sherpa Tensing were put into position to reach the summit in 1953.

The initiative for that recce of the Nepal face of Mount Everest belongs to W.H. Murray and Michard, who chose Eric Shipton to be leader, but neither Murray nor Shipton was to be chosen to be a member of the successful expedition. No matter, theirs was the thrill of unravelling the topography of an unknown region closed until now to outsiders, and they made marvellous use of their opportunity to cross high passes into new valleys between Nepal and Tibet.

By not being chosen for the 1953 attempt, Bill Murray turned the year 1952 to good account by writing *The Story of Everest*, a best seller perfectly timed for the news of the victorious climb. Before that achievement, however, Douglas Scott, Tom MacKinnon, George Roger and I had taken Bill Murray's advice and applied for permission to explore the unmapped mountains of the Rolwaling Gorge, first seen by Hillary at the end of the 1951 recce. We received it and, at the tail-end of the monsoon, set off from Katmandu, marched into the Rolwaling and after some first ascents crossed the 19,000-foot Tesi Lapcha Pass which led us to Namche Bazaar within easy marching distance of the Swiss expedition then attempting to beat the British by being first on top of Mount Everest.

The intention after the British recce was to launch a joint British and Swiss attack on the Nepal face of Everest, but when that plan proved unworkable, it was agreed that the Swiss should have the mountain to themselves in 1952, and the British in 1953. In two bold attempts, Lambert and Sherpa Tensing reached 28,215 feet, the highest anyone had ever been on the mountain, the Swiss summit bid being made after an uncomfortable night without sleeping bags or insulating mattresses, or stove for heating water for drinks. In his Everest book Bill Murray pays them tribute by writing: 'No more heroic effort has ever been made to reach the summit.'

However it was the same Sherpa Tensing who, with Hillary, reached the summit on 29th May 1953, perfectly timed by an accident of luck for the Coronation of Queen Elizabeth II, a crowning glory indeed! Headline news proclaimed: 'Edmund Hillary plants the Queen's Flag on top of the world.' The New Zealand bee-keeper was thirty-four years of age, and for him it was the beginning of a new life of exploration and social work to better the lot of the Sherpas. Hillary was knighted by the Queen and Tensing awarded the George Medal – the highest award Great Britain could then bestow upon a foreigner. Tensing himself was to do much to raise the standards of climbing among the Sherpas by founding a climbing school.

What a lot has happened in the world of mountaineering since we sailed home from Bombay in 1952 when the Swiss were battling in winter storms to reach the summit. What I am reminded of though, is the sail back to Britain and a fresh-faced old lady who graced our dinner table. Fifteen years earlier, she and her husband had lost everything in Australia, and had come back to Montrose in Scotland. He couldn't bear the cold and, with their last cash, returned alone to Australia. She stayed on, working in various poorly paid housekeeping jobs, till at last, aged sixty-six, she decided to buy a little shop and try her hand at selling baby linen.

She had £50. The price of the shop was £200. On money borrowed at three and a half per cent she purchased against advice, and got a stock in. Her motto was 'service first' and to give it she made many visits to Glasgow, touring warehouses for bargains, or for something special for a customer. These trips meant rising to catch a train at 6 am, not to return until maybe 8 pm. Hard work for a woman of her age. She put her faith in God. Every day she thanked Him and asked for help, and it was never refused.

Now, at seventy-one, she was on her way back from visiting her husband in Australia having achieved her ambition to keep her husband in comfort and see him again, probably for the last time. Her little shop had prospered. Her debts paid off, she had sold it at a handsome profit just six months previously. As there wasn't enough money to keep them both in Australia, she was going back to Montrose to work, probably in what had been her own little shop. A small, rather frail woman with a fresh face, and hair that was still brown, she told me she regarded the last testing fifteen years as the richest of her life.

I write of her now because she reminded me of my mother in her lack of self-interest, though it was not until I was handed a telegram in 1960

73

telling me of her death I realised how much my mother had meant to me. It was passed to me in a remote part of north-east Greenland, at Latitude 72 degrees north in the high Arctic, where I had been expeditioning for two months.

My diary for 25th August 1960 reads:

It was good to get in, cook a meal, get inside our sleeping bags for four hours. Lovely evening when I looked out, in time to see Dick dancing with delight because the Polypen [the expedition boat] was on the horizon. Great joy with heads popping out of tents and revolver shots and verey lights firing.

My own jubilation was short lived, for the Skipper had a telegram for me, telling that my mother had died suddenly. It was a shock on this lonely beach and I knew a deep sadness to the point of tears, even letting out a howl of anguish. Strange, when we so seldom saw each other, but I felt we had come closer in the past eight months of my first year of marriage. The burial had taken place on 23rd August. I had sent a letter on 17th but it is unlikely that she got it. How I wish I had written earlier. I feel a great ache as I write this, thinking of the unhappiness she must have suffered in the last weeks of her life, in pain and loneliness. I loved her more than I thought. She was good to me and tried hard to please me, but little appreciation she got. I wish I had been kinder to her.

And again on 26th August:

Couldn't sleep for thinking of Edgefauld Road [in Glasgow], and all the events back and fore in the last ten years which have been so eventful for me. Also, our doctor, Davy Jones, snored worse than any pig, so I pushed into another tent at 2 am and slept until 9 am. Wind sprang up around mid-day, then in evening turned right round and blew a full gale, whipping sand from the glacier-snout to spatter like hail on the tent, forcing us to get out and pin the canvas with big stones. Inside was a shambles with a film of fine grit over cups, plates, sleeping bags and stoves.

What I was thinking about was the time I picked up my mother from our old Glasgow house and brought her for dinner to Loch Lomondside on 29th December, which was my birthday. It was a terrible night of wind and rain and we were just at the main course when the telephone bell rang, and I left the table to answer the call. It was the police, telling me the Edgefauld Road house had been broken into. I said nothing as I came back to the table intending to wait until the meal was over to break the bad news. But my mother's eyes were looking at me searchingly. Perhaps because of her increasing deafness she had an uncanny knack of being able to read my thoughts. 'Has the house been burgled?' she asked. I tried a calming answer, but she was on her feet, reaching for her coat, and off we drove into the storm to learn the worst from the two policemen guarding the broken door of the ground-floor flat.

She rushed past them along the lobby and into the best room, shifted a chair and pulled open a door to reveal shelves crammed with brown paper parcels. Finding the one she wanted she thrust it into my hands and said: 'Thank God. It's yours, I hid it there for safety.' Once the policemen had sealed the door and we had driven back to Gartocharn, and were inside by the fire, I opened the parcel. To my dismay I found it contained all the money I had given her over the years to pay the rent and keep the house going while I was away expeditioning in different parts of the world.

The amounts were still in the original bundles. What made it even more touching was that a new kitchen cabinet she had bought had been obtained on the hire-purchase, yet with all that money she could have paid for anything needed. I am sure she had it fixed in her head that anyone living an insecure life like mine would be sure to have bad times in the future, hence she regarded the money I had given her as my nest egg and not hers.

Her death had taken place in a middle-door house, on a landing one stair up in a three-storey tenement, with neighbours on each side of her. It was a 'Granny Flat', a single room with a bed at its far end, living space in the middle and with kitchen sink and gas-cooker by the window. She had moved into this from our larger Glasgow house not long before I went to Greenland. Her neighbours had become concerned at not seeing her go in and out. When they pushed open the unlocked door they saw a letter lying on the floor, addressed to her. It was the one I had sent from Greenland.

Inside, my mother was lying on the floor where she had slid off the sofa, with evidence that she had been sick by the vomit on her clothes. A teapot slightly off the gas-ring told its own story. Tea-water had boiled over, extinguishing the flame, and although the emerging gas was at its lowest peep, its fumes had overcome her. The official verdict was accidental death; there was no question of suicide.

In lieu of a will was a wee note leaving everything to me. Her total estate amounted to £889, inclusive of insurance policy money and dividend on purchases from Cowlairs Co-op. Among her papers was a plastic envelope containing her marriage lines, her birth certificate and a faded yellow sheet so fragile that it nearly came apart when I unfolded it. It was an official army pro-forma letter which read:

Ref. 2/13588/16. Infantry Perth, 5th April 1916

It is my painful duty to inform you that a report has this day been received from the War Office notifying the death of No/s 6405 L/

75

Cpl Thos. Weir, Royal Highlanders, which occurred at Persion Gulf on 13 March 1916, and I am to express the sympathy and regret of the Army Council at your loss. The cause of death was 'Killed in Action'.

Mrs Weir, 310 Springburn Road, Glasgow.
Signed by Major Farquharson for Officer
in charge of Records, No. 1 District.

It forced my mind back to the first time I fully realised how lonely my mother's life had become, for I had just returned from the country where my father was killed by a sniper's bullet on the River Tigris, then a part of Turkey which became Iraq when the borders were redrawn. I remember my arrival home vividly, because I had forgotten my house key, and when I got no answer to loud rings on the bell, I suspected it was because my mother couldn't hear them for she had become increasingly deaf.

Ours was a gable-end house, and I soon shinned up to the window ledge for a view into the living room. What I saw was a white-haired old lady staring into the flames of the coal fire. Knocks on the pane evoked no response, so I blocked off as much of the evening light as I could with my body and quite slowly she turned her head, started for a moment, then when she realised who it was the most lovely smile lit her face.

It was shortly after this glad arrival that she began to suffer terrible facial pains, diagnosed as a rare disease known as trigeminal neuralgia. When it was most agonising, her cheek became flushed and she was in misery. Then the pain would go away, only to return again. The only hope of a cure was to have a brain operation to cut the fifth cranial nerve. She decided to have it. It was not successful and left her with facial paralysis; her eye was affected too. She had always taken a pride in her appearance, but now became shy of company. She was only seventy-three when she died, a brave little woman like the lady I met aboard ship.

6

To the Sea beyond the Sunset

I had not thought of the upper reaches of the Tigris for mountaineering until my old expedition comrade, Douglas Scott, gave me an illustrated article which he had found in a German Geographical Journal of 1954. The writer was Dr Hans Bobeck, and Douglas was excited by his description of two ranges of jagged peaks separated by a deep gorge close to the Iraq–Iran border of Turkey. One range was named the Cilo Dagh, the other the Sat Dagh and the highest peak of the two ranges was given as the Geliasin, 13,674 feet.

More information about the approaches to these peaks was at hand, because in the Edinburgh Botanic Gardens was a botanist by the name of P.H. Davis who had recently collected in this area. He and another botanist had managed to get permission to travel through these ranges, but warned us that even with permission we could be turned back if the local Governor thought it unsafe due to strife between the Kurds and the Turks.

What he did tell us of Lake Van and Turkish Kurdistan made us all the keener to push our luck. We wrote to Foreign Secretary Selwyn Lloyd and were granted permission to explore east of the Euphrates and Tigris subject to such restrictions as the Turkish authorities might impose on us in a sensitive border area.

It was 11th June 1956 when we left Glasgow on the overnight train for London after a hectic week, getting inoculations, chasing up tents, buying basic foods and cramming everything into four kit-bags and four rucksacks. As usual I told my mother I would write, but as we would be away from all roads and communications she might hear not very much, and was not to worry. It was on the following day we boarded the Oriental Express and settled down to three nights and four days crossing Europe from Calais to Istanbul. From being a great electric express for first-class passengers only, its length grew shorter and shorter as we progressed east, until, eventually, it was no more than one coach sandwiched between wagons of a steam train.

It was hay-time when we left England, and the peasants of Europe were at the same job, with the same background of bird-songs bursting from the woods, except that the tractor drivers of England had been replaced by groups of peasants in brightly coloured smocks, getting in the hay with sickles and rakes. The freedom of leaving the train to take a quick look at Verona, Milan, or watch the gondolas and launches zipping up and down the colourful canals of Venice, ended beyond Trieste, in Yugoslavia, where police with guns stood ready to shoot down any who tried to make unauthorised entry to their sacred soil. But the Slovenes are considerate people. The Bulgarians were not, wakening us in the middle of the night to note our camera numbers, take our passports from us, examine our money and make us sign forms.

For us it was a journey in time as well as space, a step backward as we went from Serbia where the Morava River swept down in muddy red among green cultivation plots. Oxen harnessed to ploughs or carts; women with machetes working in groups in small fields, were signs of a more ancient agricultural order. But standards of housing were not so low as in Bulgaria where portraits of Marx, Lenin, and a benign smiling Stalin ribboned in red, looked down on a dejected populace of unsmiling people. We felt a definite lightening of spirits as we entered the flat lands of Turkey.

The Turks interested me as a race, never having heard them described in my youth as anything but 'the terrible Turks'. In fact we found them almost embarrassingly friendly, so hospitable even in Istanbul that they would join us at table, offer us a cigarette or order glasses of tea: the men, dark-haired and moustached for the most part, sallow-skinned and not so unlike Italians. In restaurants servants invited us into kitchens so that we could inspect the full range of kebabs or chicken dishes on offer.

Three days in this sprawling city of two million people made us realise what a bustling place it is at 8.30 of a morning as we watched the paddle-steamers whisk north and south of the Galata Bridge dumping thousands of lightly clad men and women every few minutes, against a sunlit background of sparkling water and mosques gleaming on every hilltop; and always before us on the water vivid-hued fishing boats hurrying under the bridges out to sea.

All too soon we had to forsake Grecian columns, the Roman walls, famous St Sophia and the Blue Mosque, turn our backs on Europe as the sun set in gold over the Sea of Marmora, and in an overnight train journey we reached the capital, Ankara. There we were obliged to seek out the British Embassy to collect our official permit and get it translated from English to Turkish. Then the bad news: floods had swept away a rail bridge, so we would have to make our own arrangements to reach Kaiseri, 2,000 miles east by bus. We got there at four in the morning, and stretched out until the train going east arrived at 9 am. Thirty-six hours later we were disembarking at Kurtalen, the end of the line.

Anatolia in June is not a dusty desert. It is a garden, green with grass and vivid with flowers. Buffaloes wallow in the streams, herds of goats, flocks of sheep, packs of fine horses, even gaggles of geese graze beneath rock outcrops. But the most astonishing feature of our 1,000-mile zig-zag crossing was the extent of the land under cultivation, the most conspicuous buildings in the landscape being the tall red cylinders of grain silos built by American Marshall Aid and still going up. Always, there were birds of prey or vultures in the sky.

It was late afternoon when we disembarked from the rail terminus and, to our delight, there was a small bus waiting at the station to transport passengers travelling north-east to Lake Van. We were on our way within the hour, rising rapidly to a ravine of waterfalls spouting between great crags. Trees growing up to the tops of the pinnacled hills showed that Anatolia is very much the Scottish story over again of man's destruction of the accessible forest. Terraces of rice grew on wet hillsides as we followed the tumbling river to Bitlis. That stream had a special meaning for me, for it was the infant Tigris on its way to Mesopotamia and the Persian Gulf. The thick walls of the fortress town of Bitlis testify to centuries of war and murder.

At 10.30 pm we were more than ready for bed in the tiny hotel of Tatvan at the ferry terminal, all set for the next part of our journey, a sail across Lake Van which the ancient Assyrians called 'The Sea Beyond the Sunset'. We saw it in the gold of dawn, and found it hard to believe we were 5,700 feet above sea-level and that the snowy cone of Supan Dagh was over 14,000 feet and second only to Ararat in height. The legend is that the ark came to rest here, before the waters rose still higher to deposit it on Ararat. The subtly changing shades of blue and brown and grey, echoed in the loch, made it easy for us to understand why experienced travellers have called it the Scotland of Turkey. Its fabled blueness stems from its high percentage of alkaline salts, which make it buoyant and cleansing. Only one fish can thrive in it, an endemic Chalcaburnus tarichi, known as tarekh.

The sail was a delight, among friendly Kurds, with short stops here and there at Hebridean-style piers; indeed the feeling was of being in the Scottish islands with rocky skerries and snow-capped peaks like those of home in springtime. On an island we saw, distantly, the famous sixth-century Armenian church of early Christian history. But gradually another famous landmark was drawing closer, the Great Rock of Van, with walls and minarets perched on its bald crown dwarfing ancient mosques under it. Five kilometres from it was our destination, the new town of Van.

In quick time, on landing, we were installed in the best hotel, costing roughly seven shillings in British coin for a room with two beds; no food supplied, but with a boy in the corridor to go out and fetch anything we wanted. I don't know whether it was the sour and greasy soup we ate, in what was praised as the best eating house, that did it, but I felt far from well

79

the next morning when we rose at six to visit Old Van and explore the bird life of the marshes surrounding it.

My diary records:
It was one of the best and one of the worst days I have spent in a foreign country. The birds made it the best, with thrills galore, black-headed wagtails, great reed warblers, black-winged stilts, marsh harriers, Caspian terns, little terns, Brahmny duck, little egrets, rock nuthatches, lesser kestrels and many another. Soldiers from a nearby camp were bathing and gave us cheery greetings. But I was aware of two great urges, one was to visit the lavatory, the other was to lie down. I did both the moment we returned to the billet, but neither eased the headache or the ache in the stomach, so I swallowed some sulpha drugs and hoped for the best.

In bed I was afraid to move because the immediate reaction was diarrhoea and vomiting, so between rushes to the toilet I just lay in a fever with a parching thirst. Next morning I was obliged to go with Douglas to see the Governor for authority to purchase tea and paraffin, which were rationed. We also wanted his good-will and help in getting transport to Hakkari.

Our meeting with this small and friendly official could not have been smoother. He greeted us warmly, immediately ordered tea, never asked for passports or documents, merely said he would wireless Ankara to confirm authority, and do what he could to fix us up with transport on the atrocious road to Hakkari. A lorry was expected in a few days, and he would contact us.

I was feeling much more like myself now, and after a wet afternoon, which brought a skirmish of new snow to the hills, we packed camping equipment and some food and headed off for the marshes below the Great Rock of Van to be out early in the morning for some birding. Frogs were croaking and a cicada chorus sounding as we just beat the darkness getting the tent up. I lit a candle inside to enable us to lay out the bedding and immediately a growth of mosquitoes formed a smudge on the canvas, so I quickly extinguished the light.

Heavy, thundery rain fell in the night and by 5 am, as we boiled our eggs, the sun was rising and we saw that the lake was no longer soda-blue but mud-brown with silt carried down by the streams. Birds were everywhere; dragonflies flitted round us; tortoises sunned themselves nearby. Creeping to try for a photograph, a grey snake thicker than an adder glided across my path. It left behind it a newly cast skin, quite complete, even to jaws and eyelids.

It was the mixture of mountain and marsh birds that was so intriguing; alpine swifts zooming overhead, and swooping about, picking from the surface of the water, and close to where they skimmed, green sandpipers

80

and black winged stilts, Caspian terns, stiff-tailed ducks, egrets and herons of various kinds; march harriers balanced over the reeds, black vultures sailed high and great reed warblers sang all round us as we wound our tortuous way over swollen streams to the ruins of Old Van and the Great Rock standing above, shaped like a battleship from this angle.

This fortress, above the ancient ruins, gets its first mention in the fourteenth century BC. Climbing crumbling staircases we were led to the mouths of man-made caves at different levels, making it a tenement stronghold that was fought over by Persians, Armenians, Sassanians, Tartars, Kurds and Turks of the Ottoman Empire. The Kings of Urartu occupied it in the eleventh century BC. On the south side of the cliff the best evidence of antiquity is a cunieform inscription incised on the rock face, well out of the reach of vandals. We photographed it, and I'm told it reads: 'Here lived Xerxes, Son of Darius, King of the Earth.' Xerxes was King of Persia in 485 BC and after mighty conquests met the usual fate – murder.

I returned another day, by myself, since Douglas was laid low by the same bug that had smitten me, but with the addition of a sore throat. So after I had got him breakfast, I made off for a photographic session with the Kurdish herdsmen around the Rock, watching their sheep and goats and water buffaloes, some with carts with solid wooden wheels pulled by oxen, and behind them colourfully dressed women carrying huge baskets full to the brim, the weight secured by head bands that kept the loads on their backs. At another spot men were making square mud-bricks to build a house. All were friendly and full of laughter, but I could have done without an ever-growing tail of children dancing around me.

Back at the billet I found Douglas much better, and after tea-time as we were walking along the street we were stopped by a lorry driver who was looking for us to give us news that he would be leaving at six in the morning for Hakkari. So at once we threw ourselves into a bout of shopping, getting flour, rice, margarine, potatoes, salt, dried fruit, dried milk, shell-beans, onions, cheese and fifteen black loaves.

The lorry was a Fargo, a six tonner carrying seven tons of cement and a cargo of passengers, six of them soldiers in charge of a prisoner fitted with a ball and chain round his legs. I can tell you we were grateful for our tough Scottish upbringing in bothies and camps. We certainly needed all our resources, whether sleeping out the hours of darkness beneath the stars, or below the lorry to keep the rain off. Patience is not so much a virtue as the lesson experience teaches.

One passenger said he would cut off his hands if this vehicle ever reached Hakkari. He said it was too wide to go through the tunnels, never mind pass through the narrow gorges of the Great Zab. Other critics agreed with him, and we wondered if we should have taken his advice to wait for another vehicle, when we stalled at the first hill and all of us, except the prisoner, had to get down and push. Before the next few hours were over we were beginning to envy that prisoner!

Going slowly had its rewards, however, especially when we came to the towering ruin of a fortress perched on a rock commanding the watershed between Armenia and Mesopotamia. It was the castle of Hosap with below it a bridge over the loop of river. It was there the Assyrians, under King Shalmaneser the third, retreated after their failure to conquer the country, and in more recent times it had become a stronghold of rebel Kurds under Khan Mahmud.

It was hereabouts we saw our first eagle-owl flying alongside on great rounded wings, to alight on a post and study us with huge glaring eyes, ear tufts erect. We saw nightjars dust-bathing on the road, and soldiers fired at, and just missed, a wild boar jogging along in front of us. Here also was the beginning of a series of exciting incidents that were to last for the next twenty-four hours as the road disappeared under the rubble of landslides, and driver and mate went off to examine where best to tackle the obstacles. To the question: 'When will we get to Hakkari?' the driver looked up to heaven and replied, 'God alone knows!' It was not an oath.

But that swarthy driver, who had driven 750 kilometres from the Black Sea to reach Van, was no defeatist for, as one problem led to another, and we churned over boulders forming the stream bed of the river blocking our path, he broke into song, thus restoring the sinking morale of our despondent party who feared a watery demise.

I've written enough about this journey, but the man who said he would cut off his hands if the lorry ever reached its destination was very nearly right. We did stick at the tunnels, but a Jeep came to our aid, took us to Hakkari and brought help to reduce the width of the lorry by removing some of its superstructure. What we did not expect at the end of that rough road was a well-laid-out administrative village complete with a hotel for visitors.

It was to this remote region that Kurds, fleeing from poison gas attacks by Saddam Hussein's weapons, sought refuge in 1990, and endured a bitter winter. It was with some trepidation we sought the Governor next day to present our official permission to explore in his area of the Iran and Syrian border. We knew that an exploration party before us had been turned back despite having a permit. With an interpreter we had taken along, we explained ourselves, told the impassive official of our past light-weight climbs in other remote regions and our reasons for coming to this little-visited area.

Not only was permission forthcoming, but we were asked to wait for two days, when he would arrange transport to a village by the name of Yutsekova, where we would be given a military escort. It was here we were introduced to a ragged-looking pair of Kurds, Bahri and Mehmet, by name. Inspecting our kit they said we would need four horses not two as

82

we proposed. We thought it a ruse to get twice as much money out of us, but in days to come we blessed their wisdom as we forded rivers on horseback that could not be crossed on foot, and rode at twice the walking speed of a man over the undulations between us and our mountains.

We were to develop not only respect for these able Kurds, but a deep liking: Mehmet, forty years old, with shaven head and half-shut eyes that didn't inspire confidence on first sight; Bahri, the boss, in city-style lounge suit jacket and baggy trousers. Both had rubber goloshes for footwear. I wish I could say I liked the Turkish soldiers as well. We took the bold step of dismissing them after two days in their aggressive company.

For me, who had never ridden a horse in my life, it was a tough introduction to pony trekking, akin to crossing the wildest Scottish mountains on horseback, except that these foothills were knee-deep in red poppies and purple vetches, beautiful to behold, yet nothing compared with the alpine meadows we climbed to, slopes of yellow primulas being the ones with the sweetest scents among a host of plants more familiar to us in other high mountain regions. Up there the air was frosty, and the act of riding through big patches of unmelted snow made the horses break into a trot when they reached dry ground, then to a gallop. Even when my hat fell off there was nothing I could do except hope I wouldn't follow the hat. It was a relief when the ground steepened and the leading horse slowed down.

Ahead of us was a wall of red rock, cut by a U-shaped cleft, the Demirkapu Pass – the Iron Gate – perfectly named for its narrowness. For us it was entry into another world. There was no gradual unfolding of a view on the far side. One moment the horses were snorting up a snow-gully between red pinnacles, the next their heads were hanging over a great drop, and before us, as suddenly as a colour picture on a screen, was the mountain range of the Cilo, its beauty unexpected, its form and composition a horse-shoe of shining glaciers flowing between slender spires, with a stream discharging from its centre.

The view was both a revelation of beauty and a climber's despair, for we had not expected peaks quite so perpendicular. Nor could we spend long with binoculars looking for possible routes, for we had to get down to their base by alarming-looking slopes of rock and rubble. The Kurds knew how to cope. Each of us took a good grip on the tail of a horse, and with Bahri hanging on, we did the same, acting as human brakes behind the sliding horses. It worked, and soon we were contouring obliquely, leading them over gullies, until at last we were at the glacial stream to the sward we had seen from above, and here on its alpine meadow pitched three tents.

Watching moonbeams stream out from jagged crags filling the glen with silver, we agreed our first day should be a reconnaissance of the great glacier blocking the head of the horse-shoe. Frost whitened the grass in the morning and walking was a joy as we headed towards a bulging ice-fall whose background was a surround of rock towers. It was obvious to us that these porcupine crests were untraversable, that summits would have to be taken as direct climbs and two looked likely.

The big thrill that day, though, was to see our first Syrian bear mountaineering its way across a steep snow-gully above us, and climbing faster on four paws than any man on two legs, thrusting along like an escaped zoo animal and impressively large and brown, its great head turning towards us occasionally. We were shortly to have an adventure with one of them.

We did not climb next day. A weird sky with rain and low clouds banished the thought, so we made do with the fine alternative of descending the gorge to a Kurdish encampment of black tents perched in the throat of the ravine. With the greeting of 'Merhaba', hand touching the breast, they gave us welcome and invited us into their tents, squatting down beside us in their loose and colourful clothing and wool boots. They had the open expression of frank men, and we looked at them with interest, conscious that we were speaking to semi-nomadic men of a fierce and most ancient race – an independent people who have resisted all change, and survived the passage of all the invaders of this most ancient part of the ancient world.

These were true mountain Kurds, of the kind the Turks would like to suppress. It was one reason why we dismissed the soldiers who had been less than agreeable to other encampments encountered in less wild areas we had passed through. This tribe flaunted weapons which are forbidden. They could be free with our own two Kurds and with us.

We were in the company of a pastoral people, whose livelihood lay in the animals, sheep, goats and cows all around us. As we talked, yoghurt was being shaken up in a skin bag, while a tall woman, beautifully dressed in white blouse and graceful baggy trousers, organised a feast for us. She was queen of a host of not-so-distinguished-looking women, and in due course we were ushered in to a ceremonial tent, seated on carpets, and a huge tray was set down bearing delicious new bread and butter, fried meat, fried eggs and yoghurt, round which we all sat cross-legged and dipped in as we felt inclined. No plates here, or knives or forks. They were neat with their fingers, a lesson to us, and when you had had enough you withdrew to make room for someone else.

These Kurds were oriented on Iraq rather than Turkey, though their village was in the Hakkari region. They got their clothing, cooking pots, and no doubt their ammunition there, for they were hunters as well as herdsmen. Within minutes of handing them our binoculars they were pointing out family parties of bears, and herds of ibex on the crags. Luckily we were able to return their hospitality with gifts of sugar and tea, while the numerous children each got sweets and chocolate. We became such

84

firm friends that this tribe used to come and visit us, and we felt proud to be on such good terms with a people whose forbears had lived in these mountains for 2,000 years before there was a Persia or a Turkey. Except in outlandish places such as this it looks as if the Turks are absorbing the Kurds, but we were able to see a few more wild tribes clinging to their independence before we left the mountains.

Altogether we spent a week in this charmed camp spot 1,000 feet above the Kurdish camp, and the quality of afternoon light was a constant delight, especially around 4 pm when the meadows and pinnacles shone in the lowering sunlight and the tents gleamed orange against a blaze of alpine flowers – colour all the more vivid as the huge mountain wall above us became luminous, and stray sunrays filtered between the pinnacles. We had climbed two good mountains named by the German explorers, the Eckfeiler, 3,700 metres, and the Seespitz, 3,460 metres. It was on the first of those we had our too close encounter with a Syrian bear, huge, brown and growling. We were in a gully on steep frozen snow, nicking footsteps with our ice-axes, when out from the rocks across our path charged the bear, mouth open. We didn't even have time to be frightened as it shot across our bows, skidding on the frozen snow, but getting a better claw hold when it climbed vertically upwards, until it stopped for a breather, turned its head and stared down at us, pointed ears erect. Shouting at it, and blowing a whistle, we sped its departure. Only then did we realise what a good photograph we had missed.

On our climbs we looked hard at the highest peak in the massif, the Geliasan, 4,170 metres rising in 4,000 feet of steep rock above its glacier. It had never been tried from Bear Meadow, the name given to where we were camped.

In fact, we saw bears every day we were in these mountains, thankfully from a distance. They heightened our pleasure, as did the flowers which surpassed those of the Himalaya in their variety. They even bloomed through the snow: pale pink crocuses, primulas of many colours lining the banks of streams, geraniums and sweet peas, while amongst the rocks were cushions of alpines, white and red. The birds too were a delight: rock thrushes of orange and blue, red billed choughs, ortolan buntings, flocks of vividly pied snow finches, dippers and wagtails on the rivers, even common sandpipers as in Scotland. Soaring over the peaks we could see lammergeyer and griffon vultures of nine feet wing-span, familiar to us in the Himalaya.

The time had come now to move out by the way we had come in, and to look at the Geliasan from its other side to see if we could find a route to its top from there. So it was up in the morning before 5 am for the 3,000-foot climb to cross the numerous spurs separating us from its eastern side. The journey took two days, with descents to terraced fields and the sad ruins of Nestorian Christian settlements whose folk had been murdered in recent times by Kurds, just as these assassins were to meet the same fate at the hands of the Turks. Of human life all we saw was one camp of semi-nomads with hundreds of sheep, goats and cattle.

In the morning we saw the pass we had to cross, a snow-crest gleaming in the sun, and the way to it was by a rocky zig-zag to ice-covered lochans, the bleaker for not having sunshine. But from its high crest we got what we wanted, a view of the whole east ridge of our mountain rising above a contortion of green ice-falls and a crevassed glacier. To gain the ridge would mean a rock climb up a rock-wall of 2,500 feet. It looked uncompromising, but you can never judge a mountain wall until you rub your nose on it. Down we went for 3,000 feet to camp among a tumble of gigantic boulders.

Descent to that camp site was in heavy rain, so it was good to get in, put the horses to graze, and set about making some pancakes as a change from eating stale bread, so hard that we had to chop it with an ice-axe. It was the rawest weather we experienced in Turkish Kurdistan, low clouds swirling round the crags as on a bad day in Scotland. But we enjoyed our wild situation, especially when, 200 yards from us, a mother bear with two cubs was rooting amongst the stones. Mother was light brown with a dark back; the youngsters were darker, and we watched the parent turning over stones, licking them and chewing as if she were getting grubs of some kind. Alas, our Kurds started shouting to drive the bears away, and the speed at which the parent climbed the rocks to get out of our vision was a revelation, the cubs doing well to keep up with her.

A glorious moon and clear sky that night promised well, so we were away by 4.30 in the morning to cross a snow-bridge over the river and get to work on the grey wall rising like a skyscraper over our heads. Like most rock faces, however, it was not as vertical as it looked, but was so deficient in ledges that we deemed it safer not to wear the rope until the rock-strata changed, and it was possible to get belays that made it possible to hold a man if he slipped.

Bahri had pointed out to us where the Austrians had attacked the peak, and this was roughly our line which gave a superb climb dangerously loose in its lower section, then it became sounder as it steepened in a series of rock towers, involving some airy traverses, one across a great wall, and it was a relief to find it connecting to a chimney leading to another tower with a tricky vertical descent. At each tower we expected a cut-off, but always the weakness we followed continued, the skyline getting nearer until at last the angle eased back and we topped the ridge after four hours of really interesting rock climbing.

Above us, blocking the ridge ahead, was a rock peak marked 3,750 metres on the Austrian map, a black tooth quite vertical with no cairn on top, and whose north side fell to a much crevassed glacier. Now we moved westward on a narrowing ridge between precipices. Along this we went

86

for a mile, making height steadily to phase three of the ascent, a high-angled snowcap, where the ridge bent north-west and became broader, so we were able to avoid fifty per cent of the large quantity of snow lying on it.

Views from up here were spectacular, southward past a plunge of pinnacles to terraced fields where houses were perched, while to the north and west savage crags dropped in pink walls to green ice and crevassed glacier. We felt at this point the wearisome grind of putting one foot in front of the other would never cease, as beyond one snow hump there was always another. Then at half past one in the afternoon we were there, looking down on the glen from where we had so often looked up at this peak. Now we could see escarpments of mountains far into Iraq and round to where Iran and Turkey merged. The most inaccessible summit in Asia Minor was ours, to be savoured as an uncontaminated wilderness – as yet.

After half an hour trying to imprint the panorama around us in our minds, we turned our thoughts to forsaking the route of the morning, for descent of a steep snow-slope leading into a wide basin, from which we intended to climb directly to a far point on the long summit ridge we had traversed. This went well, but the descent proved slower going than we expected, taking 2,000 feet of rock a rope-length at a time.

It went well at first, but with high-angled frozen snow mixed with poor rock it demanded care and vigilance and must have been testing for Douglas who was feeling unwell, especially when we had to chimney between rock and snow, wondering all the time if there would be some impasse that would block our way and force us to spend a night out. But there was none. Dusk was drawing to darkness as we got to the foot of it, and the light was just good enough for us to see two bears scuttling below us.

Stumbling over moraines it seemed we would never get to camp, crossing snow-gullies and boulders, then suddenly we saw a light far below – the tents – and simultaneously we heard a whistle, faint but heartening. Indeed we were still fumbling through crags when a shape materialised near us, not a bear but Mehmet, who had seen our light and climbed up to help us down. How good to be led back to camp where Bahri had the kettle boiling and welcome tea quickly in our hands. We were ready for our sleeping bags, feeling that the Geliasan had certainly given us a climb to remember.

Unfortunately the desire for a rest after the big climb had to be quenched if we wanted to explore the peaks of the adjacent range, separated from us by the formidable gorge of the Rudbare Sin, for our food supplies were getting low and so was our cash. We had travelled with a minimum supply of money because of the danger of being robbed by Kurdish brigands. Our dilemma was whether to plunge directly down to the gorge, or traverse into it from the ridge above at 10,000 feet where mountain flanks were of softer form.

We chose the latter, and it led us to meadows, carpeted with flowers, and a lochan 2,000 feet above the gorge, where we camped looking out on a range of fantastic pinnacles and trench-like valleys rising on the other side. They were to prove even wilder than they looked. First, though, we had to drop from refreshing alps into a slot of enervating heat, a world of sterility and fertility. The fertility was in the oak and walnut trees, the tropical flowers, and small terraced fields where streams pouring off the peaks gave life and irrigation channels. Precipices sawing the air and hemming the torrent told why this region is inhabited by Kurds so independent that they are almost a law unto themselves.

To our regret we saw only a few of these mountain dwellers. The villages were empty. Their inhabitants were away to higher pastures, and their well-built stone houses were securely locked. We guessed why, with biting flies driving the horses nearly crazy and perspiration dripping off ourselves. This was no place to be in summer, though the woods were busy with birds, woodpeckers, golden orioles and such familiar homeland species as chaffinches and wood pigeons, dippers, grey wagtails and jays.

There was a bridge of interlaced twigs enabling us to cross the deep river, but the horses had to be swum across assisted by the Kurds who had each one on a rope. It was surprising how little persuasion they needed. They certainly needed none once out of the water and climbing out of the zone of flies for 2,000 feet! My diary records a few anxious moments, contouring rocks, with a track zig-zagging up a huge moraine where snow formed a natural bridge over the stream and two fawn-coloured ibex with smooth pelts and big curving horns looked down on us, before elevating their black tails and springing lightly from rock to rock.

Our camp that night was a real eyrie, looking out through the sword-cut of the gorge to the peak of the Geliasin. Of this I wrote at the time:

> Wonderful to have climbed it. This is really one of the best camp spots in my experience. Celebrated arrival by a good meal of oxtail soup, pork, potatoes and onions, rice pudding and apricots, then fresh pancakes and tea – both piping hot.

Moonlight and a dawn alpenglow on the Geliasin made this camp even more memorable, and so did the climb ahead, involving us in making a path for the horses on the ice and rubble of a dying glacier that led via a wide bowl of high-angled snow to a frozen lochan below a ring of rock spires – the perfect base camp for the Sat Dagh. The best peak we climbed was the Ciae Dis, 3,360 metres.

Up there we were filled with admiration and envy of the Australians, led by Dr Hans Bobek, who had made the first penetration of these mountains to map them twenty years earlier. It was a photographic copy of their map we were using, and we found it accurate in every detail. But for them we would not have known to come here and carry exploration a stage further, as had another Austrian party before us. We were less than four miles from Iraq, looking into a great escarpment of limestone frowning down on Mesopotamia.

In the direction of Mosul, the sky had the pale look of the Sahara, in contrast to the cloud-flecked blue of Persia and Turkey, telling of a more congenial climate. Our desire was to drop south, progressing by remote valleys of Iraq where few Europeans have ever been. The terrain is so rough that horses cannot be used for travel.

We had to be content with going east, however, across the next mountain ridge to see what lay beyond. The memory of that crossing is of hosts of gentians in deep blue clusters; and of a rock where we found Stone Age drawings of figures with bows and arrows, and representations of animals incised on flat rocks, some recognisable as deer and ibex. It was the last link we needed to complete our picture of the Ancient World, for we had seen fragments of every other developing civilisation from Hittite lions and cunieform writings of Babylonians to a hilltop temple of early Christians.

This crossing revealed the astonishing climbing possibilities of the highest peaks of the Sat group. The two peaks we chose were on steep sound rock as good as any in the European Alps. After crossing three more passes we had the proof that travelling in the Sat Dag is more difficult than in the higher Cilo Dag, yet we came across more Kurdish camps, and it was pathetic to see some Kurds remove their turbans and substitute cloth-caps at our approach, Kurdish dress being forbidden by the Turks.

Our very last pass was almost as dramatic as the first one at the beginning of our journey. Instead of mountains we looked down on the first flat plain we had seen since leaving Anatolia. But this was no prairie, it was a huge wet marshland 6,000 feet above sea-level. Our descent to it was by a succession of grassy downlands then almost suddenly the horses were belly-deep and struggling to make progress. We could only hope they wouldn't flounder and leave us stranded. This flat is known as the Gevar-Ova, and it was home territory to our Kurds who saw us safely across, stopping off at a little village on the way.

Bahri waved us to dismount at a mud-house built on a rise, and invited us to enter. Going through the door we found ourselves in a dimly lit long room which in contrast to the heat outside felt deliciously cool. Within moments its owner was welcoming us and leading us to a carpet where we all sat cross-legged, and I became aware that we shared the room with a horse and some young calves. There was also a cot, and when our host saw me glancing at it he waved me over to look within.

With a flourish he removed the covering to reveal a small baby, and rattled a string of walnuts to make it smile. Swarms of flies buzzed out at each shake of the rattle, but there were still enough left clustering round the baby's eyes almost to obscure them.

W.ving me back to the carpet, he disappeared for a short time, and came in with a pail of sparkling snow, offering lumps to us, and to some of his children who had gathered about us. Its dazzling purity was in contrast to everything else in the room. 'From the Sat Dagh,' he said, pointing below the house where his underground storage system must have been good. Dim as the light was, we could see fleas jumping on the carpet where we sat.

Then in came his wife with a meal of new-baked bread, yoghurt and fried eggs, and we were given wooden spoons to eat with, the Kurd sitting down with us and encouraging us to eat our fill. His house could have been a mansion and his easy manners worthy of one. To a gift of a tin of sweets for the children he bowed his head in acknowledgement, refusing at first to take it, nor did he open it to see what was inside.

Exit from the mountains was all too speedy. One year earlier it would have taken us four days to reach Baskale. Now a motor road to the Great Zab got us there in five hours by lorry. So it was farewell to Bahri and Mehmet who had served us so faithfully, and we looked our last on the mountains that had given us so much.

Returning from the exhilaration of high places into Turkish Armenia, the hills which had been green were now withered and brown. Where we had plunged through mud in June we now had to put handkerchiefs over our mouths to keep the dust out of our throats in late July. From Van we had permission to board a bus that took us 750 kilometres to the Black Sea, with never a dull moment, though plenty of sleepy ones, through vast armed camps in this part of Turkey bordering Russia. Ack-ack guns, Jeeps, lorries, artillery stood at the ready; watching eyes directed on Georgia.

The Turks reckon that whether you are a Scot, an Indian, a Japanese, an American, an Australian or of any other nationality, you will find a bit of your own scenery in Turkey. Erzurum is Indian with blowing dust, but when you climb northward over the mountains you enter Switzerland as the valleys deepen and forests of pine and spruce stand above chalets on cultivated alpine meadows.

This is the attractive Pontic Taurus where children crowded our bus, at stops, to offer capfuls of cherries, peaches, pears and apricots from their own trees. It was over these wooded hills that Zenophon's weary army straggled on their long retreat from Mesopotamia, setting up a loud cry of: 'Thalassa, thalassa' – the Sea – which spelt home to them after years of battling in a foreign land.

The sea spelt home to us too, as we zig-zagged down and down to Trebizond after two days cramped in the bus, and in harbour there, ready to sail in twenty-four hours, was a passenger ship bound for Istanbul on which we booked a passage. Sitting in deck chairs next day, among the well-dressed tourists, we watched the famed Black Sea coast drift by, seeing in imagination the great Anatolian Plain behind these green forests stretching from Armenia and Syria to the Persian Gulf, land of war and bitter struggle described as the 'Cradle of Civilisation', but getting further and further away from that description every day.

It is in that 'Cradle' my father is buried, but has no known grave. His only commemoration is on a panel with a list of names at Basra, sixty-four kilometres from the mouth of the Tigris where it enters the Persian Gulf. I got this information from the Commonwealth War Graves Commission in a letter informing me that a large proportion of the records of soldiers killed during the period 1914–20 were totally destroyed by enemy action in 1940, and it would seem that S/6405 Lance Corporal Thomas Weir's was among the records lost.

Can it be that there is indeed 'a divinity that shapes our ends'? I think I prefer the guid auld Scottish aphorism, 'Whit's fur ye, will no go by ye.' But maybe it means the same thing.

I wrote the above before it was reinforced by this story I now tell, which begins on an evening in 1985 when I opened the door to a well-built stranger, swarthy of face with a black tooth-brush moustache and alert brown eyes: 'I want to shake your hand. On television you have said good things about my people. I am from Kurdistan. My name is Nabaz Malaly, from Slemani.'

I held out my hand, and after it had been taken, invited him in. As I introduced him to my wife, she asked politely if there was someone else in the car he would like to bring in. His answer was a smiling: 'Yes. It is the girl I shall marry in a week or two.' My wife went out and ushered in an attractive Glasgow lassie. 'This is Joy,' he said with pride. 'As Joy Malaly she will go with me to a job in Saudi Arabia.'

The television film that had stimulated Nabaz's desire to talk to me was *Tom Weir at Seventy*, an hour-long interview with Magnus Magnusson looking back on my life. As I talked, film clips and slides I had taken were shown against various episodes I was describing. Of my various mountaineering expeditions I pin-pointed my trip with Douglas Scott to Kurdistan as being the most interesting of them all, not least because of the colourful Kurdish tribesmen living the nomadic lives among beautiful and inaccessible peaks beyond reach of their Turkish and Iraqi oppressors.

To make him feel at home I showed him some pictures of Kurds we had met and peaks we had climbed, discovering that his passion, apart from fighting for a 'free Kurdistan', was true mountaineering on rock and ice. He talked with enthusiasm of the Glasgow Lomond Mountaineering Club, and climbs he had done with its members in Glencoe and Ben Nevis. But now he was having to leave Scotland for a job in microbiology in Saudi Arabia.

It was by no means the last I heard of him, for he sent me postcards from the Middle East, telling me of the excellent rock climbing he was finding when he had time off from his hospital job. In 1988 he had raised the Kurdish flag on a hitherto unclimbed peak in the Pakistan Himalaya.

His last letter to me was dated 18.3.93. It read:

The Friends of Kurdistan Society (Scotland) on behalf of the Kurdish community have much pleasure in inviting you to join us for our Kurdish New Year (NEWROZ 2693) celebration in Glasgow on Tuesday 30th March, 7.30 to 11.30 pm.

An invitation card showed a programme of Kurdish music, dancing and food. Alas, I didn't go.

However I did see him at the Lomond Mountaineering Club dinner, when the Glasgow club celebrated its sixtieth anniversary, and I was Principal Guest. He was working in Glasgow Royal Infirmary, and I would hardly have known that his serene and confident blond-haired wife was the same shy and immature girl who had come to our house. She was now the proud mother of three children, Jwan, Dilan and Daran, and Nabaz was insisting that my wife and I come as guests to their house, meet the children and partake of a real Kurdish meal cooked by Joy.

On wall-boards behind the dinner table was a photographic display of Lomond climbers in action, and Nabaz showed me ones of him climbing. He told me he was away most weekends: 'To live properly, a Kurd must have mountains to climb.' From when he was very young, his father had taken him and his brother Yasser on long hunting expeditions, and as he grew up he became politically active in the Kurdish struggle for independence. By March 1974 he had joined the Kurdish Liberation Movement revolt against Saddam Hussein, and was soon a leader, administrator and freedom-fighter.

Sadly the revolution ended in defeat in the spring of 1975, when he returned to the university in Slemani to complete his final year and graduate with an Honours Degree, obtaining a PhD at Glasgow University in 1981, when he returned to Iraqi Kurdistan to find that his brother had been murdered by Saddam's secret police. He himself, to avoid having to serve in the Iraqi army then at war with Iran, returned in haste to Glasgow. His words to me in my house on our first meeting was that Scotland was heaven on earth, apart from the weather!

Then one day in mid-April of 1993 I got a shock on opening the *Glasgow Herald* to read a short paragraph under the heading:

Doctor Dies on Ben Nevis

A doctor died of head and chest injuries after falling 400 feet on Ben Nevis. A Sea-King helicopter took Dr Nabaz Malaly, of Ferncroft Drive, Glasgow, to Belford Hospital, Fort William on Sunday. Dr

Malaly, a microbiologist, died during a helicopter flight to the Southern General Hospital, Glasgow.

Nabaz was seen falling by other climbers and they summoned the helicopter. He was making a solo ascent of a hardish climb that was well within his capabilities. But new snow had fallen and it could have been that the underlying ice on which he had to depend was weak. A radio telephone in the mountain hut summoned the helicopter.

What happened to cause the fall we shall never know. Words spoken at his funeral service by a Kurdish relative translated into English read: 'In his heart Nabaz felt that by climbing high he could convey the suffering of the Kurdish nation closer to the heavens in the hope that one day justice and peace will be bestowed on them from above. As a climber he was brave and keen, without fear of danger or risk. He lived for the mountains, and it was the mountains that took him from his family, friends and country. In Kurdistan he will be remembered as a man who dedicated his life for the freedom of his people.'

But what about his young widow, and the children without a father to share their lives? Climbing can never be a safe activity, for the more proficient you are, the harder you climb, trying to find your limit. Without the danger element that brings out your best, there is not the same exhilaration, and that is the drug factor in what is too dangerous a sport to exercise alone.

7

All Over the Place

Variety's the very spice of life,
That gives it all its flavour.
                    William Cowper

In 1992, at a reunion of surviving members of the 1950 Scottish
Himalayan expedition at Inveroran Hotel, Graham Little, the mountaineer who invited us, had brought along his projector and screen just seven
weeks after his return from climbing Panch Chuli. He wrote of it
afterwards:

> The three living members of the 1950 Scottish Himalayan Expedi-
> tion watch as Chris [Bonington] and I make a final climb along 'a
> shining chisel blade of ice' to the summit of Panch Chuli 2. Forty
> years have elapsed and yet time is reversed: they are there again,
> looking over the greater Himalaya, sharing the magic, reliving the
> joy that is forever within us.

On return from our 1950 expedition Bill Murray had written:

> One could not find mountains more worthy of ascent. The final peak
> of Panch Chuli stood right before our eyes, a shining chisel blade of
> ice. So thin were its upper edges that over a stretch of a thousand feet
> we could see the sun shining through.

Panch Chuli translates as the Five Fires, highest of the group is No 2; its
summit 6,904 metres. The snout of the Uttari Balati Glacier is one of the
lowest in the Himalaya, where base camp was situated at 3,200 metres with
a height difference to the summit of 3,700 metres, more than Mount
Everest from its base. The 'fires' relate to the glow on the peaks at dawn
and sunset. Our 1950 attempt on the mountain was from the east. Theirs
was from the west, the route recommended by Bill Murray following his
recce before we left the 'Fires'.

Bill was a trainee banker before the war, but even at school he wanted to
be a writer. Call it bad luck if you like that as Captain Murray he was taken
prisoner in the western desert and had to face three years of prison camps,

94

with their lack of privacy, starvation diet, and above all their fearful confinement. Yet he found a way to live more in the mind than the body and set himself to write *Mountaineering in Scotland* on stiff brown toilet paper. He had completed it and stuffed it into his battle blouse when he was moved to another camp policed by the Gestapo. He was searched, the manuscript scrutinised, taken away, then, believing that it was a secret code for Czechoslovakian Partisans, it was never returned to him. But as the allied advance on Germany moved closer, the prisoners were moved again, this time to a camp well provided with amenities and real paper for writing on, so he rewrote the pages which became *Mountaineering in Scotland* and reviewers who forecast that time would prove it to be a literary classic were correct. It was just after he had finished a sequel with the title *Undiscovered Scotland* that Douglas Scott invited him to join the first Scottish Himalayan expedition.

In 1992 both of these books were published in one volume. After his Scottish Himalayan expedition book, and his explorations in the Everest region which led to finding a possible route to the South Col and the summit, he had the subject for his fourth book, *The Story of Everest*, from its discovery as the highest peak in the world to the first attempts in the 1920s, a period when it was unknown if man could survive at these heights, despite successive attempts with bottled oxygen – all from the Tibetan side. Then the British explorers were forced to stand aside when the Swiss were allowed by the Government of Nepal to make the first attempt from their side.

The thorough Bill had to hedge his bets: leave open the last chapter and have it ready for a Swiss victory and, when they failed, keep it open for a possible successful attempt by Sir John Hunt's party. First published in April 1953 after the Swiss failure, it was reprinted in May, revised in July and reprinted again in August. A real scoop, from first attempts to final success, it went into eight foreign translations.

In life you never know what is in store for you, and as Rabbie Burns put it: 'The best laid schemes o' mice and men gang aft agley.' At the time when Ed Hillary and Sherpa Tensing were reaching the top of Mount Everest I should have been fulfilling a long-held dream, traversing on skis and climbing peaks on the high-level traverse route between Chamonix and Zermatt. Instead, I was coming back to the hills after being avalanched near the summit of a Scottish peak in February three months earlier. Ironically I had returned from the Everest region just before New Year.

February had brought superb conditions of sun and frost and four of us looked forward to a classic ascent of the 'upper couloir' of Stob Ghabhar. Alas, overnight there had been a drastic change. Snow was falling out of low yellow mist and as we got up the wind became unpleasant. Black crags were hung with ice-falls and we sank deeply at each step. We reckoned it must have been snowing up high for several hours.

The couloir is a narrow cleft between two rock buttresses abutting directly to the summit. We roped up 600 feet below it to combine the lower couloir and its icy rocks with the upper.

I didn't like the looseness of the snow on top of the old hard stuff, fearing it would slide off. I thought it would be safer to leave the gully and tackle an ice-fall flowing over the rocks. Technically it was difficult, and now and then I had to hang on as fierce blasts of wind and spume struck. It led us close to the summit, but the way ahead was so steep that I could almost touch it with my nose, and even shovelling away with my axe I couldn't get down to the safe hard stuff. I tried tramping out a groove. I knew that my second had a good ice-axe belay. The other two were about eighty feet below him.

I had plunged my ice-axe up to its head, and gave the shaft a tug. Quite silently, and with irresistible force, the whole slope heeled over, hurtling me down. My second man was torn from his axe so firmly planted in the hard snow. The two others saw a great snow-tide advancing on them and tried to hold. They were lifted bodily and hurled down with us. My first reaction was that we were going to be smothered. I was in the air turning over and over. Things hit me and jarred my ribs (the rope joining us) I was a detached spectator who sees himself in a dream hurtling to death, and wakes in nightmare.

Then suddenly I began to slow up, and at once started a swimming motion to keep on the surface and not be buried and suffocated. I came to rest beside my second and I feared he was dead. His face was covered in blood, but he answered my question and said he thought he was all right. My leg was numb from the thigh downwards and I felt it trembling with shock. Blood spurted over my jacket and hands. It was then I realised that my own face was covered in blood.

Then there was a shout from above. Neither of us was capable of rising as yet. The other two joined us. The nylon rope had snapped between us, hence their coming to rest at different points. All were concerned for my eyebrow which had split open.

We reviewed the damage. One was almost unscathed. The other two were badly bruised and in considerable pain, one with twisted ankles, the other with a back that was agony. I felt sure that any man left out on the mountain would surely die in conditions of wind, blowing snow and cold. We must move as fast as our injuries would allow, for we would have to steer a compass course right round the mountain. At 6 pm we were only two miles from the car and almost at the track. We left the sound man to help our companion with the twisted ankles, and the two of us went ahead. We were lucky to find the keeper at Forest Lodge at home. He had a van and off he drove to pick up the other two where we had left them.

Soon we were assembled in the keeper's kitchen and plied with tea by his wife. They could not have been kinder or more understanding. There is always a fortunate side to any unlucky event. Ian, my second man, could drive the car, and we had hotel-owning friends only twenty miles away at Inverarnain. There we had baths, a hot dinner, bathed our wounds and one man went to bed. We drove on to Glasgow and Ian dropped me off at our tenement building at 2 am. I just managed to climb the two stairs and no more, my leg was now so badly swollen and stiff.

I had hoped my mother wouldn't hear me come in, but she had been waiting anxiously wondering why I was so late. Now she was shocked at my appearance, and I am afraid I was a bit curt in ordering her to bed. She would have been more worried had she seen me trying to get into my own bed, every move torturing my ribs. But once in, I was asleep within minutes, and groaned when I had a call from Dr James Kerr in the morning, telling me that Ian had phoned him and he was bringing an ambulance to take me to the Western Infirmary for an X-ray.

The injuries took longer to heal than I expected, and on that morning when Tom MacKinnon came into the Glencoe hut telling us that Everest had been climbed, I celebrated my return to the hills by climbing Archer Ridge on Aonach Dubh, and next day took my doctor friend, James Kerr, up a climb on Buachaille Etive Mor, as thanks for visiting me nearly every day I was in his hospital.

My loss of that high-level ski-traverse, however, was the gain of the friend who took my place. On the other hand the period of inaction made me settle down and tell the story of the Scottish Nepal expedition of 1952, resulting in the book *East of Katmandu*, published in 1955 and reprinted in 1981. I also busied myself with some photo-features for newspapers and magazines. A Scotsman, Alex Connor, proved a good friend, and after his death a few years ago his son sent this piece about me he found among his father's papers.

I was in the office one day when a smallish sparkling-eyed man in his late 30s I reckoned, breezed in. 'My name's Weir – Tom.' It meant nothing to me but soon, throughout Scotland at least, it became as well known as that of his famous sister, Molly of war-time Itma fame. Tom's enthusiasm for the things he was doing showed in his eyes. He had thrown up his job in the Ordnance Survey in order to indulge his passion for climbing and the greater freedom of the outdoor-life generally. But he still had to earn a living and he saw that coming from article work for magazines on mountaineering and the challenge of the peaks. Later, with age, he literally came down from the clouds a bit with a never-ending stream of contributions describing the joy to be found in the Scottish scene at an altitude more suited to the ordinary person.

He was on a market recce, I adjudged. I was able to tell him that pre-war I had earned a good living as a freelance and that there was a market. It was obvious he could write and that he could use a camera to advantage as a supporting tool.

Mountaineering was far removed from mining, the subject I was spending more and more time writing about. By chance, I was that day fixing a date for a visit to Brora Colliery, Britain's most northerly and oldest working pit amongst the country's thousand or so. It was a Brora distinction like its one-time modest alluvial gold discoveries nearby.

Tom saw this as a new and novel experience for him. Could he come with me he asked. Being an outdoor type he said he would bring his tent. Off we went by car, found a camping spot behind the shelter of a wall taking the brunt of the cold wind blowing from the North Sea and presented ourselves at the colliery in the morning. It was all a new world for Tom, underground with the miners, and having preplanned and prepared, he took out his camera and captured facial expressions of true-like reality, black faces and all, as they worked. Certainly a contrast to the Himalaya.

In Scotland I discovered there was no end of picture stories to be picked up, so much was changing in a post-war world of opportunity, in contrast to the bleak 30s. It was Alex who persuaded me to put my profits into buying a motor car, and not waste precious time depending on public transport. But new cars were in short supply, even the Ford Popular, cheapest at £400. I didn't want anything second-hand for fear of breakdowns on the road. Then one day I was offered the new Austin A30, price £520. I paid cash, and on Glasgow Fair Saturday, a shop-keepers' holiday, picked up my butcher pal, Matt, and off we drove to North Berwick in the hope of getting on to the Bass Rock where neither of us had ever been, but were eager to see its famous gannet colony.

On the pier as we got out of the car I was hailed by a man I knew, John King, a history master of Edinburgh Academy who shouted: 'Are you coming over with us? You could be of help ringing gannets and shags. We'll be leaving in a few minutes and we should have six hours ashore.'

Luck indeed. Even as we sailed, a dullish morning was giving way to sunshine, and in half an hour we were under a veritable blizzard of white wings whirling round what is the stump of an ancient volcano projecting in rock-ledges 321 feet high above the Firth of Forth.

What a photographic day I had there, edging out on the ledges high above the sea, and seeing these oceanic birds really close for the first time, coming and going to feed young birds at all stages of development. A good natural history story needs people, and here were boys and masters in airy places catching these huge birds, skilfully holding them so that their beaks could do them no damage while rings were fastened to their legs. Young birds were ringed too, as well as shags nesting at the foot of a precipitous gully which had a chain in position to make descent safer.

The rock had lighthouse keepers resident on it at that time, who told us the story of how when the Bass was a prison for Covenanters, and then also for Jacobites, four of them overpowered their guards and held the rock for James VII until 1694. So this was the last part of Scotland to surrender to the Union and become part of Britain.

The story I did that day paid the cost of the Austin A30 within one year, and in successive visits to the Bass I added to the account as more and more was revealed of the life story of the gannet. I was so eager to see the results of that first day that whenever I got home I loaded my developing tanks, cutting the time of development slightly to lessen the contrast between white birds and bird ringers, so that printing would be simplified.

Next day I had a big session at the enlarger making dozens of 10" by 8" prints and captioning groups of them, varying the treatments so that no two sets were the same. Then came the tedious bit, putting them in big envelopes stiffened with cardboard. That done, the bundles were posted so as to arrive in newspaper offices in England and Scotland on the same morning, in the hope that a goodly number would be featured. In fact the success ratio was ninety per cent.

The period from the end of the war until the 1960s, when so many developments were taking place in Scotland, was hard to keep abreast of if you were out of the country for any length of time, and I tried to make the most of it in picture stories. At the same time I realised I was in my physical prime, and that I should grasp every opportunity to climb and explore in the mountain ranges that had fired my imagination by reading or hearsay. So while I used the period usefully while the patella was mending, I was arranging a trip to the Julian Alps of what was then Yugoslavia with two companions, one of them Dr James Kerr who had visited me so often in the Western Infirmary.

Here is what Dr Tom Longstaff answered when he was asked for his opinion of the Julian peaks:

It is a fact that they have become for me, after forty years' devotion to scenery, the most desirable of all mountains. I want to revisit them more than I desire to see any other region of the Alps: more than the desire to see the frosty Caucasus, or Himalaya, or the mountains of Canada and Alaska, or the ineffable light of the low sun on the fantastic peaks of the Arctic. I believe this feeling is greatly due to their surprising quality of mystery. By comparison the Dolomites are obvious. Surely there is no other mountain land like this.

My first impression of them was mysterious enough: forked lightning stabbing, thunder growling, and rain with tropical force battering the windows of the railway carriage. Then, as it passed, wild tatters of cloud ablaze with sunset parted slender towers and spires – verily 'Castles in the air' stood revealed. As I was to discover, the Adriatic does for the Julian Alps what the Atlantic does for the rock peaks of the Cuillin of Skye, except that the Julians are three times higher and tall forest trees surround their base.

Jalovec, the Queen of the Julians, stands at the head of the Planica Glen, where the Tamar Hut, close to the Italian border, provides bed, two blankets and simple meals for a few shillings, or did in 1953 when I was guest of Professor Avicin and Dr Daro Dollar, two of the leading lights of the Alpine Club of Slovenia at that time. With us, too, was Dollar's girl-friend.

I had been introduced to them the night before in Ljubljana by a gentleman who had boarded the train at Trieste, had noticed my rucksack and that I was reading an English book, and discovering I was Scottish, had announced that he had trained in Glasgow's Western Infirmary and was Marshal Tito's physician. When he found out that I was not on my way to meet friends but was proposing to climb alone in the Julians, he took me in charge the moment we got off the train. He led me to a hotel, and said he would return in six hours with some alpinists who would be able to help me.

We had a jolly evening, eating and drinking too much, resulting in my being sick in the night, and not feeling my best when the Professor arrived at 8 am on his motorbike to take me sight-seeing round the town and do some shopping for food. Three hours later we were boarding a train for Ratce, almost on the Italian frontier in an alpine zone of pine woods and green alps, with the spiky peaks of the Julians towering up in razor edges, and giant limestone rock buttresses.

The walk to the Tamar Hut at 3,600 feet was a joy, and on it I had my first-ever sighting of a chamois, slender-antlered, its fawn coat tipped with ebony along the spine. Interesting birds kept popping up: red backed shrikes, crested tits, black redstarts and nutcrackers. On the alpine meadows sky-blue gentians and cushions of pink moss-campion mingled with silky edelweiss.

That chat in the hut was good. My friends had all been partisans, and all were agreed that since the swing away from Russian communism to the more democratic order under Tito in 1948, life had become easier, with a slackening of police control.

Up at 3 am next morning we were away within the hour as rays of bright orange touched the tips of the peaks, and filtered through mountains where our target, Jalovec's east wall, rose in two leaning steps for 5,000 feet, the first 1,500 feet, the second overhanging, and the Slavs chuckled when I said I could detect no way through that upper section. 'You will see,' Avicin said.

They were certainly first-rate rock men, wriggling up cracks, swarming up chimney clefts, traversing narrow ledges, searching for lines of weakness of slabs until we were immediately below the section which looked to me unclimbable.

'Now,' said Professor Avicin, 'you must lead us from here.' They were enjoying the look of incredulity on my face as we changed the order of the rope and I set off on the only way one could go, by an exposed traverse on the tilting edge of the wall with nothing but fresh air below. But the hand- and footholds were reassuring. On I went, losing sight of the others as I angled round and found myself facing a natural tunnel piercing the overhang and offering an easy passage. I could hear them laughing, enjoying the surprise I must be feeling after that sensational traverse.

The difficulties were over, and perched on the edge of the big overhang once we were up the wall, we arranged ourselves on a sloping slab to have breakfast and enjoy the view. Swinging off his rucksack, Dollar laid it down and disappeared to do an urgent job for himself. On his return, he leapt down from the small cliff we were using as a back rest, tipping his rucksack with his foot which started it rolling. Diving after it he missed his footing, sprawled out of control, and just managed to turn himself stomach down and hands above his head clutching for holds as the sack went over into space; Dollar very nearly did the same! He was visibly shaken when he hauled himself up – and so were we at such a near miss. His worry now was the loss of his identification papers, which would be troublesome for him unless he could retrieve them at the bottom of the east face.

Up there on top of Jalovec we were in a world of monochrome, grey rocks, uplifted, twisted, folded to splintered edges, and no friendly sound of rushing mountain torrents. The Julians are silent mountains. Two soaring golden eagles were the only birds. Our way down was marked by splashes of red paint, pointing a way that led to steel cables and iron pegs, then a long traverse to a rocky gully with more of the same artificial aids, and a descent of 500 feet to slippery snow and ice. The climb had take us eleven hours up and down. Now we spread out above the Tamar Hut to hunt for Dollar's rucksack, but he was without it when I left next day.

As in other mountain ranges, the true enjoyment to be had out of the Julian Alps is to be found travelling among them as much as in the climbing of them. It was dawn when I left the Tamar Hut next morning when these gaunt peaks were blood red on their crests. I climbed steeply to a pass on scattered rocks to strike down into a corrie, and with no human soul to break the spell I felt that sense of wonder that comes of being among new mountains. To prolong the moment of deep contentment I lit a fire and boiled up some water for coffee and ate a second breakfast. I was thinking of the country I was in, dominated for over 1,000 years by invaders from Austria, yet its people had retained their Slav speech and habits. Now that they had nationality again they were proud of it.

My hut that night was the Erjaceva Koca, where I was to rendezvous with James Kerr, whom I had left to enjoy himself in Split, and another friend, Leslie Duff, newly out from Britain. Like me they were delighted with the splendour of their surroundings under the fine peaks of Razor and Prisonjnk but less thrilled to find that difficulties had been tamed by high explosives and staircases of metal pegs. These amenities are symbols perhaps that these are the Peoples' mountains, not merely reserved for the agile few, but made accessible for an Alpine Association which has 65,000 members and beautifully sited mountain huts like the one we were in, and others we were to use on our traverse of the range.

After I had left James Kerr in Split he had visited two hospitals and was impressed by the dependence they placed in British medicine. No German books were in evidence, but both had a magnificent collection of British books. James, who served as a doctor in the Dolomites just as the war ended, speaks fluent Italian, and one day when he was mistaken for one by a dour-looking bar attendant, the man's face became all smiles when he realised he was English. A deep and undying ill-will towards neighbours surfaced all too quickly with the death of Tito, the breakdown of law and order and the barbarous civil war that still goes on as I write this in 1994. Bill Tilman of Nanda Devi fame, who fought in the First World War, was parachuted into Yugoslavia to fight with the pro British partisans and every year a Tilman Day is celebrated in that part. Readers interested should read *High Mountains and Cold Seas*, his biography by J. Anderson.

The classic book on the exploration of the Julians is *Alpine Pilgrimage* by Julius Kugy who climbed with chamois hunters who knew the secrets of these mountains before the beginning of alpine climbing. He camped with them under the open sky, and every page of his writing evokes the joy of discovery before they were defaced by mechanical aids to make the summits accessible to everyone. The Slavs I climbed with on Jalovec were climbers of high calibre, who used pitons only where no natural belays were available, but they had no prejudices hammering in pegs in lieu of natural holds, if there were none.

In fact ironmongery was just beginning to creep into Scottish climbing and is very much part of the world of mountaineering now as harder and harder ways are challenged on overhanging rock and ice.

8

Harum-Scarum Days

As I was writing that last chapter there came in a letter from the Secretary of the Lomond Mountaineering Club explaining that it was celebrating its sixtieth year with a special Club dinner and asking me to be its Principal Guest because I grew up in Glasgow and began climbing in the early 1930s. I was just a bit daunted however by his request that I should make the subject of my speech 'The History of Scottish Mountaineering'.

Since my background was working class I thought it better to pitch the history from a significant occasion when round a camp fire a fair-haired young shop-assistant by the name of Jock Nimlin enrolled twenty of his pals and founded the Ptarmigan Mountaineering Club. The date was 1929, and for a year before Jock had never spent a weekend at home.

What was new in Scottish mountaineering when this club, which was named after the hardiest bird of the hills, was formed was its approach. 'Aye,' said Jock when he looked back: 'We were a bit harum-scarum, I suppose, delighting in caves where we slept like tramps, taking pride in hard living, but being as comfortable as circumstances allowed. Not for us the kind of equipment people take for granted today. These were weekends of simplicity I would not have missed. Climbing was a healthy outlet. The early 30s brought hard times, unemployment or dead-end jobs. Just to have a job was happiness. We climbed for adventure because we needed it.'

Jock's philosophy of hard living and hard climbing caught on. In 1930 on the Campsies a group of Clydeside shipyard workers, their leader Andy Saunders, named themselves the Creag Dhu. My pal Matt and I saw much of them on the crumbly face of Slack Dhu where they were as sure-footed as cats. That Club lives on today, and has a comfortable hut merging unobtrusively below the face of mighty Buachaille Etive Mor, and some of the hardest climbs ever done on that rocky peak are theirs. A lot of cash had changed hands too, gambling at cards while waiting for the rain to go off!

The Lomond Club, formed in 1932, was the inspiration of a lithe, black-moustached climber, Johnny Harvey by name, with a gift for

103

organisation. He was its first President and remained so for thirty years. It differed from most clubs in that it admitted ladies. It still does, and the present membership is around sixty.

The 30s and 40s were decades of cheap and plentiful public transport because car ownership was rare. To meet the sudden surge towards the great outdoors in the 1930s the railway companies ran special rambler tickets, entitling you to put your bicycle on the train. I did that. I got off at Inverness, cycled north to Little Loch Broom, camped, and climbed the Fannichs, An Teallach, then moved round the coast to Loch Maree and on home from there by Achnasheen with a stop off at Aviemore to climb Cairngorm. The total cost for a fortnight was £5.

The Lomond Club were innovators in the matter of cheap transport to the hills. First, when petrol rationing was in force they hired a lorry, with a canvas canopy like a covered wagon. Jock Nimlin tells the tale of one with a full cargo of climbers aboard which came to a premature halt, jamming the city traffic. The driver couldn't get it to start, and the illegal cargo peering out through peep-holes in the canvas saw tram-conductors, drivers and police lining up to push the lorry.

At the wheel the driver signalled them to be quiet, and when they complied, there was a stage-whisper from an imaginative passenger, 'If the polis ask what's in the lorry make a noise like a flock of sheep.' Travelling as freight was one way of getting to Ben Nevis, and one party camped for two days at New Year in the ruins of the summit observatory.

Then came the hiring of buses, filled with any who put their names down, Lomonds, Creag Dhu or Scottish Mountaineering Club members. One bus had a special name, 'The Mountaineer' commissioned by the Lomonds from a Charlie 'Flee-on' McAteer. Charlie could take his passengers through floods and snowdrifts like a hurdler. By 1938 he was leaving Glasgow on Fair Friday to have his passengers climbing in the Bernese Oberland by the Monday. In 1939 Lomond members had six days' cross-country climbing over several high glacier passes to bag peaks, Charlie's bus sitting waiting for them at the other end.

Actually, the very first climbers I saw with ropes on their rucksacks were members of the Tricouni Club, formed in 1930, a happy band of about thirty strong, equally divided between the sexes. The only qualification for entry was the ability to traverse the three peaks of the Cobbler. More important than climbing ability was an agreeable personality. That seemed to be its downfall, for the Club died when all the men married all the women.

Among the 30s' climbers I knew, climbing styles had not changed since the era of the Victorians who had formed the Scottish Mountaineering Club in 1889. We climbed in nailed boots, and eighty feet of Alpine Club rope was deemed sufficient between three. It was not until the 1950s that I heard the sound of metal pegs hammered into rock on the crags. One of the pioneers of the steeple-jacking approach was a tall teenager by the name of MacInnes, who launched the Greenock Mountaineering Club in 1949, and whose ambitions lay beyond the ordinary.

I remember this lanky innovator of pitoneering bearding me in Glencoe to ask about the cheapest way of mounting a trip to the Himalaya: 'None of this official expedition stuff,' he said. I told him how we had done it, using equipment more or less the same as for Scotland or the Alps.

Not so very long after, the young Hamish MacInnes was marching for Mount Everest with fellow member of the Creag Dhu, John Cunningham. Both became professional climbers. Alas, the superb mover on rock and ice, Cunningham, was drowned attempting to rescue a rock-climbing student on a Welsh sea-cliff who had been swept off by a freak wave. On joining the Antarctic Survey, experimenting with front-point crampons and a dagger in each hand, he had found a fast and natural way of climbing high-angle ice up ninety degrees if the arms and leg muscles were trained to it. The method is now in general use, but a short ice-axe with curved blade in each hand has replaced the daggers.

MacInnes, writer, film maker, and mountain-rescuer extraordinary has been honoured by three universities and in 1992 was awarded a DSc.

In the 50s the Cairngorms were explored as never before by a wave of young Aberdeen climbers, not so different from those of my own generation, but with more free time at their disposal than we had in the hungry 30s. Tom Patey's spectacular rise was meteoric. From being a hill-walker with the Boy Scouts, to sharing a rope on sea-cliffs as practice to enable him to cope with the ascent of any peak in Scotland, he sprang to fame literally overnight when he forced a way up the unclimbed Douglas Gully in winter, acknowledging that he had to get up as the only alternative was to fall down, since he had no hope of reversing what he had climbed.

His last true mountain climb was with me, on the Cioch Nose in Applecross, just six days before he was killed abseiling from a previously unclimbed sea-stack off Whiten Head in Sutherland.

The year was 1970, the month May, and the night before our climb we had talked right through the hours of darkness: it was only when the whisky bottle was empty we drew the curtains and saw it was daylight. He had played his accordian, sung a dozen or more of his witty ballads, philosophised about men and mountains, then off we drove for Loch Kishorn in heavy rain turning to wet snow high up. Other than a couple of rope slings we carried no gear, just a full-weight 150-foot rope.

Wise men would not have set off, but Tom was enthusiastic about the route which he and Chris Bonington had pioneered, and he wanted me to lead because I'd never done it. As we went up he was telling me of his intention to solo the Eiger North Face later on in the year, to move fast and do it in a single push.

That day I asked him if he had any regrets at sticking to medicine when he could have been a Chris Bonington, since he had proved himself on some of the hardest routes in the Alps, in Norway and on the previously unclimbed peaks, the Muztagh Tower, and 25,550-foot Rakaposhi in the Himalaya. His answer was: 'No. Climbing is not a good reason for living. Providing a good medical service to a remote region like Ullapool and the far north-west is as important to me as any climbing. I've worked hard to build up the practice, and I've enjoyed it, though I'd like more time for climbing.'

He was none too happy about the modern rock-climbing scene, his philosophy being this:

The magic of a great route does not lie in its technical difficulties, or even in the excellence of the rock, but is something less readily definable: atmosphere is the general term applied. A route should perform an honest purpose: it should follow a natural line of weakness up a natural obstacle and reach a logical conclusion. There are many so-called routes whose conception would not tax the mental faculties of an ape.

Dr Longstaff was one of Tom's patients, and Tom wrote about him thus in the *Alpine Journal* of November 1964:

Some men never grow old. Age, after all, is no more than a state of mind and cannot be measured in years. My late friend Tom Longstaff was one of the few who proved this argument. At the age of eighty-nine he was younger at heart than many of my contemporaries in their early thirties. The climbing world will remember Longstaff as the greatest mountain explorer of his time; those of us who knew him more intimately will remember him as one who had discovered the elixir of life. He enjoyed living as few men know how to.

These final words could also be applied to Dr T.W. Patey even although his entire life span was no more than from 1932 to 1970. But how he lived it up! And how well he told his story in *One Man's Mountains*, which he never saw in book form, but which brilliantly captures the joy of everything that meant anything to a friend, whom I regard as a genius – and I do not use the word lightly. Bill Murray wrote of Tom Patey: 'He alone of the post-war generation of Scottish climbers displayed an unmistakable talent for writing. Shortly before his death he had begun his autobiography. In all ways our loss has been more than we can ever know.'

Patey had been inspired by the ascent of Parallel Buttress on Lochnagar by J.H. Bell and W.H. Murray, two of the very best of the old school, with eyes for possible lines of weakness on unclimbed faces. Both had found their own way to the hills.

Murray, who has been much mentioned earlier, knew the name of only one mountain in Scotland in 1934 – the Cobbler, when in town clothes and city shoes he set off one April day from Arrochar to climb it. His only period of fear was while kicking steps in the frozen snow of the corrie, conscious that a slip would send him sliding to the bottom. The rocks above were clear and dry, though, and after topping the summit pinnacle, he went for the harder scramble up the sharp side of the South Peak.

It was seeing the vast panorama of snowy peaks to the north that instilled in him the desire to be a real mountaineer. He knew no climbers, but joined the Scottish Youth Hostel Association, and for a year climbed alone, from the Perthshire peaks above Crianlarich and Tyndrum to the Cairngorms and the rock-banded summits of Glen Torridon.

It was in the hostels he heard of the Junior Mountaineering Club of Scotland which had been formed in 1925, its purpose to train climbers for entry to the Scottish Mountaineering Club. He gained entry to it, was led up classic rock climbs and heard lectures by eminent mountaineers, but the most important aspect of indoor meetings was making friends and arranging climbs for the next weekend. Murray has written more than once that nothing that has come to him since, in the Alps or the Himalaya, has brought such ecstasy as on hard routes with well-tried companions when he was physically fittest and enthusiasm was highest.

Although Bill is glad he started off alone, finding his own way, he regards clubs as being 'Mountaineering's essential backbone – a framework on which tradition and development naturally hang and grow.' His view is that earlier climbers probably got a bigger kick from their climbing, with nothing more than nailed boots and a single axe, than the modern generation with advanced aids. The need for constant vigilance on steep places is the hardest lesson to remember, and one which even the best climbers forget at the cost of their lives. From the danger element stems the exhilaration, based on judgement and self-reliance.

Little was known about the opportunities for alpinism in the Highlands until a gathering of professional men met in response to a letter in the *Glasgow Herald* of 10th January, 1889 with a: 'Proposal for a Scottish Alpine Club'. From this meeting arose the Scottish Mountaineering Club, and it is a tribute to the ability of its early members that from 1889 until 13th September 1930 there was not one fatal accident to a member despite forty years of enterprising activity on the biggest rock walls in Scotland in summer and winter. This fine record was broken when, on the Buachaille Etive Mor, Norman Mobray slipped to his death on unroping after climbing the renowned Crowberry Ridge.

Not until Sir Hugh T. Munro published his table of 3,000-foot

107

summits, listing no fewer than 283 separate mountains of this height, was it fully realised what scope for exploration there was in Scotland. On 23rd November 1991, a hundred years after his publication of the list, its compiler was celebrated in a unique way by a dinner attended by climbers, and their supportive partners, who had completed the 'Munros'. Numbers had to be limited to the first 250 to apply. And at a table was Sir Hugh in effigy, complete in balmoral and kilt, his favourite dress.

In Sir Hugh's time it was a considerable achievement to take in all the separate summits he listed. Now with smooth roads, fast motor cars, and a leisured working population equipped with detailed guidebooks listing all the Munros, anyone of reasonable fitness can add his or her name to the thousand and more who can claim to have done them at the time of writing. The tally is kept by the Scottish Mountaineering Club, and in the year between 1991 and 1992, a further 160 names were added.

Even Sir Hugh, who died with three of his Munros still to climb, has made a posthumous completion, thanks to Professor Robin Campbell who constructed the life-like effigy and helped carry its thirty pounds of weight and five feet of height to the top of Carn Fhidhleir and Carn Cloich-Mhuillin, finishing with Skye's Inaccessible Pinnacle, a rock climb for which many Munro baggers enlist the help of a professional guide.

Young climbers I meet often stress how lucky I was to be climbing in the 30s when relatively few folk were on the hills, and ways of life in the glens had hardly changed since Victorian times. But they have their own reward and, as many of them are my readers, I love to hear from them, as in this letter from Bill Grant, dated 1st November 1992:

Dear Tom,

What a pleasure it was to read your fine article on Carnmore in this month's *Scots Magazine*. It rekindled the exciting memories I experienced when I first read your original trip to the Fisherfield Forest in my favourite book *Highland Days*. I read this book, your finest, in Springburn Library in 1954 when I was fifteen. The many exciting trips in your book lit a flame in me for the hills which, to this day still burns brightly.

I have walked in many parts of Scotland, but I often wish I had been able to have done so during the era before hydro-electric dams, and been able to visit places like Benula or Strathmore before they disappeared under the now enlarged lochs of Mullardoch and Monar.

The Fisherfield Forest mentioned by Bill Grant is part of the roadless wilderness that stretches from Letterewe on Loch Maree to Strath na Sealga and over the shoulder of rocky An Teallach to Little Loch Broom. It was to make its exploration I set off on my second big bike-trip from

Inverness. It was May, I was on my annual summer holiday from the Co-op, and it was Saturday evening when I reached the village of Poolewe, where the postman invited me to camp in the area of his croft by the river.

He was none too pleased, however, when next day I asked him if he would look after my spare food and some baggage while I went into the hills for a few days.

'No good can come of climbing on the Sabbath. And in this cold changeable weather! Leave it until Monday if you must go.'

But I was anxious to be off, and with a lightly loaded rucksack containing sleeping bag, tent, groundsheet, stove, cooking pans and food, waved him goodbye, telling him I would be back in the middle of the week.

Following up the River Ewe to the house of Keronsary, I soon found the footpath that twists and turns between lochs under Beinn Airigh Charr and in ten moorland miles reaches the head of the Fionn Loch above which spring the crags of A'Mhaighdean whose summit is the remotest of all the Munros. It had been a bracing walk, with bursts of sun between rain and hail showers discharging from clouds moving fast on the strong wind. Just how fierce the squalls were I realised while struggling with the flapping canvas to pitch my tent. Once pegged down however and groundsheet laid, I soon had the stove going for a quick drum-up, unloaded all my gear from the rucksack in order to pack gear for the hill, and tent flaps secured, was off.

I've never been able to resist rocks that look climbable, and A'Mhaighdean is a mountain built of Lewisian gneiss, which weathers into clean-cut holds that are notably sound. I was soon moving steeply up, but getting uneasy by the clampdown of the clouds, the disappearance of sun, and thunder-claps of gusting wind throwing me out of balance at times. It was when I was being lashed by rain, and my hands were getting numbed by the running wet rock, that I began to feel I was engaged in a fight for survival.

The higher I went, the more carefully I had to judge my moves in case of being blown off. Relief, indeed, to ease myself on to the top and shelter behind some pinnacles out of the screaming wind. Map out, to get the configuration of the ground on the lee side out of the gale, I felt my way down. The worst was soon behind me, and in my chilled state as I lost height, I was looking forward to a change into dry clothes and a meal. My landmark for the tent was an overhanging boulder, but I could see no welcoming white shape. A search revealed an over-turned Primus stove, a scatter of cooking pans and a few scraps of rain-sodden food. Of my tent and sleeping bag there was no sign. I cursed myself for taking my rucksack to the hill and not leaving it behind with all my stuff inside. It would be dark soon. What was I to do?

Now, unsuspected by me until I came to the Fionn Loch, there is a house named Carnmore on the map in this no-man's-land. A house moreover from which I had seen smoke coming from its chimneys before the mist closed in. I had just time to reach it before dark if I hurried. Feeling rather like a tramp asking for shelter, I knocked at the door praying the family would not be abed. It was opened immediately and before I opened my mouth I was pulled inside.

Within minutes I was given a towel to dry myself and an assortment of clothing to put on. Then came an omelette, the king of omelettes. Warmed and happy, I could not have felt more at home with father and mother Macrae, and the two six-foot sons, Andy and Calum. I was to meet two young lassies in the morning, Katy and Mary. Over breakfast I had them in stitches with stories of life in the shop as a grocer, and giving the old man my political views on the Spanish War then being waged, everything being eagerly lapped up.

The weather was still wet and windy, and as we talked, I discovered that the family got their groceries in bulk every six months, rowing it up the whole length of the Fionn Loch by boat. To get bread or mail meant crossing the shoulder of Ben Lair and descending to Letterewe Lodge on Loch Mareeside. Andy, who had his Higher Education Certificate, was being paid a modest salary teaching his two sisters in the absence of any primary school within range of this remote house. Said Mrs Macrae: 'If one of the boys or girls gets anything, the others must share it.' I was conscious of an aura of happiness in this family that I had never met before.

In the afternoon, when the rain eased off, we all went out hunting for my missing camp kit. There is nothing like local knowledge! Mr Macrae went straight to where the tent was wedged between some rocks, and in the same uncanny way took me to where my sleeping bag lay in a narrow burn, blown up with water as if enshrouding a body. That afternoon the whole glen was roaring with falling water tuned to different pitches by the wind, an echoing sound I have always loved.

It was Wednesday morning before I could tear myself away, and when I got to Poolewe in the evening I was just in time to stop a search party. Alarmed at my non-appearance, the postman had sent round the fiery cross thinking the worst. I was mildly rebuked, but welcomed with relief. I returned to the house of Carnmore two years later, this time from Letterewe over the shoulder of Ben Lair. The family were not expecting me. Andy was at the door as I came up the path, but he quickly went inside and out came his father. 'By God it's Tommy,' he shouted as he saw me. It was a grand reunion, with the family singing and the melodian playing.

All this came back to me on 12th August 1992 when who should come to our door on Loch Lomondside but Andy Macrae all the way from Salt Lake City. He brought sad news and good news. He had flown over with his wife Bette to attend the funeral of his brother Calum. Said Andy, 'He was seventy-one, three years younger than me.'

I wanted to hear about Calum, who a few years before had visited me with Andy. He lived in Somerset, and he used to take an old man to the store every week to get his messages. To pass the time Calum had gone for a wee walk in the village, and on his way back to collect his elderly neighbour he fell to the ground. He was still breathing when folk gathered round him. The last words he spoke were, 'See that the old man gets home.'

Andy himself had been suffering heart trouble, and had had a by-pass operation, a costly affair in the USA where there is no National Health Service. Back in Scotland he had been in touch with Dutchman Paul Van Vlissingen, owner of the Letterewe Estate for the last fourteen years, explaining that he was one of the family who had been the last permanent residents of Carnmore, and with his permission would like to revisit the place with his sister and her daughter.

Said Andy: 'He couldn't have been nicer, and he has put his head keeper at our disposal. The keeper'll meet us at Poolewe next week, and take us to the Fionn Loch in his Land-Rover, and from there we'll go by boat to within a mile of Carnmore.' Impulsively I said, 'I'd love to go with you!' His reply was that there was nothing he would like better. 'If you can get to Pitlochry where I'll be staying with my sisters, we can go in the one car.'

Off we drove in the car from Pitlochry, five of us driven by Katy's daughter Rosemary, and a grey, dismal, wet morning it was climbing over Drumochter. The rain was still sending it down at Achnasheen where Katy had spent most of her working life in the post office. 'There's nothing unusual about rain in Achnasheen,' said Rosemary who was brought up here. However, within a short time of leaving the railway village, we were in Glen Docherty and descending into a different weather system. A fleecy white cloud burying the peaks, but sunshine burnishing the slopes above the pale blue slit of Loch Maree below. Then as we descended to the Caledonian pines of the shore, the white clouds lifted off the high ground and there was the summit pyramid of Slioch in pink sandstone thrusting from grey bosses of Lewisian gneiss. Slioch is well named – the spear – and it dominates Loch Maree in the same way that Ben Lomond dominates Loch Lomond, even to having archipelagoes of wooded islands stretching across their broadest surface areas. To get to the top of Loch Maree however, you have to swing away to the Atlantic at Gairloch, then climb over a pass to reach the top of the loch at Poolewe.

Already waiting at the parking place by the post office was a large-sized Land-Rover, and as we drew up, out leapt a lithe figure in knickerbockers, kenspeckle with his long wispy beard, who greeted us warmly in a Glasgow accent. He had been a steelworker in Ravenscraig before becoming a keeper. 'Dougie Russell,' he announced. As he shook Andy by the hand, we were introduced. 'I'm at your disposal for the whole day, and as late as you like, so just say if you want to stop anywhere.'

With Andy in the front seat we were off in a few minutes, following the

River Ewe for the track that leads to the house of Kernsary where a herd of Highland ponies grazed on the green just below Dougie's abode, sure-footed animals used for bringing deer carcasses down from the hills.

Then we were on a vehicle track through a wood of pine and spruce that didn't exist in Andy's day, both created by Colonel Whitbread, who sold the estate to the Dutchman. 'The trees are just about the right height now for taking down the fence so that the deer can get in for shelter without damaging them,' said Dougie.

Leaving the wood behind, we were soon on the wet open moorland dotted with the small lochs that I remembered, the track steering a way between them to get to the Fionn Loch four rough miles on, Dougie feeding us with wild-life information all the while.

'This approach is great for waders; greenshank and golden plover in the nesting season; redshank too. Red-throated divers use the small lochs for nesting. On the Fionn Loch four pairs of black throated divers each reared one chick this year, but the big surprise was a pair of red kites, and tags on them showed they were ones released by the RSPB in an attempt to reintroduce a bird that's been extinct in Scotland for a hundred years. In the air the kite has an unusual butterfly flight.'

Next came the sail up the five-and-three-quarter-mile loch of many inlets, famous for brown trout and sea-trout. Osgood Mackenzie, remembered today for his famous garden at Poolewe, described it as the best trout loch in Scotland. In his classic book *A Hundred Years in the Highlands* he wrote: 'The total weight of twelve fish caught that 12th April day was 87 pounds 12 ounces.'

It was the rocky peaks getting nearer and nearer, white clouds steaming off them, that excited Andy, well remembered, as were the glens threaded with waterfalls where he had stalked red deer. I looked on them with the eyes of a rock climber remembering the scope for exploration on their Lewisian gneiss. Then, under the steepest rock face, the white house of Carnmore came into view. Now we were all impatient to get out of the boat and take the track past a herd of Highland cattle, as shaggy as any in a Horatio McCulloch Victorian oil painting.

Katy, the wee girl in the photograph, now a granny, doesn't say much, but hers was the first cry of excitement: 'Look, the hen house that Andy made against the rock is still standing, yet it could never keep the foxes out!' It was simply four sides of corrugated-iron with a roof.

Nearer to the house is a commodious stone bothy with a new roof and a notice inviting hillfolk to use it, but not to camp, and to use the big litter bin within for rubbish. Said Dougie: 'I did most of the dry-stane walling and put on the new roof. Climbers who saw it unfinished thought we were demolishing it, and we got some bad publicity. Climbers are welcome here, and we tend to get responsible people. The only time we want them to keep off the hills is September and October when the boss is in

112

residence at Carnmore and we're busy deer stalking. Deer have to be culled for their own good, but we don't shoot the best, only the poorest beasts.'

It was good to see the wonder in Andy's and Katy's faces as they stepped inside the house and found it more or less unchanged from their memory: the same simple furniture and oil lamps. The main change was that instead of a peat-burning grate, there was an oil-burning stove, and Calor gas for boiling the kettle for tea. Before our picnic, we had a tour of the house. The major change was that of a bedroom now turned into a bathroom. Otherwise all was simplicity. 'That's the way the boss likes it. No electricity because a generator makes a noise and spoils the peaceful atmosphere.'

I was only sorry the boss wasn't with us, as he had hoped he would be, but had had to fly off to Japan on urgent business. Letterewe, across the other side of the bealach, is the main lodge, a stiff two-hour walk which the Dutchman enjoys for its wilderness quality in the heart of the deer forest. Dougie drew our attention to a colour photograph on the wall. It showed a badger looking up at the boss – *inside the house*. 'The door happened to be open and the young badger came in to say "Hello". There's a lot of badgers around here. A Natural Heritage chap who came over to check on golden eagles found a partly eaten badger in one of the eyries!'

We took a wee cruise to the causeway dividing the Fionn Loch from the Dubh Loch. The path from Letterewe runs along the top of it, a walkway with a history of trouble; a man and a horse have been blown off it, and Andy's father coming from Letterewe one stormy day had to turn back and retrace his steps over Bealach Mheinnidh to Loch Maree. 'Over there,' Andy pointed, 'just above the top end of the Dubh Loch, is where your tent and sleeping bag were blown away and you were forced to come to our door for shelter. We had been there only a year and you were the first stranger to call on us. We hadn't seen anyone at all at the house for three months.'

How I had envied them their life-style. They had four cows to provide them with milk, cheese and crowdie. From the hill came the best of meat – venison. In the loch there was an abundance of trout for the catching. Hens laid eggs for them. The moor near the house gave peat for fuel. They had a horse, and grew oats and hay. I actually suggested to old man Macrae, giving up my job and coming to live here for a year to learn the craft of keepering, saying I would pay my way.

The old man dispelled my romantic notion, telling me: 'The highest pay I ever got as a keeper was £2 a week, and it's been a struggle to rear a family of seven on that. Andy and Calum are well qualified, but they can't get jobs. Their three older brothers had to leave the Highlands. One is at London University studying to be a teacher. Of the other two, one is in the police force, and the other is a prison officer; both are in Glasgow.'

Andy had confided to me that when he got his Higher Leaving Certificate from Ullapool Secondary he had hoped to use his educational qualifications to train as a pilot in the Royal Air Force. He had filled in a form, but his father refused to sign it. Strangely, though, on demobilisation from the army his working life was to be spent around aircraft, with a staff of eighty-five working under him eventually in his capacity as a distributor of aviation fuel. He moved to the USA on retiral, to be with his children there.

With the boys away in the army it was no longer possible for the Macraes to stay on in such an isolated place, and in 1941 they moved to Achnasheen. Great was the joy of Mrs Macrae to be able to see cars passing and wave to passengers on the Kyle Line from their house of 'Druimdhu' perched one mile north-east of the railway station. That dwelling is steadily becoming a ruin. Andy had wanted to buy it and make it habitable for his retirement, but the Estate refused his offer.

I've visited Carnmore a good few time since the Macrae family left, and in 1963 I raised my voice against the North of Scotland Electricity Board's plan to build dams at the top and bottom of the Fionn Loch to raise it eleven feet, and harness it to Loch Fada, utilising the difference in level, and so connect them to an under-ground power station above the Furnace Burn on Loch Mareeside. I have no doubt the Board would have done the construction work well, but it would have taken the 'wild' out of our rarest wilderness.

Later on in the 1960s I wrote a paper on the desirability of the nation purchasing Letterewe and Fisherfield Estate to be maintained as a true 'Wilderness' if it ever came on the market. At that time I was the only independent member of Study Group 9, a Scottish Committee set up to look ahead to 'The Countryside in 1970'. The impetus for action came from HRH the Duke of Edinburgh. The Scottish remit was to examine a wide range of countryside planning issues distinctive to Scotland. England had its own groups with the His Royal Highness as general Chairman.

Our Scottish Chairman was Professor Robert Grieve (later to become Sir Robert), and we identified the issues that required action, such as environmental pressures on Loch Lomond, and the Cairngorms. Some strategy was needed, with public funding, to balance conservation and recreation. We didn't want to talk about National Parks, since they mean different things in different places. We talked of a 'Thing' that might be set up, with executive power to purchase and manage land. As for my idea of 'Wilderness', the feeling was that such an ideal was impractical in terms of management. It was agreed that the status quo was most likely to keep it that way at the present time.

In my submission I had concluded: 'Given the wrong type of owner who wants to buy Letterewe and Fisherfield in order to develop it for money-making we could lose a priceless treasure.' That the Estate had remained a wilderness resulted from the fact that its owners had been wealthy enough to sustain its quality of remoteness. The Marquis of Zetland was the owner when the Macraes lived at Carnmore. Its next owner, Colonel Whitbread, had carried on the tradition of minimum change, which Dutch owner Paul Van Vlissingen continues. Should this Estate come on the market again, the organisation I would like to see acquire it is the John Muir Trust, and I believe so would most outdoor folk who love lonely places that are becoming increasingly harder to find.

The John Muir Trust has been called 'the shy trust' because of its low profile. It does not want civilisation nibbling its wilderness properties away. John Muir, of course, was the Scot from Dunbar in East Lothian who was taken to America at the age of eleven in 1849, and by the time of his death in 1914 was the acknowledged father of the conservation movement. Tramping across the country from coast to coast, and alerting the settlers to the terrible injuries they were doing to the countryside, he inspired President Theodore Roosevelt to declare five National Parks and set aside 148 million acres of Forest Reserves. Brilliant writer as he was, Muir reckoned the hardest task he ever set himself was to find adequate words to describe the wonders of the Grand Canyon to ensure that its 806 million acres would be protected. Thanks to him sixteen other National Monuments were also declared.

It took until 1983 for a John Muir Trust to be launched, its object being to acquire areas of outstanding beauty and manage them sustainably, to keep the wilderness wild, but at the same time support those living in such areas of outstanding beauty. Its first acquisition was 3,000 acres of wildest Knoydart, including Ladhar Bheinn, the most westerly mainland Munro in a roadless peninsula. Its second purchase was across the water in Skye, 5,200 acres of the Torrin Estate, including the flanks of Blaven and the top of Gars Bheinn, outliers of the Cuillin. The third was in north-west Sutherland, 11,000 acres of grassland and coast supporting a crofting community with, at its tip, remote Sandwood Bay and the pinnacle of Am Buachallie, untouched by development. These purchases were made by moneys from individuals and outdoor organisations.

That young student Adam Watson, who had joined Douglas Scott and me on the 1951 trip to Arctic Norway, has been trying to do for the Cairngorms what John Muir did for Yosemite. His inspiration came from the books of Seton Gordon, and at the age of eight he began a correspondence with the old naturalist which led to their meeting for the first time on Deeside when Adam was thirteen, and Seton led him to an occupied golden eagle eyrie, the first young Adam had ever seen. In an early letter to his admirer Gordon had written:

It is a fine thing for you to have a love of the hills, because on the hills you will find yourself near grand and beautiful things, and as you grow older you will love them more and more.

115

The Cairngorm Hills of Scotland by Seton Gordon was Adam's Bible, leading him to make a life-long study of this true fragment of the arctic in Britain and qualify as a DSc. Alas though, he has seen the steady erosion of its wilderness qualities as from both Speyside and Deeside it has been criss-crossed by sub-standard vehicle tracks for deer stalking and mechanical up-lift for skiers. Seton Gordon died just short of his ninety-first birthday, on 19th March 1977. Adam was on the Cairngorms with him the previous year, and it was my good fortune to spend a day with him at his home in Skye a few months before the two had their last walk.

During the 1914–18 war, Gordon had been given the job of organising a secret coast-guard service under the guise of being a bird-watcher. He told me: 'It seemed all wrong that I had this marvellous opportunity to have my own fishing boat, *Lustre Gem* and sail where I pleased, landing on uninhabited islands, while friends were being killed in France.' Based at Aultbea, Wester Ross, in 1916, he met the last of the Gaelic-speaking Highland lairds, Osgood Mackenzie, who at eighty years of age and living at Inverewe was trying to write a book. Gordon was able to help him and the end result was *A Hundred Years in the Highlands*, one of the most readable of all social histories of life as it used to be in Wester Ross when people lived off the land.

Lying on the floor of a bothy at Carnmore, on one of my post-war trips, I found myself thinking of Osgood, who as a lad of sixteen had slept in this very place wrapped in his blanket. He was young then, and laying the foundation for a more intimate knowledge of this complicated wilderness in summer and winter than any had done before him, from the wooded islands of Loch Maree to Isle Ewe and the hinterland of the Fionn Loch. The title of the book derives from Osgood inheriting from his uncle the ten manuscripts of Highland Memories covering 1803 to 1860, and Osgood asked the reader to imagine he is

sitting on the opposite side of a peat fire listening to leisurely memories of one who has lived a great number of years, observant of the customs of his neighbours, attentive to the passing moment, and who finds an increasing pleasure after a life in the open air, in dwelling on the times that are gone.

Osgood Mackenzie remembers the potato famine of 1846–48:

But for the potato blight when should we have got our roads made through the country? My mother never left Gairloch, not even for a day, for three long years when the famine was at its height.

This resourceful lady put all the able-bodied men to work, building a road along Loch Mareeside, paying them a wage which enabled them to

116

live. Little Osgood was allowed to cut the first turf, surrounded by starving men.

Osgood's mother rode her horse everywhere at this time of desperation, acting as doctor, building several schools in which the Gaelic language had to come first, and influencing her people to pull down insanitary dwellings and build new ones with timbers which she would provide. Under the run-rig system houses were all huddled together because the crofting land was communally held. She reorganised the system to give each crofter a four-acre piece.

She doled out oatmeal to keep the crofters from starving, when their only standby was shellfish from the shore, boiled in milk. Yet Osgood himself forecast that more education would mean less cultivation, and in his lifetime he saw the croft system become less productive as people became less and less willing to spend their days with the foot-plough and crowbar.

The world was moving towards a money economy as manufactured goods replaced what had been natural commodities. You could buy a better rope than you could make with twisted birch twigs; nor was there a danger of having your horse's tail cut off when you could buy fishing lines which replaced horse-hair.

Yet it was the creation of something out of nothing that was the basis of Mackenzie's philosophy – the garden he created round his house at Inverewe is an example. He waited twenty years for the trees he planted to grow up, so that he could plant a garden in their shelter. And a garden that is a wonder of the world, growing sub-tropical and other exotics on a barren peninsula of Torridonian sandstone, formerly open to the Atlantic winds.

He was a creator and a destroyer. Consider his words after he gives his figures from his gamebook for the year 1868.

Grouse 1314, black game 33, partridges 49, golden plover 110, wild duck 35, snipe 53, rock pigeons 91, hares 194; a total of 1900. What a big pile it would make if all the black game I shot between 1855 and 1900 were gathered up in one heap. Now alas, there are none, and why, who can tell?

In his early days he described Gairloch as swarming with fork-tailed kites and plenty of polecats. Pine martens were so numerous that his mother was able to make 'the most lovely sables and coats with forty or fifty skins taken each year.' He robbed ospreys of their eggs, killed thirty-four golden eagles in four seasons, and exterminated the white-tailed eagle. He poisoned hoodie crows and foxes; shot, trapped and set dogs on badgers and otters. Despite all, however, he saw the once rich wild-life dwindling instead of intensifying.

117

In pre-sheep days, when thousands of wild roses grew everywhere in the Gairloch area, Osgood's grandfather, Sir Hector Mackenzie, had written: 'There was as much game as could be expected when the game-keeper was merely a game-killer and never dreamt of trapping vermin.' It was habitat destruction that made game scarce, aided in part no doubt by Osgood's gun, in action almost every day of his life.

Osgood believed he had exterminated the pine marten which he prized for its pelt that made beautiful furs. In the 1960s, when I made a visit to Inverewe, I had proof that he had not, when the caretaker told me that martens were killing her ornamental bantams. Call that tit-for-tat! Indeed, this most lovely member of the weasel family is no longer rare on Loch Mareeside and my first glimpse of one was at a litter bin at dusk in the area of the Ben Eighe National Nature Reserve where Warden Dick Balharrie carried out pioneer studies on the way of life of this elusive and beautiful animal.

In 1922, the year Osgood Mackenzie died, August was a hot and sultry month. In those days when refrigerators were almost unknown, and communication between Loch Maree and the outside world was by a single telegraph wire, the father of a friend of mine had a narrow escape from poisoning. He was one of a party of nine fishermen staying at the hotel, and they were given duck-paste sandwiches from a tin that had been opened some time previously.

All who ate these sandwiches died of botulism, except Andrew Buchanan, father of my friend Ian. He had looked forward to his picnic lunch, but after one bite no longer felt hungry, and gave the remainder to his gillie, who died in great agony. The one he had bitten he fed to gulls, and the police found the birds dead behind the rocks. The hotel proprietor never recovered from the shock of eight people dying from eating these contaminated sandwiches, and, it is said, died from a broken heart.

Andrew Buchanan felt it was possibly Divine intervention and, his son told me, gave away a considerable proportion of his income and capital to the welfare of the community, to charity, and to others in need of help. He also saw to the needs of the two unmarried sisters of his gillie, who lived frugally in a but-and-ben near Gairloch.

9

Regular Assignment

The best advertisement that any photo-journalist can have is a steady stream of work published with a name-credit to it. In the half-dozen years from 1950 onwards I think I could describe myself as being hyperactive in terms of output, working long hours at desk and darkroom, and bombarding editors with picture stories. One editor I had never met was Arthur Daw and over lunch he put a proposition to me which was to have far-reaching effect.

He had been editing the *Scots Magazine* for about the same time as I had been free-lancing and had published a few things of mine. He said: 'What I would like you to consider is writing a monthly article of six pages with photographs in the magazine. I suggest it should contain about half a dozen different subjects; maybe something about a climb you've done, a wild-life happening, some interesting person you've come across, or a case of public concern you want to air. You could also invite queries. Would you like to try it for a year?'

As I dithered, he encouraged me by saying: 'There are three people who know more about the Highlands and Islands of Scotland than anyone else writing today. The first is Seton Gordon, who lives on Skye, the second is Alasdair Alpin MacGregor who lives in London. The third is yourself, and you are the most active.'

He also offered some sidelights on my writing. 'You love climbing and write well about it. You meet a lot of interesting people, but you could make more of them than you do. Your ear for dialogue is good, but is not so sure when it comes to dialects distinctive to different rural areas. You know a lot about birds, I think you underplay them. The best advice I can give you is, get as much variety as you can into the articles.'

In the beginning I feared that I might have to struggle to get enough material for the diary which was headed 'My Month'. In fact I usually had far too much, and because I was on the move so much I learned to write it wherever I happened to be: a camp in Corsica; tents in the glens; a railway train; in a bothy or in a boat. In 1970 I had the new experience of writing in a hospital bed after a rock-climbing fall which squashed my spine, cracked a hip and damaged my ribs. I covered that period by writing a 'Portrait of the Isle of Rum', which had an unexpected result.

Rum is the most mountainous of the Inner Hebrides, and appears as Rhum on some maps. It is an island that was entirely cleared of its people. It is said that the laird, McLean of Coll, assisted the entire population to emigrate, replacing them with 8,000 sheep. Then, when the island was under-manned, a dozen families from Skye were brought in. In my article I had written: 'Maybe the pathetic tombstone in Kilmory Churchyard, erected by Murdo Matheson, commemorates a family of these incomers. It tells of five of his children dead, in two days, of diphtheria in 1873, fifty years after the original population was forced to leave.'

A letter from Miss Helen Matheson of Otago, New Zealand, gave me the sequel to the subsequent life story of that same Murdo Matheson, who was her great-grandfather:

Following the diphtheria epidemic Murdo Matheson and his wife sailed with their five remaining children to try and build a new life. One child died shortly after arriving in Otago in 1875. In March 1876 Murdo obtained a job as a shepherd on Coppersbrook Station, at an annual wage of £65, among 80,000 merino sheep.

Murdo was sent to a hirsel known as Bald Hill, and twenty years later the owner of that section was Murdo's son, Dougald, and the farm had been renamed Attadale, the seat of the Clan Matheson on Loch Carron. Dougald married in 1897 and had three sons and a daughter.

One of these sons is the father of Miss Helen Matheson, and she had visited the Island of Rum. She wrote:

I shall never forget that day, August 24, 1966. It was a perfect summer's day. It seemed an achievement to find the gravestone. But sad to think that one part of the family is buried on the Island of Rum and the remainder in the little country churchyard of Middlemarch, in Central Otago, New Zealand. It was interesting to note that the countryside where they chose to live was similar to Rum: outcrops of volcanic rock, mountains, peat bogs and tussock grass.

Before I went to the Isle of Skye, I knew the Hebrides only through the writings of Seton Gordon, whose descriptions of the views from the Cuillin I copied down; especially the thrilling words he wrote of seeing St Kilda from Bruach na Frithe. It was not until a quarter of a century later I saw the writer for the first time, on the stage of the Usher Hall playing the pibroch 'Farewell to St Kilda' on the bagpipes. My role that evening was to lecture on the human and natural history of St Kilda, in aid of the National

Camp at 4,000 ft in the range of the Aiguilles di Bavella, Corsica. 'Every day we looked from our tent on the red ball of the sun rising above the Mediterranean.'

Above: Corsica. This mountain, the Tafinato, has a great hole gashing in its upper wall.
Below: This was the first post-war Himalayan Expedition. In centre row, left to right, Douglas Scott, Bill Murray and Tom McKinnon. The six porters were Dhotials, excellent men who stayed with us for all the expedition's four and a half months.

Above: Tom McKinnon; behind him Bethartoli Himal,
above the Rishi Gorge in Garhwal, formerly British India.
Below: Darmaganga was the third of the great Tibetan trade routes we linked.
Bill Murray in cape, beside Douglas Scott, looks almost a holy figure.

Above: Sunset afterglow gilds Tibetan peaks above the swirling clouds.
Below: Rolwaling Gorge gives way to the notably difficult pass of the Tesi Lapcha, camp one. Route goes over the shoulder of background peak.
Opposite page: Camp two on the attempt on Panch Chuli, seen in background. The range rises above the Darmaganga trade route to Tibet.

Opposite above: Buddhist monks at Beding in the Rolwaling Gorge, Nepal. The small boy wears the yellow hat, signifying he is the reincarnation of a holy Lama.

Opposite below: From Beding to Namche Bazaar near Mount Everest, the high pass of the Tesi Lapcha. Camp two was below the background barrier.

Right: Dawa Tensing in 1952 with the Scottish Nepal Expedition. He was chosen for the successful attempt on Kanchenjunga in the mid 50s, a brilliant piece of mountaineering for which Tom McKinnon received the Mungo Park Medal.

Below: This shows the climb to reach camp two, a snow gully and a dangerous traverse on steep friable rock. (This route is not used now.)

Above: Kurdistan. This is the point from where we hoped to climb the Geliasin, which rises in over 4,000 ft of rock above its glacier, its summit 13,760 ft.
Below: Our nearest neighbours were in black tents 1,000 ft below us with their animals. They made us welcome in this empty area.

Above: Frosty nights and marvellous glows from hidden sunsets made this one of the most perfect of camps, with fine sharp peaks some of which we climbed.
Below: After two days travel across passes with our Kurdish guides we climbed the Geliasin by the left hand rock buttress and traversed the summit ridge to reach what is perhaps the most inaccessible point in Asia minor.

Opposite: Peaks of the Jaegervandstind in the Lyngen Fjord region of
North Norway, explored in 1951, between climbs in Lofoten.
Above: Puffins, clowns of the ocean, confiding at their nesting burrows.
Below: Stac Li of St Kilda, one of the three which form the greatest gannetries
in the world. Both puffins and gannets were valued as food, and still are in
some island communities.

Above left: Ptarmigan, the mountain grouse of the
Scottish Highlands, which turns white in winter.
Above right: Capercaillie, largest of the grouse,
whose natural home is the Caledonian pines.

Above left: The dotterel, rarest of mountain plovers, whose home is the
high Scottish hills where the vegetation is almost tundra-like.
Above Right: Dotterel chicks just out of the eggs. The male incubates the eggs and
looks after the chicks. Female dotterel are larger and more brightly coloured,
so courtship duties are reversed.

Isle of Skye. A problem rock, which vanished overnight in
the 1980s, on the Western Ridge of Sgurr nan Gillean.

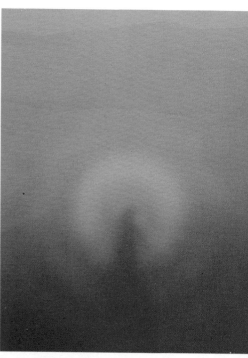

Above left: Len Lovat on Buachaille Etive Mor.
Below him a halo in the mist known as a 'glory'.
Above right: A full 'glory' with Tom Weir's shadow in centre, an effect caused
by tiny particles of mist acting as prisms when the sun is level with the climber.
It is known as the Brocken Spectre.
Below: Glen Torridon, said to be the oldest glen in the world. The peak
Liathach is composed of terraces of sandstone laid on Lewesian gneiss,
estimated to be over 2,500 million years old.

Tom Patey in Raven's Gully of Buachaille Etive Mor, one of
the most awkward rock climbs in Scotland. Taken in the 1960s.

Above: A smouldering sunset at Poolewe casts its glow east over the whole sky.
Below: A' Maighdean, over 3,000ft, is the remotest summit in Scotland. To its left is Carn More Crag, where the author's tent was blown away, which led him to a wonderful family (see black and white section).

Trust for Scotland who had come into possession of the island group at a time when a radar station was about to be built on its highest hill, to monitor rockets fired into the sea from a military base on South Uist.

I had been to St Kilda twice, the first time as a member of an expedition of scientists and ornithologists, arriving after a ten-hour sail from Tarbert, Harris, with food for three weeks, seeing Hirta as its forty-three inhabitants had known it when they were evacuated in 1930 at their own request. They left when they were better fed and better housed than at any time in the island's long history; but for them the old ways of fishing, wild-fowling, cultivating the small fields and herding sheep and cattle had lost its savour. They sailed away with some sticks of furniture and a few precious belongings, and for twenty-seven years the island lay empty; only the odd expedition of visiting naturalists broke the isolation, finding delight in the millions of birds and the unique mice and Soay sheep for which St Kilda was famous.

For our little expedition the first surprise of the island was its fresh greenery, and how little sign there was of the birds that had supported a population here for a thousand years. All you needed to do to see the birds, however, was climb to the summit of Conachar and shrink back from an edge of cliff falling sheer into the sea. Douglas Scott and I wore the rope descending this face to spend a night out on a grassy ledge two-thirds of the way down the cliff. Ten minutes before midnight, small bat-like shapes flitted past us, storm petrels and Leach's forktailed petrels, the latter distinguished by 'quick-ik-icker' cries. Then came the discordant screams of Manx shearwaters. We listened for the thuds of their landings, and caught them in our torch beams before they disappeared underground into their deep burrows to feed their young and relieve their sitting mates who would fly out to sea after days and nights below ground. Then as dawn spread its red light behind the gannet-packed rock-stacks on the horizon, Boreray, Stac an Armin and Stac Li, the sky began to darken over our heads as thousands upon thousands of puffins emerged out of the ground and took the air, all circling the same way to avoid traffic problems.

My second St Kilda visit coincided with the delivery of the first wheeled vehicles in history to arrive on the island, driven ashore from landing barges with material to build a radar station – stone-crushing machinery, an electricity generating plant and high explosives for blowing a beach-head landing strip. It was the spring of 1957 and men were working round the clock on a shift system. On the island, too, were Ordnance Survey former mates of mine, their job to tie the island into the main triangulation network of Britain on the National Grid, important for the tracking of rockets fired from South Uist fifty miles distant.

Also on the island was Kenneth Williamson, bird migration specialist, acting as warden for the National Trust for Scotland and the Nature Conservancy. He had landed with the military invaders, and in my three weeks we snared many birds of passage in mist nets in order to ring them. Ken had landed in April with the radar base construction party, to ensure that minimum damage would be done to remnants of ancient dwellings, including the hundreds of stone 'cleits' dotting the green slopes round Village Bay. In these unusual Stone Age refrigerators the St Kildans had stored the seabirds they caught, and the eggs they gathered from the nests. They were built so that the wind could whistle through them, yet the arrangement of the stones would shed the rain. Inside these cleits was the favourite nest site of the St Kilda wren – larger, greyer, with a stouter bill and louder songs than any other wren in the world. By their territorial songs the Hirta wren population was estimated at 230 pairs.

As well as two bee-hive structures with bed-chambers, probably used by man one thousand years ago, Dr Iain Whittaker of the School of Scottish Studies located a pre-Viking settlement of similar houses in Village Bay and another on the other side of the island, in Gleann Bay. Our geographer made a detailed plane table survey of Village Bay area and drew in the site of a pre-1830 settlement. These were days of discovery.

But what a difficult weather environment for the Royal Air Force construction builders – with winds of over 130 mph, so frightening according to one officer, that men were being blown over in the strong gusts, as the barograph fell below 952 millibars and the anemometer could not give a reading on the chart. The fact that Stone Age structures still stood, when the village cottages built sixty years before were falling down revealed how well early people built against the elements.

It was the inauguration of a regular tourist service to St Kilda by the MacBrayne's *Dunara Castle* beginning in the summer of 1877 that undermined the contentment of the islanders. Until then, money had never troubled them. They had no sense of its value, but the liberality of the visitors gradually destroyed their self-reliance.

Seton Gordon and his first wife, Audrey, had stayed for nearly a week on St Kilda two years before the islanders were evacuated. They had gone at the invitation of the Factor, John Mackenzie, and with St Kildans at the oars, and as guides, they made difficult landings on the ferocious rock stacks of Boreray and Soay.

When I visited Seton at his home in the Isle of Skye in the last year of his life, I told him how much his writing had meant to me, and how in the 30s I was camped on the sea-shore just below where he lived but was too shy to call upon him. The house, which had been a church manse, had seventy acres of croftland where eight or nine cows grazed with some sheep, and there was a patch of oats and some potatoes.

Sitting comfortably, while the rain lashed against the window panes, he told me how much he had loved writing; three hours in the morning, off in the afternoon for some fresh air, then another three hours after tea. 'The roads were quieter in these days, and I knew every pothole. A car was essential to go lecturing all over Scotland, Ireland and England during February and March.'

He had no self-consciousness and a laugh was never very far away as he told me many humorous stories about landowners; not for publication, for he was indebted to them for board and lodgings wherever he went.

'For me,' he said, 'writing has always been a ninety-nine per cent pleasure. As an author and nature photographer I was able to support myself, helped out by lecturing. I went to Russia in 1912 with Prince Felix Youssoupoff. He was with me at Oxford; he owned thirty-two properties and wanted me to be one of his foresters. He was the Prince who killed Rasputin and married the Czar's niece. If I had taken the job offered I might have died in the revolution.'

As Adam Watson wrote in tribute to Seton Paul Gordon CBE:

> With his passing ends the period of wholly exploratory naturalists in Scotland and their extraordinary breadth of interests. He was the last practitioner, over-lapping with the modern period when scientific method dominated ornithology. Astride two centuries, Seton had a timeless attitude, exemplified by the patched decades-old kilt he wore on every occasion, sun or snow, in mansion and bothy.
>
> Gordon continued to write books into his eighties and numerous articles into his nineties. He also gave many lectures. I remember one in Aberdeen on Hebridean birds: he followed the slides with a pibroch reverberating through the café.

In fact Seton Gordon never liked to be without his bagpipes wherever he travelled. He even took them to Spitzbergen, at 80 degrees N so close to the Pole that Spring begins in June, summer in July, autumn in August and winter in September. He was then aged thirty-five and official photographer on a high-powered Oxford University expedition and among its distinguished members was Dr Tom Longstaff. Alas, I forgot to ask Seton if the two ever got together when Longstaff retired to Coigach in Wester Ross.

One thing Seton was firm about was, that without piping and judging at competitions his life would not have been the same. I had hoped for a tune, but his pipes were away in Portree being fitted with a new bag. 'I want to beat the record of Angus MacPherson of Invershin who played until he was ninety-seven!' Sadly, his wish wasn't to be granted, but I have no doubt that the new bag was under his oxter a few times before he squeezed it no more.

Some of Seton's last articles were for the *Scots Magazine*, so it was fitting that I should make the day I spent with him the subject of 'My Month', celebrating my twentieth year as a monthly contributor to that magazine. With my piece about him I had a photograph of the young Adam Watson sitting outside Corrour Bothy in the Cairngorms, very much as Gordon had known it when he played his pipes outside in a blizzard, worried by the non-appearance of his companion who had gone to fetch water from the spring. It was the sound of the bagpipes that enabled the bewildered water-carrier to find his way to the bothy, for in twenty yards of whirling snow he had lost all sense of direction.

On saying goodbye to Seton Gordon, I made my way down to the pier at Uig for a rendezvous with the yacht *Mysie*, skippered by Graham Tiso with another mountaineering friend, Iain Smart, as mate. They had crashed their way from Tobermory through squalls and rough seas and were glad to be in harbour.

This was the first time I had seen Graham's boat, a rigged 'Fifer' ketch, thirty-six feet long with twin Perkins diesel engines, beautifully fitted with bunks, cupboards, toilet, and galley with hot and cold running water. Aloft in the wheelhouse by the chart-table were echo-sounder, radio-telephone, radar, and there was even self-steering gear – luxury indeed. Engines throbbing we turned north out of the bay next morning, and soon Graham was passing me my breakfast which I ate on deck in the warmth of the sun, observing appreciatively that this was certainly the life for an old soldier.

Our objective was the Shiant Islands, and four hours later we were under its great pillars of columnar basalt, orange-bright with lichen where puffins hurried, or perched on hanging ribbons of green sward. In the past Iain and I had camped for a week on these uninhabited islands, so the Shiants for us had the quality of a superb colour slide come to life. Anchor down, we were soon in the dinghy and hauling up on Eilean an Tighe to traverse the boulderfields of Garbh Eilean which are a warren for puffins, guillemots, razorbills and hosts of shags.

The three islands of the Shiants – the 'fairy' islands – form the northern limit of the columnar basalt, which means that geologically they belong to the Inner Hebrides, despite their proximity to the infinitely more ancient rocks of Lewis. Five hundred feet up above the organ-pipe formation we were into a different world of greensward and singing skylarks and bobbing wheatears. Ten families once gained a living on these islands, the last of them departing for Harris in 1901. One was a girl of twenty-two who until then had never left the Shiants. Her world was 500 acres, 'fruitful of corn and grass', to quote Martin Martin, who in the late seventeenth century said the cows were better than any he had seen in Lewis and Harris.

Back at the dinghy, Graham put on the outboard motor, and off we chugged to inspect the tunnel which pierces the eastern pinnacles of Garbh Eilean. In the three-quarters-of-a-mile approach we could not begin to estimate how many thousands of seabirds scuttered out of our way, diving under our bows, walking on the waters, or swimming out of reach, while

124

overhead the air whirred with fast beating wings of auks, puffins predominating.

We knew we had been in luck as we bumped back to the *Mysie* for the sea was rising: so it was anchor up and westward to Harris, to enter Scalpay's North Harbour and tie up in front of the most prosperous fishing village in the Long Island. It was Friday evening and fishermen were still working on their boats as we cooked our evening meal at 10 pm.

Ashore, we were heartened by everything we saw. Lazy-beds grew oats and potatoes. On the peat banks cows were tethered to keep them off the rocks. Children talked in Gaelic as they played. Many of the houses had well-kept gardens.

When we asked a fisherman about the chances of getting a repair done to our self-steering gear he directed us to the Red House, and the job was done in a trice by a young-minded eighty-three-year-old, by name of McLeod, who asked us into the living quarters for tea. As we sat down, in came a son of the house, who said to me, 'We've met before. I was in the fishing boat that took you out to St Kilda and brought you back.' It was Roddy Cunningham's boat, *A'Maighdean Herrich – Maid of Harris*. Truly, in the Hebrides you are never forgotten.

From Scalpay we headed for North Uist in late afternoon in the face of a bad shipping forecast. It was rough, and no mistake, before we got to Loch Eport four hour later, to put the anchor down in a bay called Bagh a' Bhiorain. It was a noisy night as the boat kept moving round its anchor with many slaps and bangs.

Thoughts in the morning were for an ascent of Eaval, 1,138 ft, and one of the most awkward hills to climb in Scotland for it is almost surrounded by water. The peak, when we got to it after a confusing walk, was a delight, shapely and steep, with a tremendous reward in the summit view over a land of water, for such is the impression of North Uist from the top. That evening became one of flat calm, and soft gold on seaweed and grey rocks. Back at the boat we boiled some mussels and ate them on deck, enjoying a vivid sunset.

It was my last night aboard. I was dropped off at Lochmaddy car-ferry terminus for the crossing to Skye, and who should be on the jetty as I stepped off at Uig but Seton Gordon. With a big grin of welcome on his face, he stretched out his hand and said: 'On the day you left I saw a little white yacht heading for the Shiants. I had it in the long glass. It was yours, wasn't it?' He listened keenly to my account of our happy trip. I then suggested, seeing he was here, that I take a final photograph of him, and as I took it I saw we were being stalked by a black-bearded photographer, well-known as an admirer of Seton Gordon, John Murray, another golden eagle enthusiast. His snapshot caught the two of us, me with my camera raised to photograph the old naturalist and time-traveller whose twenty-nine books are a testament to his constancy to all that is good. In attempting to follow his example I could not have chosen a better model.

Seton Gordon published the first of his books, *Birds of the Loch and Mountain*, in 1907, and the ninety-one photographs reproduced were taken with a heavy half-plate Thornton-Pickard camera. He was following in the footsteps of Richard Kearton whose *With Nature and a Camera* was published at the end of last century.

On Deeside the young Seton Gordon snatched his chance to explore the Cairngorms in a way that had never been done before. He investigated the snow patches that had never been known to melt, studied the alpine plants, looked at the remnants of the Caledonian pine forests and the capercaillie and Scottish crossbills that lived among them, at the greenshank in the forest bogs, but above all concentrated on the life history of the golden eagle.

In a biography, published in 1991, written by an appropriately named admirer, Raymond Eagle, Seton Gordon's life story has been well documented, and I was glad to be of some help during the years of preparation which resulted in a book with the title: *Seton Gordon, The Life and Times of a Highland Gentleman*.

10

Moroccan Odyssey

Stravaigin', stravaigin', there's naething like stravaigin',
When soond in win' an' limb.

W.D. Cocker

In 1955 Douglas Scott and I thought up a new place for our stravaigings, the High Atlas of Morocco, the tallest mountains in North Africa 450 miles south of Tangier and most easily approached from Marrakech. The translation of an article by alpinist Jacques de Lépiney suggested to us that now was the time to go, before the area was opened up by other stravaigers. Of mountaineering there, he wrote:

The subject is a delicate one, because Morocco, still partially unexplored in its loftiest regions, is hardly properly open for mountaineering or 'tourist' exploration. Very few are still the mountaineers who have climbed some peaks: immense districts, totally unknown, reserve the possibility of many surprises. Again, we must not forget that the French Protectorate has not yet entirely pacified the Atlas and that in certain parts ingress among the hostile tribes is quite impossible at the present moment.

That small extract from an exciting article in the *Alpine Journal* was written in 1928!

One alpinist of high reputation who had not been put off by the political uncertainties described was Mr Bentley Beetham, a schoolmaster who had been a team member of the 1924 Everest expedition which included George Mallory and Andrew Irvine, whose failure to return from their summit bid remains a mystery.

For several of his long vacations thereafter, Beetham turned his attention to the High Atlas, discovering a more rewarding field for mountaineering than in European Alps with which he felt over-familiar and considered tame by comparison with the delights of the unknown. Both Douglas and I had a particular rapport with Beetham because it was an interest in birds that had first taken him to the crags, before he was weaned away by the delights of climbing for its own sake.

What little we knew about the High Atlas was from climbing literature, until we met up with Alfred Gregory who had helped carry the high camp at 27,900 feet from which Hillary and Tensing reached the summit of Everest. Gregory, who was heavily engaged lecturing on the first ascent of Everest, had travelled to Morocco to give a lecture to French Alpine Club members in Casablanca, and while there had taken the chance to go climbing with some of them in the Atlas. He was so enthused by what he had seen that he was anxious to go back.

Moreover, Gregory, a travel agent by profession, could book us a cheap flight to Gibraltar, and all we need do was cross on the ferry to Tangier, get the bus to Marrakech, and we were within striking distance of the mountains. It sounded almost too good to be true, relatively unexplored mountains within easy range, the highest in North Africa at that. So we booked a flight to arrive in Gibraltar on 22nd March, and took our heavy gear down to the Clyde for transport by cargo ship to arrive a few days before us.

Alas, that is how it came about that we were in Gibraltar but our camping gear, skis, ice-axes and some concentrated high camp rations were still on the high sea. After one day hanging about Gibraltar we made arrangements for the luggage to be sent over to Tangier, and off we went on the ferry intent on making the most of our time by visiting Cap Spartel where the Mediterranean meets the Atlantic and is a focal point for migrating birds.

Little did we know that the natives of Tangier are renowned for their ability to lure unsophisticated tourists to places they do not want to go. In our case it was to a low-class hotel at a three-star price. We even let our guide lead us to another before we shook him off with scowls. Then, after a few days we were approached by smarter individuals, asking: 'You want to buy a business? Rent a flat? You want to change money? I can take you to where you will get a better deal.' We might have been interested in seeing some belly-dancing if the show had not started well past our bed-time.

That laggard ship, by not turning up with our luggage for a week, did us a good turn, for if we had been able to leave Tangier immediately we would have missed some spectacular bird migration amid fine coastal scenery at the most north-westerly point of Africa at Cap Spartel, within cycling distance of Tangier. In late March the birds were leaving their winter quarters for their nesting territories in Europe – swallows, house martins, kites, bee-eaters, storks, egrets, rollers, hoopoes, hen harriers, shrikes, wagtails and many another.

Small birds were everywhere, feeding among the low shrubs yellow with blossom. Marsh harriers were hunting over this area, and in the bushes were woodchat shrikes, Sardinian warblers, Darford warblers, linnets, cornbuntings, stonechats, willow and melodious warblers. On

128

the beach were two stone curlews and four sanderlings. Always there was a constant passage of low-flying swallows. This migration went on each day we were there, as we extended our wanderings to Cap Malabata and Donabo, where we were seeing black-eared wheatears, serins, common redstarts, goldfinches, buzzards, gull-billed terns, more burbling flocks of bee-eaters and a huge movement of pipits.

The six days between 23rd and 29th March were unsettled with heavy rain and spasmodic sunshine interspersed with windy showers, creating bursting waves crashing on the rocks and giving exciting photographic opportunities. Sometimes we hired bikes and cycled out from Tangier; at other times we used the airport bus for cross-country walks, always getting back in time to visit the Customs warehouse to see if our luggage had arrived. One day we were invited to search for it among some newly arrived cargo, and joy, oh joy, it was there!

Now we made our way to the bus station to book for Marrakech, only to discover that before we could get tickets to enable us to pass from the Spanish into the French zone, our passports would have to go to Casablanca for stamping. Maybe it was as well we were delayed, for when we did make the fifteen-hour journey to Marrakech we learned that an attempt had just been made on the life of Pasha El Glaoui and that ten persons had been killed and twenty-seven injured. Militants for an independent Morocco had tried to assassinate him because he was pro-French.

Not wishing to linger in a trouble-spot longer than necessary and, as the following day was Easter Sunday, we rose at dawn from our one-star hotel bed in the native quarter, leaving our luggage to be picked up later, and dashed off to the modern French quarter to track down representatives of the French Alpine Club. The good news was that there was a bus leaving that afternoon for a ski-lodge high in the Atlas and that it would be an ideal launching point for climbing. With maps to procure, food to buy in the market, and luggage to collect, it was a scramble, but we made the bus.

Now we could relax and take in the passing scene, flat fields, made green by irrigation channels, gradually giving way to foothills where Berbers in homespun cloaks watched over their feeding sheep and goats. Then almost suddenly the angle changed, the bus zig-zagged steeply up, to run along the edge of a ravine crested by trees. Over the ridge we met the first snow-gullies, and now and again glimpsed, perched high-up, Berber villages. Still we climbed, slanting up, or screeching round hair-pin bends, eventually to face a cleft in a rock escarpment. Through it was a green oasis beneath a pointed snow-peak and below it was the Lodge of Oukamaiden at 8,900 feet.

Inside, it was packed with young French skiers. In decor and tasteful appointments it stood comparison with any alpine hut that we had ever been in, with a fine choice of meals on offer too – at cheap cost. All the beds in the dormitory were taken, but we were invited to feel free and make a bed on the floor. We must have seemed an odd pair.

Occupiers of a floor in a packed lodge have to be early risers to avoid being tramped on. We were first up, and out into the sparkle of a frosty morn of blue sky echoed in pools of blue water reflecting the snows above. Tiny alpine daffodils of slender form edged the pools and there was a grand singing and chuckling of birds. We saw a lot – shorelarks, alpine accentors, wheatears, Moussier's redstart, jackdaws, red billed choughs and grey wagtails – before setting off with our skis on the peak, and were first to be hauled up on the ski-tow.

We soon found out why, because the snow was too icy as yet for enjoyable down-hill running: so what we did was climb from the top station to the summit and enjoy our first close view of High Atlas peaks thrusting through a white cloud-sea that lapped their lower slopes and cut them off from the valleys. There was no doubt where our first climbing strike should be, by the west buttress of a peak within easy distance of where we stood. The name on the map was Angour.

By the time we got back to where we had dumped our skis, the snow surface had softened sufficiently to delight the first arrivals from the lodge, and we made the most of it until mid-day, after which the snow had become so water-logged by the heat of the sun that it was impossibly heavy and slow. Talking with French skiers we learned much about the opportunities for touring on skis at this time of year, and we also gleaned a bit about Moroccan history.

Out of our sleeping bags before others were awake, we were away on a delightful morning to the pass that would take us to Angour, but neither of us were feeling very delightful with upset stomachs. Once on the mountain however, toiling up boulders to get hands and feet on pink rock, warm in the sun, we came to life, finding steep pitch after pitch of high interest, never easy but never too difficult; we graded what was its west buttress Mild–Severe. From the top the peak that commanded our attention was the 6,000-foot north face of Aksoul leading to a pinnacled crest.

A glance at the map identified the pass leading to it, the Tizi n' Ouadi. If we crossed with four days' food we could stay in a simple refuge at the Berber village of Tachedirt to launch our attempt on the face. It would be quite a heavy back-packing job, so back in Ouka we found a native porter, by name, Gogema, and it was good next morning to be in roadless country, grateful for the guidance of our fast-moving Berber who knew the way and seemed to be enjoying himself.

Tachedirt was our first close contact with a Berber village, built in giant steps, so that the flat roof of the lowest house was the courtyard of the one above it, and so on to the highest house, narrow alleys leading through. Our refuge stood apart from the village at 7,700 feet, containing bedsteads, a table, a few chairs and a lockable cupboard. For fuel we gathered a prickly shrub which burns with explosive vigour. Our first enjoyable task was to recce the big rock- and ice-wall, plot a possible route up, and assuming we got to the summit pinnacles and traversed them, identify an easy route down.

At 5 am the fire was lit, eggs boiled in the tea water, a quick breakfast scoffed, and with food in the rucksack, rope and ice-axes at the ready, we were away down into the depths of a gorge to ford the river by jumping from boulder to boulder, then climbing over a hill shoulder lying between us and our mountain. In daylight this took only one hour. In darkness, as were to discover fourteen hours later, it was a very different and heart-breaking story.

Everything was frozen hard, the steep snow just above the gorge forcing us to cut steps even at modest angles, then by a gully we reached iced rocks and scrambled steeply out of shadow into sunshine on a silver saddle surrounded by red rock towers projecting against blue sky. It was good to be alive and faced by a real exploratory problem on virgin ground.

Our reconnaissance of yesterday was paying dividends now. We recognised the rock rib which we knew would lead us to a bulging overhang, by-passable by going left on snow. What we had not bargained for, however, was the snow getting soft so quickly, forcing us to stay on the rocks, playing a game of hide-and-seek between the overhang and the snow, enjoying thrilling situations that continued for 3,000 feet, and led us to another of our landmarks, a rock arête which we hoped to climb for 1,500 feet to its top. It proved easier than it looked, so we were able to move together, and at 2.30 pm we stepped on to the summit, the climb having taken eight hours with only three halts for food, delightful halts on sunny ledges.

But something ominous was happening to the weather. Our immediate concern was the couloir of descent, and how to get across the rock towers between us and it, for they were more formidable-looking at close range than they had appeared from far below. Wasting no time, we dropped to the foot of the first one, saw there was no direct way up but that threading the face like a barrel hoop was a snow tilted ledge, dangerously soft and exposed to a big drop, a tense traverse that took us to the base of the second tower, where the mist was curling.

This one had an obvious line of weakness, and in forty feet of difficult rock climbing we were on easy ground leading us to an airy summit crest, with an abrupt drop to the final tower. This one we took direct by its steep arête, Scott vanquishing its overhanging edge as if he were starting the day and not on the exposed top of a remote mountain after long hours of hard climbing.

Now to get off this last one and find the couloir! In mist and snow it is hard to judge distance. We knew we should not proceed too far, so at a likely place started down, slowly at first, then when no rocks interrupted,

131

we decided it would be safe to sit on our backsides and let gravity slide us down. It was exhilarating, we were moving fast and in good control, until suddenly we had to throw ourselves back on our ice-axes and brake on the edge of a drop. Nothing for it now but to uncoil the rope, and climb down a series of awkward pitches of rock and ice.

Once down this we were in the true gully and realising that until now we had been in a side branch of it. Daylight was going fast and we fairly shot down the next 1,000 feet. Darkness was winning the race, however, not only the darkness of night but the darkness of storm. It was time to get out the electric torch, and while Scott fumbled with the battery I tried to tie a bootlace. I was aware of a flash which I thought was his light, and so did he. A crackle of thunder, following by stinging hailstones the size of small peas, told us our mistake. 'We're going to get soaked,' said Scott. He was right.

Torch in hand and blinded by frequent stabs of forked lightning, we stumbled down the gully, keeping to the centre as far as possible in order to avoid holes, like miniature crevasses, penetrating to the stream running far below.

The peaks were clear now, as we could see when each flash of lightning outlined them in quivering purple. There was a nightmarish quality about the remainder of the descent in a wet world of ravines and waterfalls, loose stones and side-nallahs which neither of us could remember from morning. It has been remarked by more than one mountaineer, that electric storms can have a reinvigorating effect on tired men. The pair of us certainly felt fresher after the storm than we had done before it, but were glad the lightning had not caught us on top of the pinnacles where there is most danger of being struck. It was a fine moment when at last the hut loomed ahead, though it had its moment of bitterness when we found we could not unlock the cupboard door, behind which we had hidden our food. We slid into our sleeping bags supperless. After all, has it not been said that to sleep is to eat!

We certainly slept well that night, and once we got the cupboard opened put the eggs in the pan and ate a hearty breakfast before taking a leisurely walk round Tachedirt to greet the villagers, have a tour around and enjoy the plentiful bird life: shorelarks, black wheatears, lesser kestrels, black redstarts, alpine swifts, rock buntings, red billed choughs, partridges, grey wagtails and dippers and woodpeckers, as well as commoner species.

There was also another peak that grabbed our attention, Iguenouane, 3,176 metres, with a fine rock buttress rising from its upper snows and leading to a pinnacled crest. The snow approach was quite long, and the ideal would have been to take skis and get a 3,000-foot run down, but as we had left them at Oukamaiden, we contented ourselves with a first-rate climb and from the pinnacles looked into the Kassaria Valley for the first time.

That was phase one. Returning to Oukamaiden, we picked up the remainder of our kit and headed back to Marrakech to rendezvous with Jim Green of the Carlisle Mountaineering Club who was working in Algiers and motored 2,000 miles to meet up with us for some climbing. It gave Douglas and me a couple of days to enjoy the sights and sounds of the old walled city, and towards sunset experience what had been described to us as one of the supreme sights of Africa – the Djemaa el Fna – the Concourse of Sinners or Place of Death.

We had never seen before such a blaze of tribal dresses or such a variety of facial skin colours of their wearers, on a great square literally moving with people of the deserts and the mountains. From a high point we were looking down on a gigantic crowd out for entertainment and the pleasures of buying and selling. Moving down amongst them, and watching a team of erotic dancers, black Sudanese in white djellabas performing intricate patterns and gesturing against a wailing of music and jangling tambourines, my eye was held by a watching youth of startling beauty. I thought at first it was a woman, but when he simpered and made a suggestive motion to me, I knew I was looking at a male prostitute.

On looking into a booth, an Arab tried to interest us in a girl. At another booth we saw men lying back in chairs, their eyes glazed as they sucked at the stems of long clay pipes with tiny bowls, lost in the dreamland of opium. We were invited to try. We watched snake-charmers, three-card sharpers, a magician, jugglers and wished we could understand the professional story-teller who commanded easily the biggest knot of people in the square, convulsing them with laughter, or achieving absolute silence. In a land where few can read he was an artist.

Three years later I was back there, this time with Alfred Gregory, Everest climber and travel agent mentioned earlier, trying to capture the excitement of this place on 16 mm movie film we hoped to sell to television.

Independently, both of us had been trying our hands at documentary film making, and talking about our mutual experiences in Morocco, we were agreed that a film about Berber life would be an original subject. We could hire a car, drive by Casablanca to Marrakech, portray their greatest city, then cross the High Atlas and the Anti Atlas and come north again by the Atlantic coast.

This is what we did, beginning at Tangier where Douglas Scott and I had done our birding and which on 2nd May, when we began our travels, was still exciting for later migrants, such as terns and waders. There were no terrorists' problems, now that Morocco had gained its independence. Moreover we had the good-will of the Moroccan Government to make the film, and the guarantee of Government guides if we needed them.

We shot 5,000 feet of 16 mm film in colour, and in its making discovered what it is like to be 'stoned' by an angry mob who associate the camera with the evil eye. This frightening action happened in the narrow confines of a busy market. I was filming and Gregory was waving back a curious crowd who were blocking the busy scene that I was trying to portray. Then suddenly stones were being thrown, and we had just time to leap into the car and drive, with horn blaring, straight at the protesters and make them jump clear for their lives. We were more circumspect after that hostile encounter.

The desert Berbers were the most friendly, and the oases delightful places to film, with streams winding among roses and tall heads of Indian corn, date-palms and walnut trees, frogs croaking in irrigation channels, virtual Gardens of Eden, where bearded Jews worked among shady palms to the music of cooing turtle doves and the bubbling cries of hoopoes. Tall Berbers smiled greetings of *La Bas*, and left us to our filming. No one followed us or pestered us for money. The finest oasis we saw was Tinehir.

Our film captured it to perfection: the oleanders in flower by the river, and on a high tree, a Berber clinging fertilising the date blossom to ensure a good crop. As he worked he was intoning what, we learned, was a prayer for the successful seeding of the dates. From filming him at work we panned the camera to mulberry fruits, figs, apricots and peaches. The people were the handsomest we filmed.

In the region of Quarzazate oasis we sought out the Dades River to thread its miniature Grand Canyon where the river, draining the High Atlas in its course of 350 kilometres, has carved from the reddish cliffs four spectacular gorges, red walls rising as high as 1,600 feet above the gurgling stream-bed. It was not so far on from here. In the sand-waves of the desert we met a flight of locusts spattering themselves on the body of the car like hard pellets, yellow in colour, and each about a finger-length in size. We managed to get some good close-up shots of them too. A fox, greyer than the British form, with its head down, was snapping some of them up, we reckoned.

The excellent Michelin motoring map of south Morocco shows possible piste routes that are not guaranteed by reason of flood or sand. If one fails you have a choice of another, usually risky. One on which we tried to reach Safi on the Atlantic coast we are not likely to forget. After edging gingerly forward, a wheel on each side of a crumbling void below, we were just breathing easily when worse road conditions confronted us, and our thoughts were taken up with the difficulties of reversing, when coming towards us was a joyous sight, camels with Berbers leading them, and they were on their way from Safi. Relief, the worst was behind us!

In Safi, our interest was in the Street of the Potters, where we got good sequences of master craftsmen brushing artistic free-hand geometric designs on a variety of dishes and pots, working at speed too. Then we drove on for the Middle Atlas and the city of Fez, enjoying on the way a gentler landscape with vineyards and large wheat-fields on the lower

134

slopes of hills reminiscent of central Scotland. Fez, we both felt, was rather frightening in its congestion of crowded alleys thronged with donkeys, mules, beggars, itinerant salesmen, shops, factories and dealers of all kinds. As our main interest was in the tanneries supplying the finest Moroccan leather, we hired a guide, and the foul smells of the tanning process told us when we were almost there.

What a place to film, climbing into buildings by slippery staircases to look down on a vast array of vats where tanners were busy dipping and washing hides; stretched over rooftops, sheep- and goatskins were drying in the sun, in colours of brilliant reds and yellows. Fez has been called the most romantic city on earth, and was a major stronghold of nationalistic fervour resulting in the expulsion of the French and Spanish control. The trouble-spots of our 1955 trip were peaceful now, but it is to that earlier trip I now return, and the arrival of Jim Green after his 2,000-mile drive from Algiers to Marrakech.

With ten days' supply of food Douglas Scott, Jim and I set off for the Berber village of Asni, where we hired mules and engaged an ancient Berber to guard the car during the time we would be deep in the mountains. Our first base was the Neltner Hut at 10,496 feet and to reach it we had to back-pack the last bit as the snow was too deep for mules. Wonderful it was next day to fix skins to the soles of our skis and pole our way to the crest of the pass that looks south to the arid desert. From this summit of the Tizi n' Ouanoum, climbing skins removed from the soles of our skis, we swished down on perfect snow after a valuable recce of the peaks we were to climb in the next ten days.

The first of these was Toubkal, at 4,165 metres the highest peak in North Africa, below which I had my first experience of an earth tremor so strong that not only did the ground heave but so did my stomach in momentary nausea. We realised it was not imagination when stones from the mountain came rattling down. Our route to the top was by the arête first climbed by Bentley Beetham, a long mixed route by chimneys and narrow edges to a square-cut tower demanding an abseil. It was snowing on top, and even wearing all our jerseys we were cold.

Following the ascent of Toubkal we went for Afella n' Ouanoukrim, trying a line not shown on our guide-book, an arête promising an airy crest if we could keep to its edge. It took us most of the way until it became dangerously loose and we moved east to gain point 4,040 metres on our map, and marked with the word Clochetons – pinnacles. They were a joy, exposed to a drop of 2,000 feet, and with wonderful holds on most vertical rock; mountaineering at its best.

The time had come now for us to move back to the Berber village of Imlil, where we had left a cache of food, for entry to a remote valley reached by a 2,500-foot uphill slog, then 1,200 feet down, to enter a ravine of waterfalls and cedar trees above which stands the Lepiney Hut below the

135

great rock wall of Tazerhart. The snow-gullies seaming this face give winter climbs in mid-summer. Our intention was to go for its Median Arête which is graded *très difficile*.

Jim opted out of this climb, rightly, for he judged he was less fit than we were, and the two of us would be able to move faster than any party of three. That climb extended us, forcing us at one point on to its smooth east wall by a snow ribbon adhering to it like wall-paper, a dangerous traverse on high-angled softish snow where we moved one at a time, looking for any breach that might lead us to the top, now very close. There was only one possible crack-line, which neither of us would have chosen if there had been an alternative. Douglas led it, moving with the utmost caution, each move carefully considered. If he came off he would land on the snow-ledge. My job would be to hold him on the rope before he went over the edge of the precipice. Up and up he moved until there was very little slack left between us. Then came a shout that he was on a belay and it looked OK ahead.

That was a very hard pitch. We had been in mist for much of the climb. Incredibly we stepped into sunshine on the top. We were indeed lucky, for Tazerhart's summit is a plateau, and that evening it looked like a Greenland ice-cap in miniature. We were privileged indeed to walk over it, and even select a route down before we were enveloped in falling snow. So dim became the visibility that we had difficulty in finding the hut where Jim Green was keeping warm for us a huge pot of soup and spaghetti.

We slept like babes that night, and looking out in the morning saw the snowline had crept right down to the valleys and that we were in for a strenuous traverse back to Imlil. The following morning was perhaps the most sparkling we had in the High Atlas: the Berbers, in their monk-like hooded robes, taking their sheep and goats to the hill; women carrying water from the well; a villager inviting us into his courtyard to drink mint tea with him. It was a morning for a photographic prowl and we made the most of the flowers, the sparkling waterfalls and, at a water-wheel, a Berber grinding barley.

Now it was time to hire mules to transport our skis and luggage back down the valley to where we had left the car in the care of the old Berber who had volunteered to watch it while we were away. He was there, and beaming happily even if his job had come to an end. It had been agreed that we should travel together to Algiers where Jim would drop us off and Douglas and I would make our way home by crossing the Mediterranean to Marseilles, take a train from there to Calais and travel north from Dover.

It was broiling heat all the way on the 2,000-mile journey to Algiers, and we didn't envy Jim the country where he was working, while we were going home to the finest month of the year – May – in Scotland, where the cuckoo and swift would be newly arrived and ptarmigan and golden plover would be brooding their eggs on the hilltops. Daffodils would be in bloom, the trees would be in blossom and the bird-song at its best.

We were well content. We had the feeling of having travelled through several centuries in terms of way of life. We had been exploring in mountains where there were no other climbers, and the only guide-book was rudimentary.

We blessed our good luck at being there before the High Atlas became written about in an increasing age of tourism from the 1960s onward. But there is much still to be discovered, even if you have to look harder for it.

11

Singing for My Supper

O wad some Power the giftie gie us
To see oursels . . .
                              Robert Burns

Thus did Mr Melville Dinwiddie, Controller of the BBC in Scotland, head an article in the *Scottish Field* of January 1952. About this quote from Robert Burns he wrote:

> The prayer of the national bard is coming true 156 years after his death when, by a modern miracle of communication, we will be able to 'see oursels', and also enable others to see us. It is significant that it is through the pioneering work of a great Scot, John Logie Baird, that we will be sitting in our own homes and viewing events that are taking place many miles away . . . Now we will both hear and see the actual occurrence, and be able to share much more completely in it.

It was not until the mid 1950s however, when the BBC had the rival Scottish Television beaming out programmes, that sales of sets soared, and my first appearance on the screen was in a chat-show talking about recent explorations in the Middle East. I enjoyed it more than being on radio, talking freely without a script. It resulted in me being called in more and more on a current affairs programme, *Here and Now*, that went out five nights a week between six and seven o'clock, peak viewing time.

Observing that still pictures were often used in the absence of movie film, it struck me that if I bought myself a Reflex Bolex, with turret head, and shot at 16 frames per second I might fill a gap. I sold the very first one I offered.

It happened after a big New Year blizzard had paralysed the Highlands, cut isolated villages off from supplies, and resulted in deaths by exposure of four Glasgow hill-walkers on Jock's Road between Braemar and Glen Clova. Communications were still in a chaotic state when I went to Glasgow Airport expecting to fly to Wick and travel on to Dounreay where I was due to lecture that evening to the staff club at Dounreay Nuclear Power Station.

At the airport I was taken to Edinburgh and put on a plane with only one other passenger, who happened to be an airline pilot bound for Aberdeen where I had to change planes. Gaining height as we crossed the Firth of Tay with ahead of us the Grampians looking like the Greenland ice-cap, I got the camera out of the case, arousing the interest of my fellow passenger. I told him I just wanted to get some shots of farms, cut off from the outside world, and if possible the area where the four ramblers died.

'You'd be better in the cockpit,' he said. 'I'll have a word with the pilot.' So into the vacant seat of the small plane I went, and he flew a line that would take us up Glen Clova and over the scene of the accident into Deeside and on to Aberdeen. I finished off my roll of film by shooting the plane for Shetland taking off in the mini blizzard whirled up by its propellors. In Wick in darkness, the road to Dounreay was so icy that the bus slid into a snowdrift, causing such a delay that I was nearly late for my lecture.

Back in Glasgow next day, I handed in the undeveloped film to Scottish Television, accompanied with sufficient detail for a voice-over, and in a friend's house had the pleasure of seeing the film in its entirety as I had shot it. Payment was eight guineas – worth perhaps £100 at the 1992 rate. Not bad, I thought, for an apprentice. I shot a few more news items at the same rate, each lasting perhaps two minutes on average on the screen.

Now that I knew a wee bit more of the craft of ciné-filming I set about making a wild-life film, aimed at a popular programme presented by Peter Scott, bird painter and son of Captain Scott of the Antarctic. Its title was *Look*, and I burned up a lot of energy and wasted a lot of colour film on mountain birds.

I could hardly have chosen a more inaccessible subject, or one so prone to the uncertainties of Scottish hill weather. Laden like a Sherpa with camp kit, tripod, camera and hide, and pitching the tent at 3,000 feet, I scoured the 3,000–4,000-foot level of the Drumochter Hills and the high Cairngorms to portray the lives of dotterel, ptarmigan, dunlin, golden plover, red grouse, golden eagle and any animal that fitted in to the script: red deer, mountain hare and stoat. My butcher pal, Matt, and my girl-friend, Rhona Dickson, did yeoman work in the labouring.

Much easier to get on film were Hebridean birds, and in one week in Tiree, thanks to the tireless Matt in camp with me at Ballaphuil, I got pretty well everything from red necked phalaropes on the wetlands to ring plover, oyster catchers, peewits, little terns, arctic terns, twites, skylarks, fulmar petrels, guillemots and razorbills. The flower-studded machairs were at their colourful best and the early June weather could not have been better.

I didn't edit any of this material. I'd left that to the BBC specialists, and came the day when I was invited to screen it and have it judged for suitability by the producer, Miss Irene Adair. We must have looked at two hours of film before she sorrowfully communicated her verdict: 'You have some lovely and unusual shots that must have required great patience to get. You have some material that a wild-life film producer would jump at if it fitted what he was looking for. What you have is a series of shots, but there is no story line. I'm not saying that it would be impossible to get something out of all your film, but it would be a very big editing job beyond our resources. It's tragic, with all the hard work you've done, that you didn't go to a film school and learn the basics of filming. If you had done that you would have shot to a story, and let the pictures tell it with the minimum of words.'

In fact the BBC purchased some film clips from these attempts, and so did Anglia Television for their *Survival* series. Scottish Television bought some too for an environmental special. The film of Morocco, made with Alf Gregory, was on a much more organised basis, yet we made some fundamental mistakes, because we were both amateurs in ciné-photography.

With hindsight, what we should have done before setting out to make a film in Morocco was arrange a consultation with the BBC or ITV, explaining what we had in mind, and finding out if either company had a programme slot for the kind of film we intended to make. In that way, we could shoot to their requirements, and negotiate a fee covering movie making and travel expenses. Our biggest mistake after it was made was not getting the 5,000 feet of colour film professionally edited.

I left it to Gregory, who was confident he could make a sale of the version he produced, and got copied for his use in lecturing. As one who lectured on the Kodak circuit, it went well with audiences. But with the BBC and ITV he had no luck, so he began using the master film instead of the copy, because the original was so much superior in subtlety of colour.

His lecture series over, he passed the original film to me, so that I could try my contacts in the television world. The Head of Programmes of BBC Schools service, Miss Peggy Broadhead, liked it and said it could be cut to fit her *People of Many Lands* slot. She invited me to come to London and write a script to go with the film for an overall fee of £425 plus travel and accommodation expenses. In accepting this, and working under her direction I learned much in three busy days about how to write and deliver a commentary.

At that time, in the late 1950s, BBC methods were much more primitive than they are now. My introduction was done, not in a studio, but in a corner of a large hall, where an easel with a large-scale map of Morocco was pinned to a board, and beside it was a pointer, so that I could address the camera as if talking to a school class, and point out the route of travel on the map. There was no tele-prompt, but thanks to Pelmanism's mind and memory training I was confident that I would remember the words of introduction I had memorised.

But before I had got beyond: 'Hello, I've been to Morocco twice, the

140

first time before the country was independent, and again, after independence,' there was a cry of 'cut'. The sound-recordist could hear the mechanical whir of the film camera. I had hardly begun the second 'take' before I was stopped again, for a change of film position for a technical reason. A third stoppage involved a long delay while a fitment like a balaclava was fitted over the camera to deaden its sound. The fourth cut was due to me: 'Could we have a bit more smile. You're looking just a bit too grim. Look as if you're enjoying it and really look forward to showing them some pictures.' It was hard after that not to have a fit of the giggles.

We had started about 9.45 am. By 11.30 Miss Broadhead was satisfied with the intro and after lunch I was taken across London to a little theatre and placed in a telephone-box-like booth with a well-lit lectern, above which was a tiny green light. The green light was my cue. Every time it flashed I had to read the passages appropriate to the pictures appearing on the screen, which meant getting the pace absolutely right.

Sometimes I was a bit bamboozled by the green light, wondering if I had missed one, or if I was at the right passage, but it worked, and the recordings we had taken of market sounds, the music fitting the movement of the dancers in Marrakech's Djemaa el Fna sounded better than I ever imagined it would. My pleasure was short-lived, for owing to a techinical flaw, I had to do the whole commentary again.

I think in all modesty that the colour film we made on Morocco was good, and although it lost a lot, seen in black and white on the television screen, it was an effective schools programme, which I had the pleasure of watching in Glasgow with some senior secondary children. Ian Wishart of the BBC in Scotland arranged the visit, and I had a very enjoyable discussion with the pupils about the film after it was screened.

Before there was such a service as Schools Television, I had made some story material from slides, at the request of Common Ground, London, to be copied and sold as film strips, with a written commentary to be read by the classroom teacher. Such titles as *Mountain Life in High Asia, Sherpas of Everest, Berbers of the High Atlas, Life in the Lofoten Islands, Sea Birds*, and material on physical geography were among those I had the pleasure of compiling.

Lecturing to mountaineering clubs was fun, and a good way of getting to meet climbers who were famous names to me through the reading of their exploits in books and journals. I went the rounds of annual dinners, showed slides, gave the obligatory after-dinner speech, and made friends in such clubs as the Yorkshire Ramblers in Leeds, the Rucksack Club in Manchester, the Fell and Rock Club in Keswick, the Carlisle Mountaineering Club, the Karabiner Club, and the student mountaineering clubs of Oxford and Cambridge Universities.

Not so enjoyable was working for Foyle's Lecture Agency, mounting the platform twice a day sometimes; a school or lunch club in the afternoon, followed in the evening with a talk to a literary society or Arts Guild. Travelling to such places as Kendal, Harrogate, Ilkley, Sheffield, York, Brighton and London in the course of one tour was time-consuming and unprofitable, since you paid your own expenses and lost a lot of writing time. It was also exhausting, and rather lonely once you were off the platform. True, I met some very fine people, but was glad to give it up.

One lecture I did look forward to was in Cork because I had never been to Ireland, and by flying from Glasgow to Dublin I could visit somebody I very much wanted to meet again. That man was Jack Sutton, whom I first met in a Youth Hostel in Achnashellach when I was twenty-two. I'd cycled down the length of Loch Maree in torrential rain and was glad to get inside and meet a one-eyed Irishman who like me was waiting for the rain to go off. Indeed the man with a smoked glass over one eye was as pleased to see me as I him.

Soon he held me enthralled with his blarney. At twenty-eight he was six years older than I was, and we forgot the weather as he told me of a bold plan he had to build a caravan and explore every corner of Britain and Ireland, paying his way by repairing broken furniture, fixing farm gates, and buying and selling tweed.

I told him of how my butcher pal Matt and I had talked about how marvellous it would be to have a travelling van, fitted out with meat and groceries, selling round villages and estate houses of Wester Ross.

Jack, discontented with his city job as a tailor, wanted to see the world, and with the passion of an Irishman soon convinced me that we should pack up our jobs, join forces and begin by walking across Europe. To pay our way I would take photographs and write articles for newspapers at home. Jack, with his skill at woodwork and trained tailor's hands would find jobs wherever we felt like settling for a spell.

That was in 1937. Alas, the trip never came off because Jack had fallen in love with an Irish coleen, married her, and devoted himself thereafter to helping build Youth Hostels in Ireland when he was not building a home for his wife and family.

For myself, caught up in the war, I didn't meet Jack again for ten years, when he journeyed to Glasgow specially to see me. Food rationing was still in force, and when I took him for a ramble on Loch Lomondside found that he hadn't come empty-handed. With a smile he brought out of his rucksack a whole roasted chicken and a large piece of ham. Next came a large tin of pineapples and a tin of evaporated milk.

I lost touch with Jack. Then he surfaced to my mind in the most remarkable way on one of my journeys to St Kilda. I had been on the island for a fortnight with a party of naturalists. We had hired a fishing boat from Tarbert, Harris. The island was then very much as the islanders had left it and it was all ours, until one afternoon a twenty-four-foot fibre-glass yacht nosed into Village Bay, dropped its anchor, and I

142

watched the dingy being lowered, two men getting in, and I helped them beach their boat on the sand. The larger and elder of the two had a ciné-camera. 'Where are the birds I've come all this way to film?' he said in a strong Irish accent.

When I explained that they were on the cliff-face on the other side of the Village Bay and that you had to climb for them he looked so disappointed, I said that if he cared to give me the camera for a couple of hours I'd get shots of puffins, guillemots, razorbills, fulmars, seals, and a general panorama showing his boat and the abandoned houses of the village street.

He gave me the camera. 'You'll come back to the boat for a meal. We've got some lovely steak and a lot of whisky bought at duty-free prices in Norway.' They certainly did me proud, and were surprised that a man as travelled as myself had never been to Ireland. To that I answered: 'In fact I know only one Irishman, and he's a tailor in Dublin by the name of Jack Sutton.' The big man, who was a surgeon in a Dublin hospital laughed. 'Well, well. Imagine that. Jack Sutton. He makes my clothes.'

So, before I went to Cork to give my lecture I called on Jack's Dublin tailoring establishment, and there he was, inch-tape on neck, spruce owner of one of the finest tailoring establishments in the city. Father of four girls, eldest fourteen, youngest three, and with a fine house in the country handy for work, and a weekend cottage in the Wicklow hills. Prosperity had not changed him, nor had his appearance altered greatly, except for a deepening of the lines in his face and whitening of the hair.

We had much to talk about round his fire that evening in 1959. 'You've been a free man,' he said, 'and did what you wanted to do. The trouble with my business is that it is too good. I have a staff of sixty-two, but I have to make the personal contacts. People who want a top-quality suit expect to get personal attention from me. So I have to be there. I can't get away even for a few days with you, though there is nothing I would like better.'

Having dropped in on Jack without much warning, I had not expected him to be free. Anyhow my plans were laid. Have a look at this fine city, go by train to Cork, then hire a car and head off into the wilds of Kerry to explore the Dingle peninsula, the parish nearest to America from where Brendon the voyager set sail for the New World, via the Faroes and Iceland.

Before I left Jack had introduced me to some of his friends who argued hotly, but with humour, over a pub lunch. Jack had ridiculed the idea that I would find people in the Dingle area habitually conversing in Gaelic. 'They speak it only when there is a Government inspector about, for they get £5 a head from the state for every Gaelic-speaking child. Irish is a dead duck and should be allowed to rest. Don't listen to these Nationalists who would sell you the moon,' pointing to his friends. 'Now you go down into Kerry and tell us when you come back what you have found.'

The Nationalists he was good-naturedly disparaging passed an address to go to in Dunquin, saying: 'You'll see the name in large letters on the guesthouse, "Krugers", he is the man to tell you the truth of how things are in the peninsula.' And it was in that direction I headed, by Killarney, after picking up a hired car on the morning after my lecture.

Spinning along, I had that grand feeling of adventure as green slopes gave way to the russet of autumn bracken, hedges pink with fuchsia flowers and a constantly changing scene below the highest peaks in Ireland. I was ready for a stop when I came to the South Pole Inn, since just the evening before I had heard a little about its history.

It was built by Tom Crean, whose name in Ireland is forever linked with Captain Scott of the Antarctic who, with his polar party, died of hunger and cold only a short distance from base. Crean, unable to get a living from the land here, joined the Royal Navy. Selected by Scott for the Antarctic, he had saved the life of Evans by a remarkable feat of endurance when he alone was strong enough to walk over the polar ice for help. It was Tom Crean who found the bodies of Scott and his companions in the death tent. He built the South Pole Inn with his own hands on retirement from the navy in 1920, and I drank a glass of porter to his memory.

West of this I saw a village school disgorging its pupils, and not a shoe among them as they ran barefoot to their croft houses, a sight that used to be common in the Scottish Highlands. Near Slea Head I had another rare sight, a flock of whirling black birds with red bills and red legs, red billed choughs, cliff-dwelling acrobats of the crow family outlawed to only one or two places in the Inner Hebrides, Isle of Man, and Wales. I was thrilled by their mad antics and piercing cries like whoops of joy.

But something was happening to the weather over the Atlantic: black thunder clouds sweeping veils of rain were advancing on the coast, and soon I could hardly see through the windscreen, and for safety I pulled the car off the twisting road and listened to the drumming of the heavy rain on the roof. Then almost as quickly as the darkness of the storm came, the heaving sea reappeared, and a rim of sun gradually enlarging to a golden ball threw a quivering rainbow over the whole parish of Dunquin, white croft houses and emerald green shore taking on a pink sheen.

The red sun was in a clear slot balanced on the horizon and its full blaze before sinking slowly out of sight is something I have never forgotten. It was one of the most dramatic manifestations of calm after storm that I have witnessed in my lifetime. Darkness was nigh by the time I saw the house with 'Krugers', writ large. It was a lady who opened the door. To my request she said, 'Sure we'll put you up for the night dear.'

And even as she spoke she was joined by the man himself, grey-headed, burly, cap at a rakish angle. 'I saw your car back the road and wondered who you were.' I told him how thrilled I had been at the wonderful transformation when the sun blazed before dropping below the horizon. 'You're Scots. Do you have the Gaelic?' When I shook my head, he held up his hand. 'Pity, I would have liked a bit of Scots Gaelic. Come round the back with me into the shop and we'll have a talk until the tea's ready. You'll be a Protestant? You can have some rashers to your supper even although its Friday. Sure now wasn't it the Protestants who made the greatest stand for Irish Nationalism?' It was news to me.

Inside was a low room as full of character as its owner. Sides of bacon swung above sacks of flour and sugar, and beyond the low counter were boxes of every kind of food, from sausages and sweets to barrels of porter and bottles of Irish whiskey. My room lay eight paces along the lobby from this hub of activity and, as I took a lighted candle and jug of water to it, I could hear customers arriving and talking to Kruger and the language was nothing but Gaelic.

Soon Kruger called me through, and while we talked, a small boy came in, muttered something in Gaelic and went out with a loaf. 'That boy was once called "the loneliest boy in Ireland", for he was the last child on the Blaskets. There is not a living soul there today, though there were hundreds getting a living from the sea and land when I was young. Great Blasket Island is only three miles out from Dunquin, and it was evacuated in 1953 because there weren't enough young people to man the boats. The old people would have been happy to stay, but they had to leave.'

The story Kruger told me had an all too familiar ring. But he had an original way of phrasing it. 'Country people here, as everywhere else, hanker for the towns, especially the girls. A young man who wants to marry here has no prospects. He will be forty or more before he is able to afford a wife, and by then he has lost the notion. The Irish in Ireland are a race of bachelors. If they can't get a weekly wage in Dublin or Cork they go to Scotland, England or America, and that's the reason why the population of the twenty-six counties keeps around three million. If we had stayed at home instead of emigrating, the population of Ireland would be over twenty million, by the laws applying to the rest of Europe, and where would that get you except the poor house?'

Kruger himself had emigrated when he was fifteen in 1909. He got the nickname Kruger because, when he played as a boy on the hill they had a game about the Boer war, and he always wanted to be Kruger killing the English. He had gone to America and became a reporter on the *Newhaven Times Leader*. He returned to Ireland in 1929, 'one of the grey geese that came home'. He built the house himself.

'The place has flourished, thank God. Everybody who stays here wants to come back. We have ceilidhs, songs and dances, and if you can speak Irish and love a good story, this is the place to come. For years before the evacuation of the Blaskets scholars and students lodged there to study the language at its purest. The oral tradition still persists.'

I would have given a lot to be able to speak Irish that evening as the back shop-cum-pub filled up with Irishmen dark-visaged as Spaniards. 'The subject is politics. It's easier in the Gaelic, that's why they're all so talkative,' said Kruger. 'The venom against British imperialism comes not from the Irish in Ireland, but from third-generation Irish across the water.'

Before leaving Dunquin I had the notion of descending to the small harbour used by the Blasket men when the weather allowed. I was in luck, three men who remembered me from the previous night were in the act of carrying their canvas curragh to the water. They told me they were going over to look at some sheep, and that there was room for me if I wanted to join them. I was tempted, but as there was no knowing when we might return, I declined. I have been sorry ever since that I did not take their offer, especially after reading Tomas O' Crohan's classic *The Islandman*, first published in Irish, taking the reader from his birth on the island in 1856 to 1926 on Great Blasket, where he died eleven years later. It is not only the story of his life but delineates 'the character of the people about me so that the record of us might live after us, for the like of us will never be again'. He forecasts that 'One day there will be none left in the Blasket of all I have mentioned in this book – and none to remember them. I am thankful to God, who has given me the chance to preserve from forgetfulness these days. Since the first fire was kindled in this island none has written of his world.'

But Great Blasket did produce another writer in Maurice O'Sullivan, whose book *Twenty Years A-Growing*, published in Irish in 1933, is also a folklore masterpiece. Born in 1904, these years when he was growing up on the island are imaginatively recreated. As a young man he left to join the Civil Guard. Alas, he drowned while sea bathing on the Connemara coast in 1950. How miraculous that one small and remote island should produce two inhabitants with such a natural gift of writing that both books are classics, and in translation are in paper-back published by Oxford University Press after many reprints.

Lively smiles were on the faces of the Nationalists when Jack and I sat down in the Dublin pub, and I told of my meeting with Kruger, and his Irish-speaking customers whose English was not always easy to follow because it was a strange tongue. I don't think you would sell many lounge suits down there,' I told Jack.

As a reward, one of the Nationalists, a son of Thomas Mason, gave me a book his father had written, *The Islands of Ireland*, written in the 30s but republished for the third time in 1950. It favoured the return of the six counties and a newly united Ireland, but by the political process, not with the bullet and the bomb.

12

To the High Arctic

To Tam the Climber
from Jack the Rhymer

Say Tam ma man ye've cast year fear
An risked tae mak a mistress Weir
Tak tent O Tam she'll prove yer peer
An' maybe mair
She'll shin pit ye in lowest gear
Sae have a care

Those crusted bachelors there I see
They yince were four an' noo but three
Their smiles may show a glint o' glee
Yet fears corrode
That days when they were young an' free
Hiv nearly goed
Yet aw' yer friens will wish ye weil
An' that the years ahead may seal
Yer bond o' love
Till faur ower Everest ye speed
Tae realms above

These verses, in the couthy language of Scotland's National Bard, Robert Burns, dated 23.7.59, came from J.S.M. Jack in the month I married Miss Rhona Dickson in Aberfoyle Parish Church. Indeed it was fear of going into lower gear that had held me back until I was at the dangerous age of forty-five. Stuart Jack was President of the Scottish Mountaineering Club in 1952 when our band of four had newly returned from the Nepal Himalaya, hence the reference 'yince there were four'.

147

A member of the SMC from 1919, he had received the unusual honour of being elected Honorary President of the Club in the year he wrote the humorous verses just quoted. At his invitation I visited him at his home in Elderslie in 1966 where he lay in bed, very ill, but wanted to show me his photograph album and talk about the mountains of Scotland which were his life-long love. Ill as he was, his eyes brightened with enthusiasm as he turned over the pages of his album and reminisced. He was eighty-three, and he lasted only a week or two after my visit.

He nodded with approval when I told him my life was enlarged by marriage, and not inhibited by it; that it was more of a pleasure living in a cottage on Loch Lomondside than in a Glasgow flat. That above the house was a marvellous wee hill which I climbed every morning as my wife went off to teach in the village school, while at weekends we often went off together camping, exploring the Highlands and Islands, discovering rewards other than just mountaineering.

It was mountains that had brought us together, when just after the war, at a time of petrol rationing, climbers hired buses, and thanks to the mountaineering grape-vine, they were always well filled. One evening as we, a group of disparate climbers, waited for the bus home, I noticed that a rather sweet-faced lady was soaked in her lower half. Discovering that she had no change, I offered her a dry pair of trousers. She took them gladly, and came in person to the house a few evenings later to return them.

She was then, and still is, a member of the Ladies' Scottish Climbing Club, which has always had close links with the Scottish Mountaineering Club. From Shawlands Academy in Glasgow she had been taken to the hills by her English teacher, Miss Barbara Macfarlane. Eldest of a large family, her father had been a seagoing Captain in one of the ships of the Donaldson Line before becoming Dockmaster of Falmouth, Cornwall, where she had lived from the age of seven to fifteen, when she moved back to Glasgow to finish her education. There she came under the influence of Miss Macfarlane, then President of the LSCC.

We hit it off from the very beginning. Like me she had changed her profession in mid-stream, by leaving a good job in Barr and Strouds, renowned optical instrument makers, to train as a school-teacher. So I had the house to myself for the solitary occupation of writing, and the companionship of Rhona in the evenings. Weekends were less important than when we lived in Glasgow.

During the 1950s, between climbing expeditions, I'd become thirled to the Gartocharn area for bird-watching with Matt. In the past we had explored Loch Lomond for its hills. Now it had a new meaning for us, following the roadless shore to the River Endrick where it meanders sluggishly through marshes before discharging into the sandy spit known locally as the 'Ring Point', where Matt had added many exciting birds to the Loch Lomond list. It is a little wild-life world of its own, unique for flowers and wader habitats, and its rich variety of nesting waterfowl.

One day when I had become interested in looking through the *Glasgow Herald* at houses for sale, I saw this notice: 'Country cottage for sale on Loch Lomondside, three bedrooms and garage, first £2,000 secures.' Its address, Gartocharn, is the village nearest to the marshes. Without telling Rhona, I fixed an appointment with its owner to view the place and took with me a climbing pal, Frank Nelson, who was a Clerk of Works. He was immediately impressed by the thick stone walls of the hundred-year-old cottage, noticed there was some wood-rot in areas of the roof timbers, that at ground level it could do with a damp-course, but he thought that these minor disadvantages were outweighed by its advantages of situation, not least that immediately above the house rose Duncryne Hill, 463 feet high, commanding from its bald top what I believe to be the finest panorama obtainable of the rise of the Highlands from the Lowlands.

'Buy the house if Rhona likes it,' advised my friend. She did. Immediately the sale was clinched and we commissioned a builder to carry out some internal alterations, so that I would have a study facing west, and a bit taken off the kitchen to make a darkroom for my photography.

The name of the house was Fir Tree Cottage. Its commodious front porch had been the village post office in the First World War, and next to it was the old smiddy, where, in bygone days, horses were shod, carts repaired and agricultural implements such as harrows, ploughs and other early agricultural implements were made serviceable. The village itself had evolved round four small quarries amidst a farming community. Our house in its early life had been occupied by a quarry worker's family.

It was during our first winter in Gartocharn I received a letter which jolted the even tenor of the country life we were enjoying so much. It was from Sir John Hunt, inviting me to join a strong team of climbers for an expedition to Scoresbyland in north-east Greenland at Latitude 72 in the High Arctic. The unusual feature of the expedition was that a large senior team was to be supported by approximately twenty juniors selected from the 150 or so who had earned the Duke of Edinburgh's Gold Award.

I was invited, I think, because I had some association with the Award Scheme, having taken some aspirants climbing on the Arrochar Alps. I had also talked to them about wild-life and expeditioning on some of their Scottish endeavours. What I liked about them was, not only their enthusiasm, but their idealism. They felt a sense of purpose in their lives, and having passed the bronze and silver tests, had set out to earn the Gold, which as well as testing such abilities as proficiency at a hobby, skill at games, general physical fitness, and service to the community, involves a back-packing expedition over fifty miles of wild country with camping kit, as an exercise in living together as well as route-finding.

From Scottish Mountaineering Club friends I had heard much of the glorious peaks of the Stauning Alps in north-east Greenland, which had suddenly become accessible in 1958 by the setting up of a Danish lead mine with an airstrip at Mesters Vig. Douglas Scott had been one of the first explorers of these peaks, whose glaciers calve their icebergs into some of the finest fjord scenery in the world – moreover it is a region of such fine weather that it had become known as the Arctic Riviera.

Offered such a splendid opportunity I could not let it pass, and was almost immediately co-opted into helping plan the journey and equipment necessary to carry out an ambitious programme mixing climbing, exploration and surveying with the study of natural history. Moreover I was selected to be one of the four Scots who would fly direct from Glasgow in advance of the expedition to prepare an advance base, thus I would get virtually the full breeding cycle of the birds and animals in an area where spring, summer and autumn are compressed into three months of intense activity. And while the expedition made its plans, my wife was making hers, to visit Iceland and cross the lava desert on horseback.

Our first meeting with the whole expedition was to take place in the Cairngorms as a training-meet, and on Good Friday 1960 Sir John Hunt was welcoming eleven seniors and a score of juniors at Luibeg on the Glen Derry side of the Lairig Ghru. Gathering us around him he began: 'This is the first time we have come together. It is an exciting moment for me. The birth of an expedition is always exciting, but this one is especially so because we shall be trying the unusual experiment of seniors and juniors working together as an exploration group in difficult mountain country, where one team will support another. This weekend is our first chance to work together. I think we are going to have a wonderful time.'

Our Quarter Master's store was deer stalker Bob Scott's stable, and the scene as kit was handed out was a flash-back to my army days, as each group was issued with boots, snow-goggles, pullovers, string vests, socks, sleeping bags, ice-axes, maps, compasses, stoves, boxes of rations and mountain tents. It was a glad moment for everyone when Primus stoves were purring and smells of soup and lamb-chops filled the air, for most had travelled overnight from England to Glasgow, thence by special bus to Braemar and the Linn of Dee to Derry Lodge.

With permission to camp among the ancient Caledonian pines our eleven orange tents made a brave sight, strung along the river bank, but not too close together to lose the feeling of privacy. I was lucky to have senior Youth Leader Dick Alcock in my group. Dick is not a climber, but is a real outdoor man who soon had our six boys comfortable, while I worked out a plan for next day. It was to cross to the Shelter Stone of Loch Avon, climb a snow-gully to get to the top of Ben Macdhui and return to Glen Derry by the Lairig Ghru.

The morning could not have been better, the air frosty, and the sun splitting the trees as we followed the Derry Burn for Coire Etchachan. I guessed the boys would get a shock of surprise when they rounded this corrie into an arctic snow-bowl, so dazzling that they had to fasten on their snow-goggles. At 3,000 feet there is a loch here, but it was invisible because it was frozen over and snow-covered. Above us was the gleaming dome of Ben Macdhui, new moulded in the snow of a recent blizzard.

Now we swung rightward and dropped steeply down to the black slit of Loch Avon hemmed in by fierce snow-walls and icy cliffs. Down here ptarmigan were croaking and creeping about, hardly getting out of our way, true arctic birds feathered to the soles of their feet, hardiest of all mountain birds. The Shelter Stone is an enormous boulder which rests sufficiently high on smaller boulders with a natural lobby leading within to sleeping space for half a dozen or more – a life-saver in time of need. There were no residents. We had the whole policies to ourselves, including the white groove of Castle Gates Gully, twisting out of sight through the battlements of the Shelter Stone Crag. Linked by 240 feet of climbing rope, I led, kicking steps for 200 feet, but gradually as the snow hardened, every step had to be hewn by the ice-axe. The boys knew now that an axe was not a walking stick, but a tool without which ascent of this gully would have been impossible. An impression of verticality was heightened by lumps of ice bouncing down from the huge crags in the sun over our heads, while we ourselves were in shadow.

The boys were whooping with delight as we lifted our bodies over the cornice. I knew they had been roused by the excitement of moving up together. Said Youth Leader Dick: 'Funny thing, Tom, I hate being on heights, yet I loved every minute of that. Time seemed to stand still. I wasn't scared, just exhilarated by everything: the steep climbing, the fantastic rock scenery, the sight of the loch right below our heels, the thrill of seeing that summit pinnacle get nearer and nearer.'

Not far to the top of Ben Macdhui now, only two miles and 400 feet of climbing on a snow surface that was still reasonably crisp despite the warm sun. Mountains were springing up all round us as we gained height, west to Ben Nevis, south to Ben Lawers, northward to Mam Soul of Glen Affric, and Lochnagar on Deeside. Our top, when it hove into view, was thronged with bodies, most of them potential Greenland expeditioners, some in shirt sleeves, a few with their shirts off getting the first touch of colour on their winter-white skins.

It was 7.30 pm when we got back to camp after ten hours on the go. Dick cooked my supper that night from the Greenland rations, soup concocted from a packet of oxtail to which had been added powdered chicken, powdered meat, yeast extract and beef cubes, yum-yum. Then

151

we had corned beef, potatoes and peas, finishing with fruit salad, tea, biscuits and cheese.

As next morning was Easter Sunday, Sir John conducted a short service under the pines, reading three texts from the Bible, then each party went its separate way. My plan took us across the lonely little pass of the Clais Fhearnaig for descent into upper Glen Quoich, one of the less visited of glens, to camp by the river among the Caledonian pines. I had arranged to meet there with New Zealander George Lowe, companion of Ed Hillary on the first ascent of Everest, each playing lead roles. Once the tents were up, off we went to the north top of Beinn a' Bhuird, descending by the steep face above the Dubh Lochan.

The icy wall hemmed by crags looked pretty fierce as we hacked steps down it, revealing to the Gold Award lads that it is trickier to balance down a frozen slope than cut your way up it. Then when we were below the steepest section, where there was a clean sweep of snow falling away for hundreds of feet, we could glissade safely, by sliding down on our backsides, warning them at the same time that you do not glissade unless you are sure there is a smooth run-out on rock-free ground at the bottom, in case you lose control and do yourself an injury, as has happened to careless glissaders. The most elegant way is to slide down upright, like a man on skis, guiding yourself with your boots and braking with your ice-axe, but this requires practice on small slopes before you try big ones.

Just three months after that I felt I was emulating a space man: on the hills of Angus one day, flying to Iceland the next, and two days later flying over the solid pack ice of the frozen sea to Greenland with three fellow Scots, Malcolm Slesser, Iain Smart and Roddie Cameron, the date 8th July 1960.

In Iceland, haymakers were busy on their crofting strips working against a background of blue sea and rolling hills. Our various jobs done, we took the tent and headed for Thingvellir, where the Vikings had established their code of laws and held their outdoor parliament called the Althing – said to be the oldest existing in the world.

The curator of the Museum in Reykjavik, who advised us to camp by the lakeside of Thingvellir, certainly did us a good turn, since from the tent we had the company of several red necked phalaropes, one with chicks which have been well described as 'bumble bees on stilts'. On the water was a whooper swan with cygnets. Whimbrels were sounding, skylarks and meadow pipits singing. Climbing up the edge of the big waterfall nearby we found ourselves in a hanging valley of blue geraniums. One day later we were flying over the frozen sea.

I won't forget my first sight of Greenland, huge glaciers flowing down from 10,000-foot ice-caps to the frozen sea edge, then the sight of the Stauning Alps, Malcolm and Iain pointing out to me the bristling alpine summits some of which they had made first ascents of two years earlier, and named after such Scottish castles as Dunnottar, Dunvegan, Duart, and so on. Straight towards them we flew, to begin losing height and plane down to the airstrip on King Oscar's Fjord.

How wonderfully fresh the air felt, stepping out of the DC4 into a land of snowdrifts, the surprise being the dozens of men and a few women from the Danish mine. Moving forward to meet us was Link Washburn, an American geologist who had befriended the Scottish Greenland expedition two years earlier. He loaded our gear on to his truck, and, over a meal with his wife and family, explained that the snow had been thirty feet deep in May, and that even now it would be strenuous to travel, even on our skis, because of the softness of the snow and the innumerable melt-water streams, some wide and fast flowing, that would be difficult to cross.

He was all too right as we poled along on our first carry of food and equipment which included the bulky frame of a collapsible canoe and paddles for erecting and launching on King Oscar's Fjord nine miles distant. In fact, the nine miles took six hours, and as the fjord was frozen solid without a single black lead of open water, all we could do was throw our bags off with relief at 2 am, lean with our backs against them, and enjoy the midnight sun tinge the trapped icebergs and throw their blue shadows on textured pack-ice.

After a wee meal, Roddy and Malcolm started back to fetch another load. Iain and I, as ornithologists to the expedition, were eager to track bird sounds of dunlin and ring plover coming from the tundra near us. They led us to some turnstones in the contrasting black, white and chestnut of breeding dress. In this wintry July it was going to be very interesting to see how the breeding birds would cope at a latitude where spring, summer and autumn are compressed into three months. Meantime, if we were to complete the main task of the advance party, the ice would need to break up to enable us to launch our canoe, paddle up King Oscar's Fjord to the Skeldal River, get across it, and build a jetty so that a cabin cruiser would be able to land stores and equipment when the expedition members arrived at Mesters Vig.

While we were camped at King Oscar's Fjord, Roddy, who would be in charge of the cabin cruiser as Skipper, was examining it at Mesters Vig, employing his engineering skills to ensure it would do its important ferrying work when the main body of the expedition needed it. The first water leads in the ice occurred on our fifth evening, on 14th August, when the tributaries of the Skel River gleamed invitingly, and off went Malcolm and Iain in the canoe, taking thirty pounds of food, but for safety's sake leaving me where I was.

Cold drove me into my sleeping bag, but a jubilant shout nine hours later roused me. It was Iain and Malcolm, in high spirits after some exciting man-hauling of the canoe over ice, threading water leads, and finally shooting right across the Skel River on to the gravel where they found a

153

good place to build a jetty. Their timing had been neat, for the sea-ice closed in once more and it was three days before we were able to launch the canoe again, this time with the three of us in it.

It was a weird, misty experience, threading the pack, ice-axes at the ready to hook a floe, while a man leapt on to it, to try and pull the canoe through a narrow lead impossible for paddling. Now and again we had arctic terns, long tailed skuas and glaucous gulls for company. There was never a moment when you could relax concentration.

But we got to the river and across it, and as we landed a party of eleven barnacle geese sprinted away from us over the snow, unable to fly because they had moulted their flight feathers. Camped on a small patch of snow-free tundra, we had views of red throated divers and flighting long tailed ducks, the latter making splendid bagpipe skirling sounds, hence its Gaelic name, the piobran. Next day we busied ourselves gathering stones and building a serviceable jetty for Roddy to tie alongside and land stores. Then, satisfied at having achieved the main task of the advance party, we relaxed.

'Man proposes, God disposes' is an old and true aphorism, but there seemed something almost miraculous when on 22nd July, the very date on which Sir John Hunt and the main party were due to arrive, the fjord ice, which had threatened all his plans, had moved out and left the seaway open to our jetty. Indeed, we had just justified our existence when over the mountains came the plane bearing Sir John and his thirty-three followers in an assortment of gear from Tyrolean hats to woollen balaclavas.

They went off to a camp spot immediately, while we, of the advance party, began the first ferry of food and equipment with Roddy at the cabin cruiser helm, bound for our jetty. By midnight on the 23rd, the complete party and their equipment were at the Skeldal base. Hardly were the tents pitched than it began to rain, and it didn't let up for the next twenty-seven hours, resuming again for most of the following week which, we gathered, is almost unheard of in this part of Greenland.

While the seniors and boys were suffering their endurance test, and carrying heavy loads, Iain and I had paddled a heavily loaded canoe for a prolonged camp on Menanders Island where we would be studying the breeding cycle of arctic terns from the laying of the eggs to the hatching and flying of the chicks. Despite the rain we had surveyed every place where terns could nest. The favourite sites were on rock ridges. The hollows, lined with willow twigs and leaves, were ready to receive eggs, but none had been laid. We gave each of one hundred nests a number, inserting a tiny wooden plant label as marker. These were promptly removed by the occupying terns, so we had to use pieces of paper hidden under some stones.

As day after day the rain fell, our hearts bled for the climbers whose well-laid plans were going agley with new snow piling on the mountains. However, they were active, climbing a total of seven good peaks, including a major trophy, the Hjornerspids, second-highest peak in the Staunings and, until then, unexplored. It was climbed by Ian McNaught-Davis and Malcolm Slesser, with Sir John Hunt and John Jackson in support. The route chosen lay up a mile-long ridge, a ridge with 'some fourteen major gendarmes and at the end the problem of the main peak itself'. Once we had seen this ridge no other approach to the main peak seemed worth considering. Only the thought of thousands of feet of first-class rock climbing could make the packing of seventy-pound loads during the past week seem worth while.' That quote comes from McNaught-Davis, the best rock climber on the Greenland expedition.

The camp from which the summit pair launched their attack was on a wind-swept col, involving heavy carrying up 1,800 feet of ice climbing at an angle of over 45 degrees. On it, 750 feet of fixed rope was left so that Hunt and Jackson could do a second load-carry. It took Slesser and McNaught-Davis seventeen hours of hard climbing to step on to the summit at 4 am. Their descent by another route took them another nine hours, twenty-eight hours of exacting climbing – a major triumph for all four climbers.

This achievement gave a great fillip to the boys and men who had laboured through the rain. They had all contributed to its success, but now the party was split, the seniors descending westward by a difficult glacier to Alpefjord. The second phase of the expedition was an exploration of the South Staunings, penetrating into hitherto untrodden glaciers, and making first ascents of four peaks, the highest of them 8,000 feet. This, Sir John reckoned, was the most worthwhile piece of pioneering achieved by the expedition, in which junior members of the party played an important part.

My own role at this time was to sail with McNaught-Davis and join the climbing party at Alpefjord who were champing at the bit to assault some of the sharp unclimbed virgin peaks here. They also needed food, and off we sailed in an eighteen-foot wooden boat, powered by two outboard engines, towing behind us an aluminium boat loaded with ration boxes, spare petrol and paraffin.

It was no pleasure cruise for non-sailors in a sea so cold that survival is calculated at ten minutes if you fall in. Also, it is a notoriously dangerous coast because of sudden winds that rough up the sea in minutes. Nor can you keep as close to the land as you would like, because of reefs and ice-cliffs which may break off and cause tidal waves.

It was on our third day, when we had pulled into a particularly barren bit of shore to thaw out with some soup, and fuel the boat, that we saw coming towards us three figures. They were Malcolm Slesser from Glasgow, John Duncan from Alloa and Robin Brooks from Maidenhead, members of the climbing party who had given us up as lost to climbing and had decided to walk out to relieve the pressure on short rations.

155

Now they could celebrate with a meal, and they told us their story. They had crossed through ice-fields and tangled crevasses at first, then the way had lain over steep screes at such a high angle that it had been easier to walk where they ended in the sea, or rock climb where the screes became cliff. Malcolm was full of admiration for his two junior companions who had persevered for over ten hours of this difficult going, composing fresh verses of a Calypso song describing their adventures. Before they left to resume their walk, they added a fresh verse. It went:

On the morning after the night before
Our bellies were empty and our feet
  were sore;
What should we see as we bombed along,
A chicken being eaten; and behind it was Tom.

Chorus

I'm sad to say, I'm on my way,
Won't be back for many a day,
I was implored to leave the fjord,
And take a little walk along the shore.

We were able to assure them there would be no more empty bellies, for we had left depots of food ahead of them which they could not miss. Sailing on, we could appreciate the screes and the rock-wall difficulties they had overcome. Once we came to the wrinkled ice-field of the Gully and Seftroms Glaciers which thrust across the fjord, leaving only half a mile navigation channel, we had the feeling of being in a more ominous place. This is Greenland of the Ice Age and no mistake: cascades of blue-green ice on both sides of the fjord, descending from rock spires, and compressed by vertical mountain walls.

Our intention was to push through it as quickly as possible, until I saw a small island with a swirl of terns over it. Duty called that I should take a quick look to ascertain if there were any unfledged young on it. It was fortunate that we had made this twenty-minute stop, for we had resumed sailing only a few minutes when dead ahead of us there was an almighty rumble and crash as a lump of glacier front collapsed, sending a wall of water right across the narrow fjord. If we had been in its path we might have been lifted bodily in its tidal wave. As we were at right angles to it we merely caught its backlash at a mile range.

We had been sailing for fourteen hours and were thankful at last to reach the head of the fjord, our destination. McNaught, who had been in this area after his climbing epic on the Hjornerspids, thought the fjord was pretty tideless here and that we could dispense with the hard work of unloading the boats in order to pull them well up the shore. How wrong he was, he realised, when he awoke to a banging and thumping. Dragging me awake he shouted: 'The boats! Quick!' Waves were breaking over them, and the banging noise was the hull of one thumping against the other. Our petrol supply for the return journey, and some boxes of food we had dumped on the shore had disappeared.

By great good fortune our petrol can had drifted in a little further on, and we salvaged some food boxes as the retreating tide left them behind. My ciné-camera was under water, and the aluminium boat had split open along the keel. Even the seams of the wooden boat had been damaged. Ruefully we climbed 1,500 feet to the survey camp, marvelling all the same at its situation ringed round by superb Chamonix-style aiguilles.

Throughout the next two days we did what we could to put matters right, and found the survey men and the boys in good heart under the leadership of John Sugden and youth leader Dick Alcock. As well as help carrying the climbers' gear, their survey programme of measuring the rate of flow of the glacier was almost complete, and in the so-doing at 4,000 feet they had enjoyed some good ski-ing and igloo building. In six weeks of theodolite observations the glacier flow was just over eighty feet.

Our hopes were pinned on the cabin-cruiser *Polypen* arriving to evacuate the Alpefjord climbers and surveyors. As it did not, and their time was up, it was decided that a party under the leadership of John Sugden would exit over a glacier pass to be picked up at a rendezvous point, while McNaught and I would ferry the others, by making two trips from the head of the fjord to the rendezvous where we would foregather. For those committed to the sea journeys it was something of an endurance test, the sea was so rough, the weather so raw and the passengers squeamish.

However, all horrors are forgotten once you're in the sleeping bag with a tent above you. I awoke to a lovely morning and loud hails of jubilation. The *Polypen* had been sighted, and we fired off verey-light pistols in welcome. I have already described my own jubilation turning to sadness when I was handed a telegram telling of the sudden death of my mother. I discovered afterwards that her burial was on the very day when the high tide had swamped our boats, 23rd August.

I was to learn more when at Mesters Vig I had the pleasant surprise of finding my wife who had been flown from Iceland on the DC4 that was to carry our expedition members back to Britain on 1st September. Now that we were all camped together for the first time since the end of July there was much exchanging of stories, not to mention music as Roddie played his guitar and the many verses of the Calypso song, telling the whole humorous tale, its joys and sorrows.

The boys were quite an inspiration, and had acquitted themselves well, carrying heavy packs, achieving first ascents of peaks, and crossing glacier passes in previously unexplored country of the South Staunings. One ascent was not completed, when on the summit ridge a cornice broke under Sir John Hunt, and down he went for thirty feet before the prompt action of Alan Blackshaw arrested his fall.

Sir John had led a large party from Alpefjord over glacier passes into the Schuchert Valley to make the first exploration of the South Staunings, an impressive region of rock peaks, where four seniors and seven boys achieved four summits of between 7,000 feet and 8,000 feet, perhaps the most worthwhile achievement of the expedition and a great credit to the lads. While this was going on, Lady Hunt and her daughter Susan with George Lowe and Tony Streather were walking down the Schuchert for Sud Kap, where in 1958 there had been a summer settlement, but in 1960 it was deserted.

Dr Finn Salmonsen, an expert on Greenland birds, had written that the High Arctic is vacated by terns in mid August or early September. But when we left Scoresbyland there were plenty of young birds on Menanders Island not yet capable of flying, and some birds actually still sat on eggs. The Arctic Riviera did not live up to its name in 1960, but I felt privileged to have experienced it in such a topsy-turvy season. Iain had hoped to study lemmings, and continue studies he had made in 1958, but he saw none, nor did we see any ptarmigan or snowy owls. Ravens, however, arrived just as the terns hatched their young and, acting in concert, swallowed a few.

We discovered on Menanders Island that the proportion of Arctic tern nests with only one egg, fifty-three as compared to forty-eight with two, seemed to show that the cold weather was having an effect, for two is the normal clutch. To our surprise, however, the average incubation period proved to be roughly the same as for British-breeding Arctic terns, twenty-one-and-a-half days. A major difference though was that most birds began incubation with the first egg, which meant one chick hatching two days later than the other.

Our farewell to Greenland was exciting. Alfred Asmussen, air-rescue pilot of a survey plane equipped with skis, had ranged to the limit of his fuel day after day trying to find a Danish geologist and mechanic who had been missing for over a week. Their mission had been to deliver three weeks' rations of food to another three geologists, but they had failed to arrive. An American aircraft from the US base at Keflavik in Iceland was now combing the area, but hope was fading for the men missing among the huge icebergs and dangerous waters of this vast network of fjords.

Our DC4 was asked to join in the search, so instead of flying high to get above the mountains, our plane quartered the ground like a huge bird of prey, its black shadow racing over the tundra between slits of fjord where icebergs floated and rivers made estuaries. Dotted here and there on the tundra we could see herds of musk ox whose thick covering of dark wool and misshapen heads give them the authentic look of the prehistoric creatures they are.

It was an uncannily beautiful game of hide-and-seek among shores fantastic with autumn colours of red and yellow. All of us with binoculars at windows scanned the shore and sea, combing every inlet. It seemed an almost hopeless quest and it was feared that the men may have been swept out to sea in the recent high winds that we had experienced at Alpefjord. Then suddenly we fastened on something unusual, a splash of red which took shape as the sail of a boat, and we saw it had two men aboard who were waving to us. As we circled low they sent puffs of white smoke, indicating they needed help.

Everyone cheered not only because the Danish geologist Kirchner was a special friend of the expedition, but because the rescue would make a wonderful finale to the expedition. Round and round we circled, sending out radio signals to the American rescue plane which in half an hour came over the mountains to hang on our tail and release a rubber dinghy which opened up like a yellow mushroom within easy reach of the stranded men.

The north polar regions seemed very close to Scotland when, nine hours later, the pilot of our plane announced that we were approaching St Kilda. It was dusk when I saw a yellow gleam of lights on a curve below black hills – Village Bay – with, on the western horizon as we turned, the hunched shapes of the tallest rock stacks in the North Atlantic, Stac an Armin, Stac Li and Boreray, once climbed by the St Kildans to harvest the fat young of the gannets, in greater density here than anywhere else in the world. My feelings of homecoming as we left them behind was not merely sentimental, but tied up with the wonderful days and nights I have spent out on these cliffs that are the most westerly of the Hebrides and nearest to Iceland and Greenland.

I was thinking too of the barnacle geese flying around the shores of the Stauning Alps, restless with a migration urge which would make them take off and follow our route to the Hebrides, the bulk of them landing to winter on the green pastures of Islay, as would a lesser number of Greenland white-fronted geese. With a good westerly wind they could fly there in a day and a night, returning to nest in Greenland in the spring, borne on the easterly winds that blow at this time.

As for the arctic terns we had been studying, on leaving Greenland they would fly south towards Antarctica and find perpetual daylight and rich feeding on its coastal waters, the urge to move asserting itself as the South Pole daylight shortens, and the terns drift north again to nest over a wide area of the northern hemisphere, to within 8 degrees of the North Pole. Arctic terns perform the most extensive migration of any bird, girdling the world twice in a year. It has been computed that some arctic terns probably find continuous daylight for eight months in the year by their exchange of the nesting grounds in the north for the rich waters of the great white south.

I have to say, though, that these aggressive sea-swallows, screaming continually, and dive-bombing your head, wear on your nerves twenty-four hours a day. They were even noisier once the eggs hatched. Each young bird has an individual voice, which enables its parent to find it, but how it manages to pick out the sound amid the general din baffles me. One day we did get absolute silence, when a Greenland falcon dashed through the colony, pursued out to sea by every arctic tern on the island, and it was minutes before they came screaming back. Our study of their breeding cycle was not exactly a labour of love!

The most enjoyable times on the island were when the red sun was at its lowest on the horizon, staining mountains and sea crimson, and sometimes a wafer-thin skin of ice would form on the water. Then we would launch the canoe and enjoy the faint crackling of the surface-ice mingling with the breathing of seals as whiskered faces bobbed up and followed us.

I think we had almost had enough of the terns, and that Sir John did us a good turn by sending us off in different directions to aid the climbing parties, Ian to the Schuchert Valley on a long solitary walk where he located a food dump vital to the South Stauning explorations; and me to the superb Alpefjord which I would otherwise have missed.

As for Rhona, by arriving a day early she enjoyed a grand canoe trip with expert Iain Smart, and saw the rich autumn colours at their best, which nicely rounded off her Icelandic trip.

13

Unexpected Visitors

Our nineteenth-century cottage, only four miles from the A82 that twists by the west shore of Loch Lomond and by Glen Falloch to Glen Coe and Fort William, was a handy place for climbers to drop in, have a cup of tea and a chat. One of the most remarkable who was brought by a friend to see me was John Emery. The hand that shook mine had no fingers on it. His other hand was the same. His feet were odd too. He had lost the forward part of both, and wore specially shaped boots. But he was on his way to the Highlands with this climbing friend of mine, to try out a new ice-axe he had adapted for himself. He was able to wield it, thanks to a broad strap buckled on to his wrist, with two springs attached to the shaft. This, he said, would give him enough control of the axe to cut steps, and use it for balance where required.

I was glad to hear later that he had managed two fine winter climbs in Kintail with my friend, one of them the narrow summit ridge of the Saddle, the other Ben Attow, catching two days of frost and sun with magical views from the tops. I had read *The Last Blue Mountain* in which author Ralph Barker tells the story of the Oxford University Haramosh expedition which ended in tragedy, two dead and two very close to death, one of them John Emery, the other Tony Streather, who was a colleague of mine in the Greenland expedition led by Sir John Hunt.

In the *Alpine Journal* Tony described the accident that cost John Emery the loss of his fingers and toes thus:

> The evening I staggered back to Camp IV on Haramosh is one that I could never forget. We had been hit by tragedy upon tragedy. Bernard Jillott was dead. Rae Culbert was dying, and would certainly be dead before we could get back to help him – even if we had been in a fit state to do so. I was exhausted and frost-bitten, but just alive. John Emery was exhausted and very severely frost-bitten and by all rights should have been dead. He had spent last night and part of the day unconscious and wedged in the bottom of a crevasse.
>
> It was the same spirit and sheer guts which got him out of the

crevasse unaided that was to get us both off the mountain and back to base camp five days later. It has been said that I brought John down off the mountain. This is only half true. I might have been the stronger, but had it not been for John's determination, uncrushable spirit, and unfailing good humour, neither of us would have got off that mountain. It was more than any one person could face alone. But how could we give up. John never gave up.

He never gave up for one minute during the long series of operations and the months in hospital that followed Haramosh. He never gave up as he started to walk again, although his feet were such that many people would have taken to a wheel-chair. He never gave up as he started to use his hands again, although now there were no fingers and no thumbs.

John told me it had taken two years to get his fingers and feet repaired enough to try and climb again, encouraged by stories of what other handicapped alpinists had done: men such as Geoffrey Winthrop Young, who lost a leg in the war but managed difficult alpine climbs with an artificial limb, or Maurice Hertzog who lost fingers and toes on Annapurna but was able to climb and ski again.

In half a dozen years beginning in 1951, John had earned the reputation of being an outstanding mountaineer, putting some of the hardest British climbs behind him, and in three guideless seasons in the Alps had done some notably difficult routes with Bernard Jillott, both of whom joined the Oxford University Haramosh expedition.

Talking to me in our cottage he said: 'I can lead climbs up to "difficult" standard now, and can follow harder climbs under a patient leader, but not being able to grip tiny holds I am slower than normal climbers. The most uncomfortable part of climbing at the moment is the jarring on my heels coming down off the hill.' His visit to me was in 1961, two years after his marriage, and he was then doing work in Oxford University's Department of Physiology. One of his Professors had described him as 'a man who accepted his difficulties as merely a further challenge.'

In 1963 I got a shock to hear of his death on the Weisshorn. After overcoming all the difficulties of the Schalligrat and the North Ridge, he and his companion were close to easy ground when they fell, roped together, to their deaths. He was twenty-nine and left a wife and baby.

Here are some words written by John Emery around the time he visited me:

I had no hesitation in wanting to climb again; I had always considered that anyone who stops climbing after a mountain accident, unless compelled to do so by physical incapacity, had no business to be climbing in the first place, because he has either

162

failed initially to consider the full implications of mountaineering, or else he has wilfully blinded himself to them.

The device for strapping his ice-axe to his wrist seemed to have worked. He died on the longest and hardest climb he had attempted since Haramosh. His friend A.K. Rawlinson wrote: 'I think he died at a moment of great happiness.' Alas, he had joined the ranks of some of the best climbers who have died in easy places.

Just three months after John Emery's visit, who should come to the door but George Lowe, one of our Greenland party who had flown to Katmandu eight days after our expedition came home. He was just back from hunting for the Abominable Snowman with Sir Edmund Hillary. He returned to Britain via New Zealand and Tasmania after a great trip to the Himalaya with three peaks climbed, the highest over 21,000 feet.

The conclusion of their search was negative, in that no evidence was found to support the existence of the 'Yeti', either in an alleged scalp of the creature, or in the footprints. Stories told by Sherpas failed the test of truth when investigated.

Adventure began for George on his first vacation as a schoolmaster when he took a job in Mount Cook Hotel in 1947 when he was twenty-two. Between bouts of shelling peas and carrying blankets up to the huts, he began climbing. He found he was good at it, so good that four years later he was borrowing money to join another enthusiast called Ed Hillary on a four-man trip to the Garhwal Himalaya. Little did he know that he was setting off on a journey that would take him round the world eight times in seven years.

The Garhwal trip was a big success. Seven good peaks were climbed, just as British climbers under Eric Shipton were trying to find a route to the top of Everest from the Nepal side. Ed and George were picked for the climb as the world knows, and made their brilliant contribution to the first ascent of the mountain. What the public does not know about George is that this exceptional ice-climber has a semi-crippled arm. Indeed he became a schoolmaster, instead of a farmer, because of a boyhood accident which locked his arm in such a way that he can bend it only slightly. There is practically no muscle on the upper arm. George says the forearm weakness is 'due to milking cows'.

After another trip to the Himalaya in 1954, he joined the Trans-Antarctic expedition for three years as photographer. He helped drive a Sno-cat over the highest ice-fields in the world, to meet his pal Ed Hillary at the South Pole, and keep on going to the Ross Sea. Back in Britain he took a job at Repton, the English public school, and told me he enjoyed teaching seventeen- to eighteen-year-old boys so much that he wouldn't call it work.

I was keen to hear some more about the 'Yeti' hunt. Although none were seen, they discovered that the great glacier bowls of the high mountains are not deserted of life in winter, but are used by wolves, foxes and even prowling snow leopards. The most interesting items offered as genuine skins of Abominable Snowmen were those of blue bears!

A hairy skull reputedly 2,000 years old and held to be a yeti, was in fact a manufactured article moulded from blue bearskin into the shape of a guardsman's fur cap. A Sherpa was asked to make another like it, and did, using a local dye to change the bluish fur to reddish. The Abominable Snowman owes a lot, it seems, to the ingenuity of those who tell the tale.

More vital to science were the findings on the effects of too much time spent by man at high altitudes. On the 27,790-foot peak of Makalu, using climbers who had wintered at 20,000 feet, and others who had come fresh to the mountain from lower levels.

Prolonged exposure to high altitude had weakened the resistance of the wintering party, resulting in one after another going down with pneumonia above 23,000 feet. Sir Edmund Hillary himself suffered from a disabling cerebral attack, while climbers fresh from lower altitudes proved much stronger and able to withstand wind and cold better, proving that living for a long period at 20,000 feet results in physical deterioration.

One day in 1965 as I was sitting at my desk writing, I heard the door bell ring, and who should be standing there when I opened it but Sherpa Dawa Tensing, of Everest, Kanchenjunga, Daulagiri and many another notable Himalayan success. Dawa and his shining black pigtail decorated with a pink ribbon, a green tartan shirt worn outside his knickerbockers, and climbing boots on his feet. Not Tensing Norgay who reached the top of Everest with Hillary, but every bit as distinguished as a strong mountain man.

Famous now for his remarkable high-altitude performances, he was an unknown Sherpa when we of the Scottish Nepal expedition of 1952 had recognised his ability and appointed him 'Sirdar' – chief Porter.

At the same time as his beaming face was split by a big grin, he was giving me a 'Salam Sahib' with his hands together at chest height in an attitude of prayer. And as we greeted each other, out from behind the wall popped Tom MacKinnon who had driven Dawa out to be our guest for a few days. Of course I had to take him to the top of our village hill for its remarkable view of the broad base of Loch Lomond and the skyline of Highland hills, in such contrast to the fertile farming fields immediately below us. After his cry of 'Burra pokra', the 'big water', a quizzical look came over his face when he asked me where Chomolunga lay – the Sherpa name for Mount Everest. All I could do was indicate south-eastward. Folding his hands in that direction he intoned a respectful prayer for the sacred mountain whose Tibetan name is Goddess Mother of the World. Dawa had been the guest of Sir John Hunt in London, and in Wales with Sir Charles Evans. Rhona thought it was high time he was introduced to some of her village pupils, and had him swinging about their climbing frame. His smiling face won their hearts. Always willing to try something new, he had a ride on a penny-farthing bicycle belonging to a neighbour of ours, an heirloom now, but in regular use by his grandfather. It needed a leap from a back-step to get into the saddle mounted above the big wheel, and was not easy to pedal and steer, and Dawa was glad to get down without falling off.

Dawa and Tom MacKinnon were the two oldest members of the successful Kanchenjunga expedition and established Camp V at 25,000 feet. Dawa went on up to 26,900 feet, shouldering a heavy load, thus playing a big part in putting four men on the 28,146-foot highest allowable point of the Five Treasures of the Snow – the summit for religious reasons had to be left unsullied by human foot.

I hardly recognised Big Tom on his return when he walked in unexpectedly to a room where he knew a lot of his climbing friends were gathered. Slim of body and face he looked years younger. That he never got above Camp V at 25,000 feet was due to a Sherpa falling into a crevasse, and somehow or other the powerful Tom managed to haul him out – 'an extraordinary feat' according to expedition leader Charles Evans.

Fifteen years after the first ascent of Kanchenjunga, Tom was to hoist me bodily up a cliff after a fall. It happened on a carefree evening when my regular rock-climbing partner Len Lovat came straight from his work to have a few hours with me on the wrinkled schist of Ben A'an, an easy drive from our house. The climbs that we regard as 'little classics' begin low down, and follow continuously to the summit, each rock terrace divided from the other by heather ledges.

For the final wall known as the 'Last Eighty' I chose a hard variation of the normal way, involving strenuous climbing and a balancing move round an overhang to reach a knife-edge at an unrelenting angle. The pair of us, in fact, had made the very first ascent of it. Not long before I attacked it, he had been complimenting how well I was moving. He must have spoken truly for I hardly noticed the hardest move and at the top of the arête realised our rope was too short for me to reach a good belay. Normally we used 150 feet; that evening we had only 100 feet.

I took the risk of doing without a secure belay and shouted Len to 'come on'. Len is a fast mover, and I took care not to give him plenty of rope for the delicate balance move from the overhang to the arête. Suddenly there was a jerk. I tried to hold, and did for a moment, before I went out into space. As he fell backwards he saw me go over his head like a skydiver.

He explained later that he guessed exactly what had happened, twisted himself into a sitting position as he landed, grabbed what rope he could and had enough slack to twist it round a rock which acted like a pulley and

165

prevented him from following me over the drop. His problem was to release himself from the tight rope connecting us, without losing the rock anchorage securing us both to the mountain. He managed it, climbed down and found me hanging unconscious.

All he could do was straighten me up into an upright position, and wait for me to regain my senses. He told me when I did come to, in a relatively short time, I didn't seem to take in what he was saying. He stressed that I must not try to take off the rope or I'd fall to death, that he must go now to summon a rescue party. It was a night of full moon, and five hours later he was back with Scottish Mountaineering Club friends and two members of the Lomond Mountain Rescue team with their stretcher.

I remember that I could not stop shivering, that the pain in my back was agony, and that I would have to somehow turn round and pull myself into a better position, face the rock and take some of the weight on my knees to ease the rope round my chest. Body harnesses were not worn then, as they are now. Relief to hear voices, and soon Tom MacKinnon and another pal, Dr James Kerr, were down beside me, taking my weight between them, to where James waited and prodding to ascertain if I could be moved up the crag to the stretcher.

Satisfied that my back wasn't broken, Jimmy eased me on to Tom's back, and with my hands clasped round his neck, Tom climbed the rock face, safe-guarded by a tight rope from the stretcher party above. Rhona was with them, and much comforted to find me alive. At 4.30 am I was in Stirling Infirmary. My injuries were a squashed spine, a cracked hip, rib-fractures and bruises – a combination I hope never to endure again for the painful weeks between May 1970 and mid-November before I was able to climb on Buachaille Etive Mor again.

That wet cold day, climbing unroped on the North Wall of the Chasm I surprised Len by taking a vertical line on very slippery rock, which he refused to follow. When we met again higher on the wall, he said, 'Well you haven't lost your nerve anyway.' My answer was, 'That's what I was trying to prove to myself. You had more sense.'

I should put it on record that it was Len's enthusiasm and enterprise when heavily engaged in re-writing the first two-volume *Climbers' Guide to Glencoe and Ardgour* which kept me going. In the 1987 *Scottish Mountaineering Club Journal*, he looks back to 1949 when he resolved to make Buachaille Etive Mor his natural habitat. He wrote: 'Where else therefore to celebrate my sixtieth birthday in July 1986 than with Tom Weir, climbing companion of a lifetime? Though bearing no resemblance to Peter Pan, Weir at seventy-one showed that day, as he always has, an ever-young enthusiasm and energy unsurpassed by anyone I have known. Our pleasure on the Buachaille remained undiminished.'

By coincidence, both of us had married at the same time, and although father of two children, he was fretting to return to the Dolomites before he got too old, and off the pair of us went on a night flight to Venice in June 1966. I had never been to these fantastic rock spires holding memories for Len of blue skies and sun-warmed limestone.

Touchdown in Venice was magical, descending on an architectural pincushion of floodlit domes and reflected in the canals, the illusion of fairyland continuing on being ushered from the plane on to a boat that whisked through the coloured waters of the canals as the dawn began to break.

There is a grimmer industrial Venice behind the facade though, where we waited for a long-distance bus northward, and five hours later were feeling our way to the Rosetta Hut at over 8,000 feet in mist and falling snow. We had left Scotland in a heatwave, and this was supposed to be sunny Italy. By means of a cable-car we had reached this alpine hut without effort, but what had made it easy for us had made it easy for dozens of others. The noise level inside the hut was ghastly, the mob being mostly teenagers and youth leaders. Great was our joy to see them go down on the last cable-car, when peace descended in the hut and we settled down to a good meal.

Mist bedevilled us when we left the hut, plunging down 2,000 feet to locate a pass that would take us over to the Pradadili Hut where Len had stayed before and found it peacefully quiet. Not this time. In the doorway was a mountain of wet boots, and inside a mob of children and their youth leaders. To get to sleep we had to bawl angrily for silence.

Out of our bunks and away before the mob was up, Len's memories of sun-warmed crags were being jolted by rocks so cold that we climbed the Cima Wilma unroped to keep warm until increasing difficulties due to ice made us pause, belay, and move one at a time. Hands and feet cold as I belayed Len, I felt for him, leading a ninety-foot crack at a high angle. Mist bedevilled us and we got some airy surprises, abseiling into invisibility, and feeling our way up rotten rock before the mist gave us openings on the Cima Dil Lago.

The climbing was exciting if not exactly enjoyable, and that night to our joy the hut was empty. There was peace and quiet, but both of us had nightmarish dreams of getting into terrible situations above sheer drops into space, which shows the effects of Dolomitic exposure even to a climber used to it, like Len. But we did get the sun for the north face of the Spigalo of the Cima Pradidali, described in the guide-book as being on perfect rock with extreme exposure. I've never seen so much rock that looked unclimbable but which proved to be well provided with holds. Primarily it was a test of nerve, and we were sorry when it was over.

After that we moved to the Rifugio Vajolet of happy memories for Len. He remembered a hut with good food and private rooms. Now, however, the best quarters were taken and we were in an annexe. The meal of watery soup and two sausages floating in it was the poorest we had in Italy.

167

Len was disillusioned by the changes in the ten years since he had been here: too many people, and litter strewn along a path whose beauty he had extolled. You might want to admonish him by saying that he should be delighted to see so many tourists enjoying the mountain air. After all, the well-provided huts were not built for an exclusive few, nor were the roads and tele-cabins. They were put there to attract tourists, so why complain?

I travelled to Venice with Len after our fortnight was up, and sought out Rhona at the hotel where she was still asleep after travelling. I suggested where I thought we should go. I told her of meeting two Munich climbers in the Dolomites who had advised me that if I was seeking the most natural valley, free of tourist developments, I should go by train to Bolzano and take the post bus to Tiers.

It was good advice. Our enchantment grew with each mile once we had turned off the Brenner Pass. The dew was hardly off the grass as we came to the red onion-spire proclaiming the village, but already family parties of harvesters were busy, some turning meadow-hay, others with small sickles cutting barley, bunching the stooks with one hand and slicing them with the other. All wore a kind of uniform of neat blue aprons, even the children. They were fair-skinned Ladinian people of an Alpine race who speak and are taught their own language at school, as well as German.

Eventually we broke out from the Tiers Valley and came to the Alpe di Siusi, a vast meadow twelve miles long and eight miles broad where, under the pinnacles of the towering Langkofel, the peasants were busy harvesting their hay. What friendly people we found them! Living the simple life, sleeping in summer huts, milking their cows and making hay to feed them in the winter. The crop was thin, but cutting it with the scythe, they parcelled bundles into huge cloths, for carrying on their heads, and off they would go to a waiting horse and cart. Up early and bed late was the order of the day.

Difficult as it looked, the easiest way up the Langkofel was straightforward, and the local climber who explained the route enthused about what a wonderful place this was for winter ski-ing, when the pastures were under deep snow and ski-lifts made wonderful tours possible. For years it lay at the back of my mind, but it was 1992 before I went with some friends in February, and returned again with the same group in 1993 basing ourselves at Ortisei, situated at 3,700 feet.

It was not an untarnished experience however. Ortisei is a tourist trap, and is the main village of the Gardena/Groden Valley, with a capacity of 6,000 beds. Its first cable car to the Alpe di Siusi was running as early as 1935, and is now a focus for extended tours in all directions. The morning rush to get up to the heights was something I never got used to, the crush of bodies bound for St Christina, Selva, Wolfkenstein and the Sella Pass. Once that was over and you were lifted to the heights, the tours possible were beyond description in terms of scenery and travel. No need to carry heavy rucksacks, linking peaks and passes in a round of twenty-six kilometres with 15,000 feet of downhill running possible in a single day.

After that summer visit to the Dolomites in 1966, in an article about walking and climbing in these fine mountains I wrote: 'It is sad, but true to say that the Dolomites are as over-crowded as anywhere in the Alps. In this glorious South Tirol it requires little effort to reach any valley or pass, by road or cable car.'

Even my old friend Dawa Tensing became disenchanted by the streams of tourists invading his privacy in Thyangboche Monastery, where he retired to live and pray after giving away all the money he had earned load-carrying on expeditions. He disclosed his feelings to the fine American mountaineer and writer Galen Rowell, who used a sentence that Dawa used for the title of his book, *Many People Come Looking Looking*. To that Dawa added: 'Too many people no good. Some people come, GOOD.' Two chapters which amplify the title are: 'The Coming of Adventure Travel', and 'Tourism and the Khumbu'. (Rowell's book was published by Allen & Unwin in 1980.)

In 1981, the *Alpine Journal* carried a revealing article by Simon Fraser, who wrote:

> The classic books on the subject do not really prepare one for the huge scale of the Everest massif, 'vast in unchallenged supremacy . . . ' Nor do they prepare one for the litter and environmental damage to Thyangboche, or for the sight of elderly Americans, clad in down from head to foot, struggling with great fortitude to over 5,000 metres while their leader, 'Lord of all' like the mountains they have come to see, swaggers round the camp, NO PROBLEM inscribed in bold letters on his sweat shirt, giving orders to Sherpas and anyone within earshot.

Dawa died in his sleep at Thyangboche in 1985, approximately seventy-eight years of age, if, as is thought, he was seventeen when he was recruited on the 1924 attempt on Mount Everest when Mallory and Irvine failed to return from their summit bid. Dawa remembered their disappearance. This points to him being forty-six or so in 1953 when he carried heavy loads twice to the South Col to put Hillary and Tensing in position for their summit bid. Sir John Hunt singled out Dawa for special commendation.

As one of the greatest 'sirdars' in Sherpa history in his time, Dawa was accoladed in 1970 when he was made an Honorary Member of the Alpine Club. Alas, tragedy struck him six years later, when after losing his second wife and son, he gave his entire worldly wealth to the monks of Thyangboche. He was so spiritually low then, that Tony Streather who had known him on Kanchenjunga, took action to ease his life by raising a fund to pay him a monthly pension, to which I was glad to contribute.

Time healed, optimism and love of life restored, he married again, and in 1983 went on pilgrimage to India. Returning to Katmandu their bus plunged into a ravine, killing thirty-two, one of them Dawa's son. Dawa and his wife were injured. It was the third terrible event he had experienced; before this occurrence he had been accused of theft from a monastery, an accusation that resulted from a family feud. Tony Streather happened to meet Dawa at that time and had a Major in the Nepalese Army with him who took up Dawa's case, and proved the accusation false in court.

The last time I saw Dawa was on the television screen with Sir John Hunt, filmed when he was very much the Dawa I remembered, in voice and arm-waving action, but more wrinkled of face. On that programme he was lamenting the death of the old Sherpa way of life, and the sacrifice of religious traditions for worldly wealth.

Then in 1989, four years after Dawa's death, came the news that Thyangboche had been destroyed by fire, due to faulty electricity wiring recently installed. The Sherpas saw this as a sign that the gods were angry. As I write the work of rebuilding is still going on, with the help of the Himalayan Trust, formed under Sir Edmund Hillary's direction.

It was following the first ascent of Everest in 1953 the Sherpas of Sola Khumbu asked Hillary the question: 'Can you help us to have a school?' His Himalayan Trust did more than that. It financed twenty-six schools, two hospitals, thirteen medical centres and an airstrip that provides rapid communication between Katmandu and Sherpa-land. In addition, difficult rivers have been bridged, water has been piped to villages, and Namche Bazaar, formerly a trading post, is now a tourist honey-pot. From being perhaps the poorest of the hill people in the economic sense, the Sherpas are now the richest – thanks to trekking and tourism.

Since that first ascent, every ridge and every face of Mount Everest has been climbed and documented. George Lowe, the New Zealander who pioneered the route up the Lhotse Face to the South Col in eleven heroic days, described the mountain forty years later as 'the greasy pole of Asia'. In tents among hundreds of others was a large British expedition who celebrated the ascent of forty years ago by putting the first British woman, Rebecca Stevens, on top, guided by two Sherpas. Before that, on 10th May, thirty-eight made it to the summit, including former soldier Harry Taylor, first Briton to do it from the Nepal side without bottled oxygen. On the last lap, at the South Col, they would see the evidence of hundreds who have passed that way in the rubbish tip of oxygen bottles and debris including five frozen bodies who failed to return.

In the beginning, when you applied to the Nepal Government and paid the fee demanded, the expedition got the mountain to itself. Congestion began when this exclusiveness vanished, and anyone willing to pay the fee could be in competition. Hillary would like to see this free-for-all end, for the sake of the mountain. Now that commercialism has crept in, guides will take anyone who can pay them their fee to attempt the summit, without guarantee of reaching the summit. The unwary should keep in mind that over one hundred have died on the mountain to date.

With hindsight, the early explorers who caused trees to be felled and carried to the base camp for firewood, talk with sorrow of the damage done. Edmund Hillary does not exempt his own expeditions from blame. He wrote:

> You turned the corner at Pheriche and the whole place was a deep green, clothed in juniper right up the valley and beside the glacier everywhere. Now the juniper has been wiped out. The whole area is just a desert now which is all eroding.

In the mid 1970s the high area of Sola Khumbu was declared a National Park, but with thousands of travel agents encouraging more trekkers this designation may have aggravated the erosion problem.

A Nepalese ecologist has said that his country had three religions now, Hinduism, Buddhism and Tourism. Such is the Government belief in the latter that its intention is to quadruple the tourist flow to a figure of over a million before the end of the century. However, a step in the right direction is that trekkers and mountaineers must supply their own fuel for cooking, gas or paraffin, which should save the trees. One or two tiny hydro-electric units are in operation, and China has plans for a mammoth scheme to harness the waters on the great bend of the Brahmaputra, which would be the largest power-plant in the world if it comes to pass, as it surely will.

Just one year after Dawa expressed his feelings about 'too many people coming looking, looking', it was the sad duty of three Scottish Mountaineering Club men to sprinkle Tom MacKinnon's ashes round the mossy base of a silver birch near the limit of forest growth in the Lost Valley of Glencoe, on a showery November day in 1981. Plumes of new-fallen powder snow were being torn off the peaks, the gusting wind and spasmodic bursts of sun lighting the autumn colours of the gorge and producing a Himalayan landscape feeling.

Douglas Scott recalled Dawa's visit to this very place, when he was guided by Tom up the Crowberry Ridge of Buachaille Etive Mor, then driven west to the Meeting of the Waters, where cars were left and up into the gorge canyon we climbed to a cave, ideal for shelter, with wood for a fire, got it lit, cooked a meal, drank a few toasts to merry the party, and in no time songs were being sung before settling down in sleeping bags under the cave roof.

We put sadness behind us that November day, remembering Tom's paralysing stroke and long illness, when he had hardly any voice or energy to talk, yet always by his bed was a manual of yacht navigation; for after his marriage in the 1960s he had become a keen sailor and did less and less climbing. He always assumed he would get better. Indeed he did for a time, and even managed to climb the stairs.

He maintained the pretence, until one day when he had almost no voice left he motioned me to his bedside from the chair where I sat reading. In the merest whisper he said: 'I'm not going to make it, Tom. It won't be long now. I'd like you to have my collection of *Alpine Journals*.' Although I contradicted him, it was only a few days later when I had a phone call from Rowena asking if I could come and relieve her as things were now very serious. In temperament Tom was nearer to my butcher pal Matt than anyone else I have known. Charles described him perfectly, recalling him on Kanchenjunga as 'a man, extraordinarily kind, full of humour and strength and real goodness'. I'd call that a true epitaph.

14

A Team Game

That I for poor auld Scotland's sake
Some usfu' plan or beuk could make,
or sing a sang at least.
                                    Robert Burns

It is over two and a half years since I began the 'beuk' (autobiography), and trying to think back over my eighty years, I am sometimes doubtful if I have even a song to sing. Think of Burns – of immortal memory – who died in poverty and debt in Dumfries at the age of thirty-seven in 1796, who is celebrated on 25th January everywhere in the world where Scots are gathered together. Who has not heard his Tam o'Shanter or sung Auld Lang Syne?

So I use the verse at the top of the page with diffidence, realising the minor significance attached to a colour picture which appeared in the *Scottish Television Review* of 1978, captioned: 'Winners of the Radio Industries Club of Scotland television personalities of 1977 and 1978 were Tom Weir and Geraldine McEwan.' The photograph shows me handing over a large silver cup to Geraldine for her star performance in *The Prime of Miss Jean Brodie*.

The circumstances of my getting that award were casual, to say the least. It began one day with a telephone call from Mr Russell Galbraith, Head of News and Current Affairs, whom I'd known in his early days as a television journalist. He had called me in a few times for interview on the 'box'. Now he was asking me to lunch to discuss an idea for a regular weekly slot about the countryside.

What he was looking for, he said, were films of about eight minutes, or less, that could be completed in a day. 'I think you would be the man to do them. You know the countryside like the back of your hand. I'll give you a camera team. They'll come to you at Gartocharn and you can take them wherever you like so long as you do your best to get the story in the can in one day. I'll pay you £50 for each one, whether we use them or not.

'But they will be low-priority films. I'll only be able to give you a camera team when they're doing nothing else, and you would probably not know until the night before that you would be getting the team in the morning.' I said I'd have a go if I were free when the camera team was free, but it was all a bit casual. That is how it was left, and as weeks passed and nothing happened I assumed that it was another television egg that was infertile, something I'd grown used to. Then one late afternoon Russell came on the phone. 'I can give you a camera team tomorrow if you're OK.' I would like to have been able to say 'No', but as it is against my principles to refuse a challenge, I said I'd expect them about 10 am.

They were spot-on for time at the cottage, and it was a full team: director, production assistant, cameraman, assistant cameraman, sound recordist and electrician with a battery of lights. The director was a hard-boiled free-lance who had worked much abroad, and I had just begun to explain to him what I had in mind, when he interjected: 'That's enough, let's see your work-room where we've to begin.' He looked at my desk with its typewriter facing through a window to lawn and garden dyke, beyond which two horses were grazing. On the wall I had pinned a selection of large colour photographs blown up from my transparencies, some from expeditions abroad, some in Scotland. The room ran the length of the cottage but was narrow. He liked that.

He was decisive: 'We'll take the first shot from outside, see the cottage, and look in through the window at you typing. You ignore us, just carry on working. Then we'll come in and do a long shot.' That done, with spot-light illumination, I continued to type. Then came the acting bit; I had to stop, as if I were thinking, turn to camera and do my introduction, talk to camera about myself, refer to the pictures on the wall, and how years of foreign travel into some of the remotest corners in the world had brought home to me what a marvellous little country we have in Scotland, with a bit of everything, and so compact that you didn't have to go far for it, especially if you live in the Central Belt between the Clyde and Forth.

That seemed to work well. Then I went on to say why I had chosen to live here, on the gentle side of Loch Lomond. Not because it was gentle, but because from the wee hill above the house there was a unique view of how suddenly the Lowlands give way to the Highlands, and getting to the top is an absolute gem of a walk, taking less than half an hour: 'That is where I'm going and you will see what I mean.'

The camera tracked me out through the porch and locking the front door, followed me walking along a grassy track, louping over a burn, and entering the wooded lower slope of the hill. Winding through oak and ash trees into the open, all that remained was a steep grassy bump and, over the top in fifty feet, suddenly the dramatic view stretched below. The five-mile-wide broad base of Loch Lomond, spattered with wooded islands, narrowing to wind through a wall of Highland peaks, Ben Lomond on the right and the Arrochar Alps to the left.

I finished on a slow pan across the contrasting scene from Highlands to

Lowlands under my feet, saying, as the camera came in to close-up: 'We'll explore some more, so look in at the same time next week and join me on *Weir's Way*.'

I didn't find it hard to think up stories, each one with a handy series of small cards, to give to the director, showing the form and locations from opening to ending. Getting the weather for them was different, and in frustration, he said to me one day: 'You know, nobody is interested in these films except you!' Humouring him, I grinned and said how lucky it was for me to be working with him and learning so many camera tricks of the trade so painlessly! The job of the director is to direct the camera and get the most out of the story. He was good at it, but not so good at maintaining good relations with the team.

During one prolonged spell of bad weather I had a call from him. 'We're fed up hanging about the canteen. We'll come out tomorrow if you can think of a story however hard it rains.' The one I had for them, when the team arrived, was the economics of rain, and off we drove to Loch Sloy, a reservoir high in the Arrochar Alps. Impounded by a concrete dam built over a throat of rocks, the water is led out by a tunnel into four great pipes descending the hillside to a generating station 1,000 feet below, just above the Loch Lomond shore.

In swirling mist and rain, a battery-charged spotlight on my face, I had to shout my words to be heard, telling the story of this first post-war North of Scotland Hydro-Electric Board power scheme, and how a fall of one inch of rain yields one million units of electricity. We even had the amazing bonus of a rainbow, lighting the winter browns of the bracken against greenery and grey rocks, showing that even on the wildest day you can get the most spectacular effects. (In fact my best colour slides have been taken in good moments on bad days.)

By the time it came to late spring I had stacked up quite a number of short films with different directors and, assuming that they were unlikely ever to be shown, was quite relaxed about the whole business. Then one day I had a shock phone-call from Russell announcing that the first *Weir's Way* would be going out on the following Friday night to cheer folk looking forward to the weekend. 'I think you'll be pleased with them.'

Pleased! I felt dismayed, wondering where I could run to! I'd be totally exposed. I was too, but differently from what I expected. I feared I might be ridiculed. Far from it. If I went to any public place people wanted to talk to me, shake my hand, or ask me to sign autographs. At the same time I regretted my loss of anonymity.

On the whole I had enjoyed playing the team game, as a change from the lonely trade of writer. I had got back to my old desk routine, then, when winter came round, Russell called me in again, not to make a new series but to link some of the wee stories into half-hour documentaries. He had in mind a studio set up as a room in my house, with me in an Orkney chair at the fireside reminiscing to the camera between the running of the films. Timing would have to be absolutely spot-on. 'Once the films have been chosen, and timed, you'll know how much you can say between each film. Just how much he was asking I realised when I came to face the studio camera which had a clock-face parallel with the lens. A large black hand pointed to ten seconds before the hour. I was told that when this started to move, the film was running and would appear on the screen on the hour.

The test came one Saturday when I was expected to complete six half-hour films made from eighteen of the short *Weir's Ways*. I managed to get each documentary made within less than an hour, but the strain was telling, and I finished with a splitting headache to which I am not normally prone. It was due to concentration, I think, because for the linkage I depended completely on memory, and usually had to make a mental somersault to finish my fireside tale between the pointer beginning to move and end just before the film appeared on the screen.

It was for these compilations I was awarded the Radio Industries Club of Scotland Television Personality of 1977, and I was equally surprised to get this letter:

Dear Tom,
    I returned from Argentina last week to the most heartening news that you had won this year's Radio Industries Club award as Television Personality of the Year. I can only say that I was delighted, and everyone here who has been associated with your work these past few years is equally pleased. I think your contributions to our output have brought a freshness and appeal which no-one else could have managed. Enough to say that it is particularly gratifying when others outside the building are equally impressed and moved to acknowledge your work in this way. I can only hope the programmes you have made until now will be the forerunners of many more. At any rate, I would like to wish you continued success and health to wander the face of Scotland, not just on your own behalf (although I well know the pleasure this brings you) but also on ours, as well as the many fireside fans who so much enjoy your programme.
Yours sincerely,
Russell Galbraith
Head of News, Current Affairs,
and Sport

That came on top of the surprise of being awarded the MBE and of travelling to London to have the medal pinned on me by HM the Queen.

Returning to the village, to the strains of 'For He's a Jolly Good Fellow' sung by the school children, I had to tell them everything that had happened, from entering the inner courtyard of Buckingham Palace to coming out and doing the television interview which all of them had seen on Scottish Television.

It was a big night for Gartocharn, since a neighbour, Jim McKechnie was on the same *Scotland Today* programme, having won five of the top awards at Smithfield, including the Supreme Championship with his year-old steer, Fizz. No single man had ever achieved such a record in the history of this show, yet Jim rears cattle only as a hobby; he gets his living from selling fruit.

Jim could tell them about Princess Anne handing over the coveted awards at Smithfield. Now that they were in the world of Royalty on a personal scale, they were agog to hear what the inside of the Palace was like so I told them about the gorgeously carpeted art gallery of pictures into which we were ushered to await being called to the Throne Room. The time had been fixed at 10.30 am, and there were about 200 assembled when we were summoned to attention in a friendly manner and instructed in what to do.

What it boiled down to, was copying what the man or woman in front of you did. Time sped. Within one hour I was formed up with about twenty of the Ss and Ws and marched along a corridor to enter the fairyland of the huge, high-ceilinged Throne Room.

The senses could hardly take it in – a stage with a ray of crimson velvet and above a suspended golden crown. Below it stood the Queen, lit in a shower of diamond light directed from two crystal chandeliers. Then the eye took in the two thrones and rich uniforms of the Yeomen of the Guard with steel halbards – medieval figures in a setting of marble pillars and sculptures and frescoes.

I was moving forward across the room as I took it all in, enjoying the music of the strings playing a tango as I followed the kilted entertainer, Andy Stewart, neat and jaunty and showing no signs of weariness despite having travelled down overnight following two performances of his Ayr show.

A tap on the shoulder and it was my turn to walk over to the Queen, make my bow, and step up to the dais to have the MBE medal pinned on my lapel. As she did it, she asked me about my work, and where I did it, holding out her hand for me to shake. When she straightened up, I took my three backward steps to bow departure. I had the chance to see how simply she was dressed in silk frock of quiet floral pattern with a brooch at the neck and pearls.

At the far end of the room I was shown to a chair among the assembled guests who included my wife and sister Molly who had a grandstand view of the whole affair and loved every minute of it, from the bestowing of knighthoods to the final medals for gallantry awarded to soldiers, police and others. Then came the National Anthem and the departure of the Queen with her Yeomen, and we filed out.

On the stairway were the same statuesque figures we had seen on the way in, Gentlemen-at-Arms in knee-high leather boots, shining breastplates, plumed helmets and swords, holding themselves so stiffly erect and unmoving they could have been dummies. I asked Andy Stewart how he had enjoyed it. 'Very much. For stage management it was an eye-opener. You couldn't better that. What style and efficiency!'

For us the show wasn't over. Andy was doing a camera piece on the Palace steps for the BBC before flying north for two shows in Ayr that night. I did mine for Scottish Television, and in the interview was asked why I had been honoured with the medal. I told the interviewer it was for my writing about Scotland., and that it would certainly have dumbfounded my mother, who could never understand the life I had chosen. She used to tell people: 'He can be away for months, and when he comes back he just sits there, write, write, writing. Jings, he should get a medal for it.'

'Well,' I said, 'here's a medal, and I hope she is looking down from up yonder.'

To mark the occasion, STV decided to show again the very first programme I made in the *Weir's Way* series – one that began with me in the old cottage at the typewriter before setting off up the hill to look down on Loch Lomond.

Said Russell, when we met again, 'Before you made these films, Tom, you had been broadcasting and writing for twenty-seven years, and had written several books. But if I had gone into the street and asked passers-by if they knew who Tom Weir was, nine out of ten would have said "no". Today nine out of ten would say "yes", and praise your programmes.'

I was now offered a contract, extended year after year, to research, write and present a series of programmes, to include future editing and dubbing time. For this I would be paid a lump sum, without repeat fees for future showing of the originals. In accepting this form of payment I made a mistake: films I made were being shown every day during a long Independent Television strike, and are still being repeated in 1994.

I'm not complaining. I was able to use much of the research material I had accumulated in years of article and book writing, dealing with almost every aspect of Scottish life and character. I had enjoyed seeing the films I envisaged as words and pictures in my mind, coming to life on the screen. I was more in demand as a journalist and photographer than I had ever been, and I made time to visit different parts of the world with my wife on her school vacations, and rock climb with Scottish Mountaineering Club friends as opportunities occurred.

I was most sorry about a series of five programmes I scripted to tell the story of the remarkable Scot, John Muir, famous in America, but hardly known in Scotland. They never got to camera. I wanted to trace the life of the father of the conservation movement, beginning at Dunbar where he was born, and following him to the farm at Wisconsin where he was taken at eleven years of age.

It was a letter from a Mrs Hunter of Stirling that prompted the idea. She wrote: 'I wonder if you would be interested in reading books by John Muir. I heard of him when I visited America. He brought a breath of fresh air into my life. He became famous as a conservationist and mountaineer. *The Story of My Boyhood and Youth* is about Dunbar and East Lothian, and his early life in America. *The Life and Letters of John Muir* by W.F. Badie is in two volumes. You may well have read his books and know what I am talking about.'

I had not read the books, but a librarian friend got them for me from Haddington Library and I soon realised the truth of that lady's opinion. This is Muir:

Oh! that glorious Wisconsin wilderness. Everything new and pure in the very prime of spring when Nature's pulses were beating highest, and mysteriously keeping time with our own. Young hearts, young leaves, flowers, animals, the winds and the streams and the sparkling lake, all wildly rejoicing together.

John Muir was thirty when he found the high Sierra Nevada, and for five fulfilling years made Yosemite his home, learning mountaineering by forcing his way through previously untravelled gorges to climb virgin peaks, and finding moving glaciers, which even the geological department did not suspect, in the 'Range of Light', as Muir named this Indian territory.

In his first summer he worked as a shepherd, moving his sheep to the high meadows as the lower ground got burned up. Enjoying the great waterfalls, he scrambled about the rocks looking for tell-tale signs of past glacial activity, for he did not accept the theory that this dramatic valley was the result of a gigantic cataclysm. He also worked for two different hotel-keepers who were offering accommodation to the first tourists to come to the area. One who came was the American poet and philosopher Ralph Waldo Emerson, and Muir and he rode twenty-five miles through the Sierra forest, each with a lot to tell the other.

It was in 1871 that Muir found the way to write in a vivid, easy, personal style, appearing in important American magazines as a man with a message, telling of what he had seen: the fall of mighty Eagle Rock, crashing 1,500 feet in an earthquake, to disintegrate in fragments; and the effect of winter storms which made the mighty waterfalls of Yosemite sway and the trees shriek. At the same time he was urging Federal control of forests to protect them from 'the hoofed locusts' – sheep, and demanding action against those who were blasting the mighty redwoods with dynamite, treating the priceless forest as if it were inexhaustible. He wrote as one who had witnessed the deterioration of a region that until 1833 had been known only to the Mono Indians who hunted deer and other game without impinging on the environment.

His campaign led to the formation of the now famous Sierra Club in 1892, with himself as President, its purpose: 'To enlist the support of the people and the Government in preserving the forests and other features of the Sierra Nevada, and also to explore and render accessible the mountains of the Pacific Coast.' In 1903 he had the ear of President Theodore Roosevelt, camping with him in Yosemite. It led to the formation of five National Parks, sixteen National Monuments and 148 million acres of Forest Reserves. Muir reckoned that one of the hardest tasks he ever set himself was to paint a word picture of the Grand Canyon so that it would be a 'must' for protection.

Muir was born in 1836, the year Queen Victoria ascended the throne. He died on Christmas Eve in 1914, four days before I was born. My television plan had been to follow this super-tramp into the areas he loved most, and who, in describing them, urged all Americans to go, see and worship these wonderful works of nature rather than the mechanical works of man. Sadly, the millions from all parts of the earth who are following his advice are loving them to death.

Commercialism began in Muir's time. He himself acted as a guide and was employed by a hotel. Nowadays, entertainment has taken over from simple marvelling at the wilderness of the seven-mile-long glacier-carved canyon, the mighty El Capitan towering up 3,600 feet sheer, and the Bridal veil waterfall spouting 620 feet into space, a great natural wonder of the world. Visitors can have a tram tour along the valley floor, or try rafting on the Merced River with hundreds of others. There are swimming pools, ski-lifts, a golf course, an ice-rink, a climbing school, stores, cocktail lounges, large-screen television, film processing, Yosemite T shirts and souvenirs made in China.

There is more to Yosemite of course than the valley, and the goal of the Park Service now is to designate 760,917 acres as protected wilderness, never to be developed. Many commercial services will be relocated outside the park boundary, including overnight facilities. Private vehicles are likewise being excluded.

Just before John Muir died in 1914 he was writing up his travels and explorations in Alaska, which he knew as a pristine wilderness. It too has been blown open by easy access and a leisured society using airports and the New Alaskan Highway. There is also the black gold – oil – and the inevitable pollution that has destroyed so much wildlife. Planes fitted with skis land on glaciers, visitors leave behind abandoned food and human waste, even on Mount McKinley which the native Indians named 'The Great One'. Application by the increasing numbers who want to climb the 20,000-foot peak must be made to the Mount McKinley National Park Authority sixty days in advance.

15

Two Great Cairngormers

Just fifteen years after the death of John Muir consideration was given to the Cairngorms as the best area in Scotland for an American-style National Park. It had the perfect ingredients: an extent of Arctic and Alpine plateau above 4,000 feet, yet cut through its heart by the Lairig Ghru Pass, an ancient route of travel between Strathspey and Deeside, with, in its glens in Strathspey and Deeside, remnants of primeval Caledonian pine forest that once covered much of the Highlands before the arrival of man.

On the tundra of its plateau nested ptarmigan, snow-buntings, dotterel, dunlin and golden plover. Its horse-shoe corries held snow-fields seldom known to melt. Distances from habitation were long. It was home to golden eagle, merlin and peregrine. In the forest bogs greenshank nested.

The National Park never came to pass, because at that time in the 1930s some local authorities decided the Cairngorms to be too remote for the working classes. There was a fear, too, that to popularise the area might spoil its amenities for landowners concerned with deer stalking, grouse-shooting and salmon fishing.

Although the recommendations of the committee for the setting up of a Cairngorm National Park were ignored, the committee report read:

> We desire to record our conviction that such measures as we have advocated are necessary, if the present generation is to escape the charge that in a shortsighted pursuit of its immediate ends, it has squandered a noble heritage.

This was clearly a recognition that in the 1930s the first generation of working-class folk, employed and unemployed, were taking to the hills, and with such momentum that, even before the outbreak of war in 1939, ensured that the Cairngorms would be one of five priority areas recommended by the Ramsey Committee for National Park status and protected against developments deemed to be harmful to their quality.

182

In 1994 we still do not have any National Parks in Scotland. Plenty of undesirable developments have taken place. Fifty years on since the original 1930 proposal let me transport you to the Cairngorms.

Two o'clock of a June morning; the scrape of a match to light the candle and soon the purring of the Primus for a quick breakfast before setting off for the high plateau.

We were in a dark cave in Glen Slugan on the Dee side of the range, having back-packed in from Braemar. The cave had been a lucky find for we had intended to sleep out on the hillside, as the night was fine and we wanted to be away early. Our cave was below the lip of a miniature canyon where two beds of deep unmelted snow lay. Beyond that lip lay Bheinn a' Bhuird and Ben Avon, linked by a saddle known as 'the snek'.

These eastern mountains of the Cairngorms are remote, whichever way you approach them. The first contains some wild rocky corries offering hard technical climbing, whereas Ben Avon is so flat you could ride a horse over it. The amount of snow even on the south side and on the high plateau astonished us. We learned that it had been winter in the Cairngorms this year until the third week of May. We had left the cave at 3 am. Moving fast, we were on the south top of Bhuird by 4.30 in time to meet the rising sun, bursting from a point of flame to a ball of fire, and throwing our long shadows on snow dancing with frost crystals.

With the unobscured sun warming us, the air crystal clear, snow-fields stretching in every direction, suddenly we stopped with one accord, listening to a trilling sound, broken by sharper notes – the sound of dotterel, the rarest waders of the high tops. Then we saw them flying low towards us, and landing, five pairs of wings daintily upheld, one on a stone near us, brilliant eyestripe and chest band to match, a plimsoll line between delicate grey chest and warm russet belly. It filled the binocular frame, then jumped down and ran briskly to the others to engage in courtship pursuit, tripping and wing-raising. Two of the five birds were females, distinguished by their larger size and brighter colours, for in this species the cock birds are the dowdy ones, and the hens initiate the courtship. Rarest and most beautiful of these tundra-loving birds, ringing has shown that one who summered here wintered in Mongolia, and other recoveries have come from the Atlas Mountains. They shared this high ground with ptarmigan above the part-frozen Dubh Lochan.

By 8 am we were forced to wear sun-glasses, such was the dazzle from the snow. In bare places the pink of the creeping azalea showed its buds were on the point of opening. Though not so interesting as Bheinn a' Bhuird, Ben Avon is a vast hill with many tops, and it is given character by large granite tors which provide delightful scrambling. In mist there is no more confusing hill. In the heat of the sun, our problem, when we sat down, was to keep from falling asleep.

In fact we were looking forward to getting back to the cave, and in its cool recess, stretched out in our sleeping bags, we slept until 4.30 pm wakening up ravenous and refreshed; so refreshed in fact that we set off at 7 pm to look for a golden eagle's tree eyrie, and it was getting on for midnight before we returned to our shelter, delighted to have seen the bird throw itself off the nest and swerve fast through the pine trees. We investigated no further, but left hurriedly.

Since the weather appeared to be set fair, the plan now was to head for Corrour Bothy in the Lairig Ghru. On the way there we had a wonderful encounter with a pair of greenshank, pursuing each other high in the air and round the edge of a reedy loch, the air ringing with their sharp excited calls. For an hour we lay watching and listening to the thrilling song flight, ending with a catch-me-if-you-can chase on the mud round the loch margins.

Because over a dozen walkers of the Lairig Ghru had taken up most of the available floor space in the bothy, we preferred to lie outside, for it was our intention to rise, as the previous day, at 3 am and get the best of the early frost on the high tops. This time we ate our breakfast, legs in our sleeping bags, for the air was keen. Then out of the shadow of the Lairig we climbed to meet the rising sun on the rocky top of Devil's Point, and realised to the full the reward of early rising: below us a beautiful effect of morning mist hanging in the valleys, each ridge of the Grampians being outlined against it in precise recession, the highest and shapeliest peak being Lochnagar. Granite stones and snow-fields sparkled around us.

Now we headed north to Cairn Toul and Braeriach, the greatest stretch of mountain country in Scotland lying above 4,000 feet, where the Dee rises higher than any other British river and where the famous old naturalist Seton Gordon once met a dipper. This traverse round great horse-shoe corries, with snow-beds that seldom ever melt, must be one of the outstanding walks in Scotland. That day with all the western and central Highlands pin-sharp, we were seeing it at its best, every peak clear cut from Ben Nevis to Knoydart.

There is no doubt that the stream known as Allt Garbh Choire, which drains the two principal horse-shoes of this tremendous corrie, forms one of the truly splendid Cairngorm scenes, receiving as it does its waters from the Wells of Dee, flowing from the 4,000-foot plateau to plunge through the snow cornice on the corrie rim, and reappear lower down as a thundering waterfall. Considerable melting had taken place in the Lairig, but the scene from the lip was pure winter, except where edges of clean pinkish rock rose from the corrie floor in buttresses and thin rock ribs, beloved by the adventurous school of Aberdeen rock climbers.

We were on this vast crown in a silver and blue world where snow and sky met. Below us was the bouldery crest of the Lairig Ghru at 2,700 feet, and now we descended to inspect the strange Pools of Dee. The wind had

Above left: Hosap, in Turkey, a stronghold of rebel Kurds in
former times, lying close to Armenia, Iraq and Iran.
Above right: Wife of the Kurdish chief with her baby which wears a charm in its hair.
Below: Officials of Yutsekova pose with Tom, hat on knee in centre;
Douglas Scott is second from right.

Above: A Kurdish camp in the Satbazi with goat hair tents and straw huts perched above a ravine. These semi-nomads live lower down in winter but spend the summer with their flocks in the mountains.
Below: These Kurdish people who inhabit the Iran-Iraq border are the most independent tribes in the Middle East and have resisted change for centuries.

Above: Camp in the Rudebare Sin Gorge, a cavern close to the Iraq border. Travel is so difficult in the gorge that horses cannot be used. The party climbed the centre peak.
Below: Camp in the Sat Dag at 9,000ft in a sparkling world of rock peaks and shining snow. Douglas Scott cracks a joke with the two Kurds.

Above: Douglas Scott looks across to the peaks of Iran and Turkey, a view that also encompassed the hot plains of Mesopotamia. The mountain group is the Cia E Hendevade, 12,350ft.
Below: Tom McKinnon left, Tom Weir right, cooling off in the hot sun.

'Making our way to the Sat Dag in Kurdistan, through the mountains of the Cilo as the horses wend their way through masses of flowers to the snow-clad ridges.'

Above: St Kilda. Standing above Soay sound on Hirta, looking over to the Island of Soay beyond the rock stack of Stac Biorach.
Below: A whimbrel from Iceland lands on St Kilda, and gets a ring on its leg and its measurements taken by Kenneth Williamson, left, and Dr Eggeling, right. Rocket range men look on.

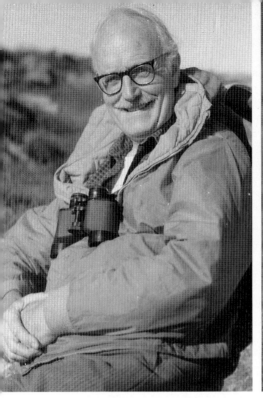

Above left: Bob Grieve in 1993—who taught Tom much about
the grammar of the environment.
Above right: Rhona on their honeymoon on the island of Foula, Shetland Islands, in
July 1959 holding a bonxie chick. Bonxie are great skuas, large birds the size of
buzzards. Foula is their stronghold with over 500 pairs of breeding birds.
Below: Tom and Rhona's wedding. Front row from left: Captain Donald Dickson,
Mother, Tom Weir, Rhona, sister Molly, Mrs Dickson. Back row: Matt Forrester,
bridesmaid, and Agnes and Willie Weir (Tom's brother).
Overleaf: Tom Weir at his desk at home in Gartocharn.

been cold on top, but off the ridge we were out of it, in a world of sun-warmed pink boulders, each offering an invitation to sit and go to sleep. A good place from which to look down on the crest of this perfect pass and see the Pools of Dee, each a little eye of blue water in a dimple of snow. They never drain away because of an underground stream, emerging soon enough to join the tumbling waters from the 'wells' some three miles lower down, and flow ever more strongly on an eighty-mile journey to the sea.

Picking our way over the boulders which litter the summit of the pass we were soon on easier walking on the descent to Corrour bothy and at that time in 1955 the mode of crossing the Dee, now a fast-flowing river, was by twin wires, top one for the hands, lower one for the feet. The secret of not falling in was to press back, using the instep of the boots, lean forward with hands outstretched, body at an angle, and sidle across. Loss of control and you'd likely fall off. (There is a bridge here now and the sport of getting safely over has gone.) We had been on the go for eleven hours when we crossed over.

Next morning we were away early again, climbing steeply up Carn a Mhaim, and by Sron Riach to look down on the second-highest loch in the Cairngorms, Lochain Uaine at 3,142 feet, snow-drifted and covered in cracked plates of thick ice. It would have been a good place to linger but for the cold wind, so we moved on over the last rise to Ben Macdhui, the second-highest summit in Scotland, graced by a view indicator.

Eyes watering, we could not identify too clearly what we were seeing, but despite some melting that had gone on for the last five days, we saw it would still have been possible to walk nearly twenty miles on snow that June. In fact we had a splendid snow slide on our bottoms down the Tailor's Burn to within a few hundred feet of the Lairig path.

On our last two nights we camped among the Caledonian pines, first in Glen Derry for an ascent of Derry Cairngorm, and from there traversed into Glen Quoich in the most magical oasis of Caledonian pine forest, on a grassy platform above the river with grey wagtails and goosanders for company. It was our last night, and next day we climbed Lochnagar from the glorious woods of Ballochbuie, following up the Garbh Allt Burn from Deeside, doffing our hats to Queen Victoria who saved this wonderful fragment of primeval forest from being clear-felled by renting it, until she was able to buy it and add it to the Balmoral Estate. She called it 'The Bonniest Plaid in Scotland'.

Although I didn't get the chance to do the John Muir story and link it to the Cairngorms, I did get permission from Mar Estate and adjacent Balmoral to make three *Weir's Way* television programmes. It took a year to negotiate, and I was lucky to get the co-operation of two real worthies of the loneliest dwellings.

Miss Nell Macdonald was brought up with three brothers and sisters in what is a ruin today, but was a snug house when, in the first twelve years of this century, it was home to Nell, and she had nothing but happy memories of it.

'Lonely? We never gave it a thought, there was so much to do and see. It was an open green place among trees, and we had a horse and cart for getting to Braemar. Sometimes we would walk the path and visit two keepers at Fealar Lodge, at 1,750 feet, the highest in the Highlands they say. We had a good croft to work with a cow and calf for milk. We grew potatoes and other vegetables. We'd fruit bushes. We cut hay in two parks to feed the deer in winter. No, we didn't want for anything.

'We loved it when the tinkers came to the door, on their way from Glen Tilt to Deeside, for farmwork – whole families of them. They came one at a time so they would all get something. I remember a wee kitten one of them carried in a basket, and us looking at some of the things they held out for sale: pins and needles, thread, and things like that. You didn't see many strangers, just odd ones, usually professional people, from the Cairngorm Club or the Scottish Mountaineering Club, looking for a bed for the night as guests. There was none of this bothying. Seton Gordon used to come about. I have a photograph of him with my father. He was the best writer of them all.'

Nell's gamekeeping family was the last to live permanently at the Bynack, and the next move was to a spot much grimmer, her home from 1912 to 1925.

'Yes and I then became known to some folk as Nell Bynack of the Derry. It seemed an awful dark place, heather and rocks, after the greenness of the Bynack. You're 1,400 feet up and it's the nearest house to Ben Macdhui, the second-highest peak in Scotland. It gets an awful lot of snow and wind. I've always loved the hills, especially Ben Macdhui.

'I've been on the top twenty-two times. I've seen the view from the summit when it was at its absolute clearest, but I've been up in the mist too, and then you have to be very careful. I got a bit wandered once, and had no idea where I was until I found the sapper's bothy. I waited and got a glimpse of Loch Etchachan then I knew where to go. There's plenty of room to get really lost on the plateau when the mist is down.'

She told me how it came about she had gone up to the 4,296-foot summit so often: with guests from the Fife Arms Hotel in Braemar. A party would want to climb Macdhui and they would send word to me asking if I would take them up. I was never out of pocket. I always went up the Sron Riach for the lovely views you get from the ridge, with the wee Lochan Uaine in the floor of the corrie below you, and Derry Cairngorm on one side and the Devil's Point and Cairn Toul on the other.'

In the days Nell was talking about, Mar Estate stalked the high ground to Cairn Toul and maintained a summer watcher at Corrour Bothy to ensure walkers of the Lairig Ghru kept to the path and didn't spoil the sport of deer-stalking parties who had tramped a long way for it.

Nell reminisced: 'There was no selling of venison in those days. It was given away. Critics may tell of low wages of long ago, but I think the old times were actually better for estate workers' families than they are now when it's all money, money, money.'

Luibeg Cottage is on the edge of the Cairngorm National Nature Reserve which stretches north over the greatest area in Scotland of arctic plateau, rocky corries, lochans and glens and remnant Caledonian pines. I took Nell up to see her old home, and looking around, she named all the hills and told me what the outhouses were used for in her day.

I also had a chat with Bob Scott, then retired to a cottage near Mar Lodge. He had no doubt that his happiest days were at Luibeg. 'Aye, I was never the same after I left.' He didn't say more, but the sale of the estate to Swiss owners, whose interest was in making money from paying guests, took away much of his carefree independence. He had a Land-Rover.

With mechanical accessibility something of his remoteness vanished. I remember a January week I spent with him after a big blizzard, and the two of us sledged home huge cuts of fallen Caledonian pines he had sawn earlier to bring along when the snow fell, the horse pulling with a will. He confided that if he had all the money in the world he would be content to buy the estate and continue to live the way he was doing, stalking stags and hinds, taking a salmon from the Dee, and enjoying the society of the climbers given the hospitality of his bothy at weekends.

Nobody lives permanently at Luibeg now. Keepers in remote places are an expensive luxury, and deer stalkers and guests don't walk as they used to have to do. They drive to the high tops on bulldozed roads. From Mar Lodge the Swiss owners built a road which leads through the wonderful woods of Glen Quoich, climbs above them and zig-zags to within a short distance of the summit of Beinn a' Bhuird at 4,000 feet. There could be as many as a hundred miles or more now of these sub-standard roads scarring the once pristine area scheduled as a future national park in the 1940s.

Bob was buried in Braemar on 30th July 1987 after enduring much suffering. His wife had died before him, and he was looked after by a daughter in Old Meldrum before going into hospital. He will never be forgotten as a father figure; kindly, but quick to give any wrong-doer the rough edge of his tongue. The deep love that Nell had for the Bynack, Bob had for Luibeg. It was in his house I met a red-haired schoolboy by the name of Adam Watson, who today is the greatest authority on the Cairngorms and the staunchest fighter to halt the damage that is still being done to his beloved Cairngorms.

Anyone, whatever his or her nationality, can buy huge chunks of Scotland. When the Swiss sold out, the next buyer of Mar Estate was an

American millionaire who soon tired of it, and when it came on the market again, conservation bodies guaranteed raising half the purchase price if the Government would pay the other half. This could have been a wonderful experiment in joint management between Scottish National Heritage and conservationists but the Government turned it down.

I devoted my last programme to the Dee side of the Cairngorms, and finished it by telling the story of Peter Grant, the Mar sergeant-major who, aged 107, was the last survivor of the 1745 Jacobite Rising. Captured at Culloden and taken to Carlisle prison where many of the rebels faced execution, Peter managed the almost impossible feat of climbing the castle walls in the dark and walking all the way back to Braemar.

King George IV was told Peter's story in 1822 when the monarch paid his historic visit to Edinburgh. His reaction was to grant Peter a pension of one guinea a week for life, adding that payment should be put into effect as quickly as possible in case the old man would get small benefit from it. On being told he was being granted the pension as the King's oldest subject, Peter is reported to have replied: 'Aye, and the oldest rebel.' At his death, aged 110, his oldest friend, aged ninety, played his bagpipes, and the tune was 'Wha widna fecht for Charlie's right?' I told the story at his graveside in the old cemetery beside Braemar Castle.

I also paid a visit to the last surviving speaker of Deeside Gaelic, aged ninety. The old language had held on in the remoter places until crofters in the high glens gave up the struggle for easier ways of living. Mrs Bain was living with her son Rob in a farm by name Ardoch, Gaelic for 'High Place', on a grassy shelf at 1,500 feet overlooking Balmoral, with a poor road climbing up to it.

Rob Bain's living was in 300 sheep and a few beef cattle. Weather-beaten, fit and in his early fifties, in answer to my question of: 'What is it like to farm such a high place on your own?' he considered the question, with a humorous twinkle in his eye. I have to paraphrase his rich Aberdeenshire dialect.

'You manage the best way you can. I'm fit for nothing else. It's hard, right enough. I don't see anybody else doing it once I've gone. I'm about the last in a place like this. The house is old and needs a lot done to it. Where I was born at Daldownie, a few miles from here up at the Gairn, also a high place, there's not even an occupied farm. I think the last man to farm there is in Glasgow now.'

The fine old lady, sitting at the kitchen range where she and the cat were warming themselves, gave me a phrase or two of Gaelic then got up to make some tea. 'She's very deaf,' said Rob, 'but she's very quick to get your meaning. She still cuts sticks for the fire and does jobs about the house. She enjoys herself.'

My next meeting with Rob was by chance. I was driving along, and he was loading turnips into his Land-Rover from a heap at the foot of his road. He gave me the sad news that his mother had passed on, and he was now alone. 'I fairly miss her,' he said.

She is remembered, however, in a scholarly work by Adam Watson on Gaelic place names around Deeside. She recalled names for landscape features that were not on old estate maps and without her would have been forgotten. She died in 1984.

With Adam Watson I went into Aberdeen to hear Desmond Nether-sole-Thompson deliver a lecture on Highland birds in the Zoology Department of the university. It was some time since I had seen him, and never before in a smart lounge suit. White beard nodding, the rebel of the past looked bland and paternal. Even at rest on a sofa he looked a well-filled-out man who took up a lot of space. On his feet his presence was commanding. At the sherry party which preceded his talk he exuded bonhomie.

An Irishman, he could make his words sing, and rush together as though he were carried away telling about something wonderful he had seen that had never been observed by any naturalist before. I can't pretend to remember the structure of that happy evening. I remember him more vividly surrounded by his young family, Bruin, Patrick, Richard, Eamonn, Katherine, and his wife Maimie, in their simple home at Ardgay in Easter Ross where he had agreed to talk to me about his work as a naturalist and writer. It was one of a series I was doing for *Scotland's Magazine* under the title of 'The Researchers'. Altogether I wrote thirty-six articles over a period of three years, using the nom-de-plume of Ward Clarke. (I did this in order to appease the Editor of the *Scots Magazine* who did not want to see my name every month in a rival publication.)

'Ask me anything you like,' smiled Desmond, puffing genially at his cheroot by the fire in his upstairs study, 'provided you don't try to make out that my life has been glamorous. It has never been that, nor is it now. It is as much a mental challenge now as it has ever been, though having filled out like Falstaff I can't do as much on the hills. I shall be quite satisfied if what I have done lights a fire for a few young men.

'I have been studying the territorial behaviour of birds all my life. And I know that animals, including the human animal, ignore the basic drives which govern man's behaviour at their peril. These drives are more powerful than reason because they reach back to his far more primitive past. I learned a lot about territory from watching a little iconoclastic snow-bunting called Baldy.

'Territory to me is now here, with Maimie: she loves, feed and bullies me, and types my tape recordings and helps me draft my books. For most of the year we are slogging away at my desk, but for six glorious free weeks we are all away in the Flow of Sutherland watching greenshanks, eagles and divers. We are like Eskimos in the spring. So now you have the mating

189

and territorial behaviour of a naturalist who has enjoyed a wonderful life and who intends to go on doing so.'

I had been talking to Desmond for two days, pretty well non-stop in his cottage at the head of the Dornoch Firth on the Sutherland border. I wanted him to rationalise for me how a man who loves Highland birds could bring himself to take and sell their eggs for gain. He had no hesitancy in answering.

'Simple. I had to live, and it can't be done without money. I came to the Highlands to study snow buntings, dotterel, greenshank, Scottish crossbills and other distinctive Highland birds. My search was for knowledge, not for eggs, but I did rob a few nests for the bare necessities of life. I grew thin from hunger and hard work tramping and camping in these hills. And when I lay in my tent wondering if it would hold against the blast of wind and rain at 4,000 feet, my anxiety went beyond the fear of the moment, for I knew if the tent was destroyed that I couldn't afford another.'

Desmond had been a schoolmaster. It was the distinguished ornithologist, the Rev F.C.R. Jourdain, who advised him to go and live in the Highlands and tackle the life histories of the most difficult group of birds in Britain.

'There were no grants available in these days of the early 30s. The birds themselves had to finance the study. But I can say that I took no more eggs than I needed, and usually from those that I knew would lay again.'

It was Kirkman, the co-author with Jourdain of *British Birds*, who inspired Desmond to initiate experiments to test the behaviour of birds in different situations. Desmond became sad as he talked of his old friend Kirkman, and with characteristic honesty said: 'There's only one thing I'm ashamed of in my life and it concerns Kirkman.'

He sat in silence for a bit, then he continued: 'Kirkman needed money to carry on his work, but there was only one source, and it was the Leverhulme Award, granted to only one person at a time. The sum was £150 for two years. I was in for it as well as Kirkman. And I got it. I took it, though I knew that Kirkman was the better man. Kirkman was poor, like me, yet he had actually sponsored me. For me that award meant I could give up egg collecting and devote myself to pure research.'

Part of Thompson's success was due to his being able to recognise individual birds by the character of their eggs, and he used this information in the way ornithologists today use colour-ringing. His classic book *The Greenshank* shows how. It was written in 1951 after sixteen years following the fortunes of this elusive species in the forest bogs of Rothiemurchus. Read how secret after secret was revealed as he tried to penetrate the inner minds of his subjects – not a dry as dust treatise, but a strange mixture of scientific detachment and emotional response to his environment.

His next book was *The Snow Bunting* which he wrote six times before it was published in 1966, the result of 263 nights spent out on the high tops of the Cairngorms and years of research. As with the greenshank book, it involved world-wide correspondence with leading ornithologists, for they are not regional studies but covered everything that was known about the birds at that time.

Basically a happy man, he has had his disappointments as well as hardships. He recalled his tough beginning in a bothy miles from anywhere on the Braes of Dorback when just to stay alive in winter was hard, let alone fight a blizzard which all but killed him when he was caught out walking home with provisions. He remembers, too, the opposition of Highland lairds who tried to keep him off their property because they distrusted his way of life.

'You forget the hard years without proper light, sanitation, no running water and little fuel, no books and absolute immobility in the dark days. But my biggest disappointment was not getting into Parliament. I fought twice for the Inverness seat and polled a record Labour vote of between 11,000 and 12,000; but it wasn't good enough. I would have enjoyed the cut and thrust of Parliament. However I could get rid of some of my fire in local affairs.

'I fought the laird's wife in a local election and won a seat on the Inverness County Council. Aviemore was a different place in 1945 from what it is now. I started a fight to transform the services in the area. Some causes were lost, but some succeeded. We got council houses, drainage schemes, grants for a Community Hall, a playing field, street lighting, scavenging, and I harnessed forces against proposed rail closures.

'What I would fight for now is a coherent plan for the Cairngorms to hold the habitats of some of our rarer birds. I'd fight for Ben Macdhui and Beinn a' Bhuird particularly, since they are amongst the most valuable wild-life places in the Cairngorms and access must not be made too easy.

'Naturalists will never know the Cairngorms as I knew them, before ski-roads, chair-lifts, chalets and tourist promoters,' he continued. 'I know now that any hardships of that old cottage which we rented for £8 annually and lived in for eleven years, were worth it. It took thirty-two years to find thirty-eight snow-bunting nests – and this is only the raw material of the snow-bunting book. But no one had discovered before the peculiar polygamy of snow-buntings which is tailored to social needs; or the polyandry of dotterel which I proved in the Cairngorms.'

He laughed when I mentioned his role of Captain in the army, and he recalled being arrested on D-Day as a spy on the Dover cliffs while he was looking for a peregrine falcon's eyrie – maybe the very one I knew myself. Marched away under escort he gave as explanation of his behaviour that he was a member of the War Office Pigeon Corps, checking up on the destruction of carrier pigeons by these birds. He emerged as a VIP, chuckling.

It was inevitable that the two greatest Cairngormers, Desmond Nethersole-Thompson and Dr Adam Watson, should collaborate on *The Cairngorms, Their Natural History and Scenery*, published by Collins in 1974 with a Preface by V.C. Wynne-Edwards, Regius Professor of Natural History, University of Aberdeen.

They open the book with the inscription: 'We love the Cairngorms and have chosen to work in them for decades.' They go on: 'We have written this book to tell you about this marvellous country and heritage of yours. We wish you to share our concern for the conservation of the Cairngorms and their wildlife. What is badly needed is a rational plan which planners must hammer out before it is too late.' My presentation copy from Adam Watson has the inscription. 'To Tom, with deep thanks for your inspiration and for many grand days on the Cairngorms.'

It is the spring of 1994 as I write this and after half a century of deliberation we still await the proposed rational plan.

16

The Grammar of the Environment

That was what my good friend Bob Grieve was enlarging upon on a December day in 1964 as we climbed towards the snowy summit of Stuic a' Chroin, and from 3,000 feet looked down on the flat Carse of Stirling, embossed with the speakpoint of the Wallace Monument and the silhouetted castle, perched on its crag like a Tibetan monastery. We relished it, knowing that a blizzard from the north was about to hit us, so we were glad to turn our backs to its stinging cold arrival and make our way down.

Resuming our conversation from where we had left off, he continued: 'Yes, understanding the environment. It was a subconscious process. Like you, I was brought up in a working-class tenement. I was studying civil engineering at night school. The only time I could get out was a Sunday, but I used to love getting away on a Saturday night, to sleep out somewhere – in the old pier-shed at Balmaha, or a barn in the Trossachs. Wandering around Loch Lomond and the Campsies I came slowly to realise that the countryside that meant so much to me didn't just evolve. Man made it what it was, just as he made the city of Glasgow what it is.

'I wanted to understand why this or that had come about. I began to see that you could change things that were bad, and keep those that are beautiful. Good taste doesn't just happen. In fact working with Sir Patrick Abercrombie on the Clyde Valley Regional Plan during the war was the most important thing in my career. It led me through the door I was looking for in my life. We began in 1944 with a paper plan. Now after eighteen years in the Civil Service I have seen much of it come to pass though much remains to be done. I now want to test every truth I have held dear.

'There is a close parallel with mountaineering, in that no achievement is possible until you can sort out the possible from the impossible. To me, being a mountaineer means being master of the environment of mountains, to feel free and at peace on them, to challenge them and know when not to challenge them. The big difference is, that planning is not a game,

193

but fraught with tremendous administrative problems and is highly political. Planning is places, work, folk, the raising of standards, the striving towards a better environment. Towns are places to live in, not just to escape from. Countryside like Loch Lomond must be fought for, preserved against developments which could ruin it for recreation. We have to work hard and think hard about how to retain what remains undespoiled. Look at the Clyde coast. We have to care about these things. The sheer growth of people, and their mobility through the motor car, poses problems of land use all the time.'

I was fairly close to Bob then, for he had appointed me the only lay member of a powerful Committee with the title of Study Group No. 9 to examine a wide range of countryside issues distinctive to Scotland. Bob was Chairman, and our task was to anticipate what would be needed for better management of the countryside in 1970 – European Conservation Year.

Over a period of several weeks we had seven meetings in St Andrew's House, Edinburgh, involving our Committee studying fifty technical papers, looking at every aspect of present legislation, and seeing what was most needed in an age of increasing leisure and ever more pressures for recreation in the countryside. Often we had guest speakers, experts for interrogation by us where understanding of issues needed explanation.

The Committee decided that what Scotland needed was a 'thing'. We didn't call it a National Parks Service – because England and Wales had between them ten National Parks, and their problems were different from ours. The thing we envisaged was an agency with executive power, armed with planning powers and finance from the Government, to purchase and manage chosen areas of outstanding beauty for recreation and wild-life.

England had its own regional study groups and it was envisaged that the various chairmen would meet with ours in London under the Chairmanship of the Duke of Edinburgh, to report and discuss what Government legislation would be needed to meet the challenge of managing the countryside in 1970 and beyond.

It wasn't just waffle and talking shop. Our Committee's finding resulted in a Countryside (Scotland) Act, establishing an autonomous agency called the Countryside Commission on 27th October 1967. Its weakness was that it was not given the executive power we had hoped for, but from a shaky beginning it rose from strength to strength as a planning and advisory body in its twenty-four years of active life, disbursing cash to voluntary conservation bodies, helping to secure sites of outstanding natural beauty, offering advice, and influencing the creation of thirty-five Country Parks adjacent to towns, as lungs for their inhabitants.

The very first of these was the John Muir Country Park, approved in 1976 and taking in the ruin of Dunbar Castle perched on a cliff (where John Muir had done his first scrambling), and from where a self-guided

Nature Trail leads along an escarpment of cliffs to sand dunes, a salt marsh, woodlands, scrub and permanent grasslands; superb habitats for birds. Even the house where Muir lived at 126–128 High Street has been refurbished in the style he knew it in 1838 and is open to visitors during the summer months.

The Countryside Commission ended its life with honour on 1st April 1992 when it merged with the Nature Conservancy Council to become Scottish Natural Heritage, with a budget of £34.6 million to dispose of under the Chairmanship of Magnus Magnusson KBE, a face known to as many millions of British subjects for his Chairmanship of BBC Television's *Mastermind*. Those of us who love the Cairngorms were looking forward to reading SNH's first Working Party Report – 'Common Sense and Sustainability, A Partnership for the Cairngorms', signed by its Chairman after twenty-one months of study.

That it was a very big let-down became clear when I was invited by Dr Adam Watson to be the first speaker at a symposium hosted by Kincardine and Deeside Council to discuss the future of the Cairngorms. As I was the person with the longest experience I looked back sixty years to then and now as a scene-setter. Following me was Desmond Thompson, son of the famous ornithologist Desmond Nethersole-Thompson, who was a small child when I visited his famous father and mother Maimie as already described. Desmond spoke as Principal Scientific Officer of Scottish Natural Heritage. His main areas of concern were:

(a) In the central Cairngorms, recreational pressures leading to erosion scars and damage.
(b) Overgrazing by sheep and deer.
(c) With 60–70,000 deer in the whole Cairngorm area, natural woodland regeneration is prevented. He saw a drastic cull of red deer as the only answer, despite the difficulties in imposing this on landowners.

He stresssed that the time had come for action, not words.

Dr Adam Watson summed up the general feeling of the speakers at the symposium when he described the finding of the Report as bogus, incompetent, and maintained that its authors should be sacked. He put much of the blame for scores of errors and lack of rigorous analysis as being due to poor selection of work party members by the Scottish Office. He called for the Report to be set aside and a serious independent review commenced, and stated that this one was an expensive flop.

The two most knowledgeable members of the Working Party, I'm glad to say, dissented from the Report recommendations. John Hunt, Senior Conservation Manager of the RSPB, called for a new authority funded eighty-five per cent by the Government, able to own land and manage it.

The second dissenter was mountaineer Eric Langmuir, one-time Principal of Glen More Lodge Outdoor Training Centre on the Aviemore side of the Cairngorms.

In the October/December 1969 Bulletin of the International Union for the Conservation of Nature Resources, Professor E.W. Swanson, discussing the economic impact of National Parks in the United States wrote:

> There is nothing in this earth today which will yield such a high non-gambling reward as proper management of scenically grand, and wild-life rich, landscape.

Professor Swanson even set a profit figure of forty times the outlay, which is reason enough why 130 civilised nations of the world have set them up.

This brings me back to Loch Lomond, and the reason why this largest surface area of water in Britain, whose 'bonnie banks' are celebrated in song wherever Scots are gathered together, is in more need of National Park protection than anywhere else in Scotland. Here is the view of Professor Sir Robert Grieve who saw this as a priority in 1946, and as chief technical planner did his utmost to protect it against unsightly developments. Take heed of the words he wrote in the 1970s:

> Loch Lomond must be a test case in our whole approach to scenic heritage, because it is as near to perfection as this world can attain, yet it stands close to one of the biggest urban industrial areas in the world, from which escape is as necessary as food. Loch Lomond is here and now, and could be ruined in the next twenty years by being increasingly regarded as an area of exploitation for one resource or another, whether for pumped-storage electricity, water supply, extraction of concrete aggregate or tourist gold.

The significant words of this paragraph are 'pumped-storage', reference to a scheme drawn up by the North of Scotland Hydro-Electric Board to create a reservoir half-way up Ben Lomond, connected to an underground power house, so that water could be pumped out of the loch 1,600 feet uphill, and brought down again, giving an output of 1,600 kilowatts of electricity. The power to shoot the water uphill would be bought cheaply from Hunterston Nuclear Power Station on the Clyde, and water would be brought down when peak load was required for sale at a higher price. Furthermore, if demand rose its output could be doubled with little more environmental damage.

Not very many years earlier, when I was writing volume one of *The Scottish Lochs* (Constable 1970), the Hydro-Electric Board had provided information on their future plan to convert Loch Sloy to pumped storage and provide a vastly increased output. To achieve this, little environmental damage would have been caused, because the power station was on the A82 adjacent to the West Highland Railway. I certainly saw no objection.

The Craigroyston Scheme was a very different story, for this steep, steep side of Ben Lomond is its priceless shore, its oak woods spanned only by paths, and would be irreparably damaged in the eight years the scheme would take to widen the existing road to Rowardennan and extend it for lorries carrying aggregate.

Moreover, years of work had already gone into converting Loch Lomond from natural water to a reservoir, with a pumping station capable of diverting up to one hundred million gallons of soft water per day to Central Belt towns between the Clyde and Forth. That water scheme itself could have been disastrous but for consultations between engineers, Nature Conservancy scientists, and boatman Alex MacFarlane whose family had kept a record of the fluctuations of the loch since the beginning of the century.

The correct minimum level had to be fixed, otherwise many of the delightful little bays would be inundated, and the shores and marshes of the National Nature Reserve at the mouth of the River Endrick, notable for rare species of flowers and a variety of wet-loving birds, could be lost. In fact, the water scheme was carried out so well that few visitors to Loch Lomond know that Loch Lomond is a reservoir.

To fight off the Craigroyston proposal a society which named itself 'Friends of Loch Lomond' was formed, its aim to raise public awareness of what this pumped-storage scheme would mean, and to contest its need. As an executive committee member I gave public lectures, wrote critical articles, appeared as a member of the audience at Hydro-Electric Board propaganda meetings, and embarrassed the public relations speaker by asking him the same questions as he went from village to village.

Probably we could have saved our breath, for what really put the pumped-storage scheme in cold storage was the recession, and a fall in demand when Britain was already vastly over-provided with electricity generators. The 'Friends of Loch Lomond', ably led by Mrs Hannah Stirling, then took on a new role, utilising their funds to initiate a whole variety of conservations tasks, using, with the addition of Countryside Commission grants, the man-power services to build paths, refurbish broken walls, restore viewpoints, plant trees, and so on.

The 'Friends' also maintained a vigorous campaign for Loch Lomond to be given National Park status. In this way they were supported by the local authorities, which led to Loch Lomond being declared a Regional Park with a Joint Executive Committee and the appointment of a first-class Park Officer in Nick Pennington, a geographer with much administrative experience of English National Parks. His remit was: 'To conserve and enhance the natural beauty and heritage of the area; to promote public enjoyment of the area; to promote the social and economic well-being of local communities.' Without adequate staff, or any financial help from the Scottish Office he was attempting an impossible task.

Then one day in 1992 I had a letter on House of Commons notepaper from Dumbarton MP John McFall (Labour) inviting me to be the first speaker at a seminar on Loch Lomond he was organising. I was allowed forty minutes to show slides of the loch and air my views on its conservation.

I was followed by Mr John Arnott, Vice-Chairman of the Countryside Commission, and ex-BBC radio producer, with whom I have done many outside broadcasts on country matters. He saw a similarity between Loch Lomond and the Cairngorms in their complexity of pressures. He talked about sustaining the different qualities of different parts of Loch Lomond, which may include discouraging as well as encouraging different uses, ranging from built-in facilities such as marinas for water ski-ing, and footpaths for walkers, to preserving places of solitude by the minimum of intervention.

Robert Maund, Strathclyde's top planner, was no less forthright. He condemned the Government for its refusal to grant National Park status to Loch Lomond, pointing out that since Strathclyde Region came into being in 1975, pressures had grown relentlessly on the bonnie banks, that there was dereliction, and land badly in need of positive management to cope with the influx of visitors. Also, there was much poor-quality development, out of keeping with the quality of the landscape. He said that prevarication and indecision still ruled. More resources were urgently required, and the way to channel them was through National Park status being granted.

President of the 'Friends', Hannah Stirling, always forceful, stated that many of the visitors would not come back if pollution and noise didn't stop. She deplored chain-saw visitors who cut down trees for camp fires, and litter louts who bestrew the shores with broken bottles, dirty nappies and beer cans. She suggested we should have a scheme to sell environmental bonds, akin to war bonds, as a way of bringing about the National Park we wanted.

What I think everyone liked was the non-political aspect of the discussion. Roger Carr, Chairman of the Countryside Commission, shortly to retire, said that although he did not vote as John McFall, he 'shared his very real concern for Loch Lomond'. The last words of the conference were his when he spoke from the heart without fear or favour:

There is a lot going wrong around here and something has to be done about it. I am becoming angry and frustrated with the Government's refusal to act. They appear to want some kind of voluntary body to look after this very fragile and beautiful piece of

198

countryside, but this is the wrong route. The case for a National Park has been made here today.

The Scottish Office seems to have a blind spot. I am afraid we are bashing our heads against a brick wall.

Ironically, when a Scottish Natural Heritage Working Party was set up to consider the 'Management of Loch Lomond and the Trossachs' the option of a National Park was not within its brief. The terms of reference laid down by the Rt Hon Ian Lang MP, Secretary of State for Scotland, were to:

1. Consider the management issues connected with the conservation of the natural heritage and visitor trends in the area.

2. Make recommendations on how improvements in management practices might be achieved *within the existing statutory framework.*

3. Consider the areas in which its findings and recommendations might apply.

These sombre words 'within the existing statutory framework', gave little comfort to those campaigning for something more revolutionary. We did not, however, take account of the steely resolution of its Chairman Sir Peter Hutchison Bt, who had good quality in his nineteen work party members to look at the kind of sustainability that John Arnott and Robert Maund had talked about at the John McFall symposium.

Between 8th November 1991 and 26th April 1993 the Working Party held nineteen meetings in a variety of locations, and as early as at the fourth of these meetings Sir Peter was writing to the Secretary of State for Scotland, expressing his concern with the current financial problems faced by the Loch Lomond Park Authority, and the greater problems likely to arise in 1993/4 when it appeared that the resources available to the Park Authority would not be sufficient to meet their commitments in the financial year.

That this was no rush job can be appreciated when no fewer than eight research projects were commissioned to assist the understanding of the Working Party. The response to the Report of the Loch Lomond and Trossachs Working Party was one of congratulation for going beyond its restricting brief. Its preferred approach was very much akin to the National Park system in England, should major legislative change become a possibility.

Striking while the iron was hot, the Scottish Council for National Parks – a pressure group – booked the main lecture hall in the University of Strathclyde to host what it advertised as: 'Celebrity lectures by Tom Weir and Chris Bonington – world-famous mountaineer and Chairman of the Council for National Parks in England'. I was to open with Loch Lomond and the Trossachs. Chris would make a case for the Cairngorms.

We had a large audience. Chris, who lives just outwith the boundary of the Lake District National Park, spoke about how effective its management was in maintaining paths, disposing of litter, curbing noisy speed boats by enforcing speed limits, and controlling architectural styles where developments were sanctioned.

Chris had a lively question and answer session, and was able to show that National Parks in England did much for long-term conservation integrated with recreation. I was pleased to hear that the Government had accepted the recommendation that all National Parks in England should be independent authorities, declaring in a policy statement 'Fit for the Future' that it regarded National Park designation as 'conferring the highest status of protection as far as landscape and scenic beauty are concerned'.

A full ninety per cent of Scots consulted at the last poll on National Parks voted for them to be set up. But we are still waiting, impatiently.

17

Foula Honeymoon

A young man married is a young man marr'd
Willam Shakespeare

To that aphorism, a father of three children exploring with me on the 1960 Sir John Hunt Greenland expedition would add 'Amen!' He believes that for marriage to succeed one of the partners has to die, usually the male. He is not of course referring to physical death, but the act of turning your staff into a stake. He believes that to stay young you should refuse to grow up. Remembering the adventures I might have missed if I had married my land girl, I felt there could be an element of truth in his cynical words.

But as the Arabs say: 'The different forms of madness are innumerable', while Samuel Johnson has it: 'Marriage has many pains, but celibacy has no pleasures.' As I left off marriage until I was forty-five I could be accused of hedging my bets since my chosen wife, a few years younger, knew the kind of man I was. She realised I would still want to go off with well-tried Scottish Mountaineering Club friends, and that she, as a member of the Ladies' Scottish Climbing Club, would continue to go out with her friends.

Another virtue was that, as a trained teacher, she could get a job in the village school and practise something she loved, while I had the house to myself five days a week, and we could make the most of weekends and long summer vacations together. Even on our honeymoon we went for wilderness rather than comfort – to the remotest island of the Shetlands, Foula, often inaccessible and said to be served once a week by island boat, weather permitting.

So after our wedding in Aberfoyle Kirk we drove in my Austin van, packed with camping kit, to board the boat in Aberdeen for the overnight sail to Lerwick, the Shetland capital, where neither of us had been before, and feeling as if we were abroad, so many boats of different nationalities packed the busy harbour. That feeling was emphasised when in a shop to buy paraffin for the Primus stove, the assistant asked me if I came from Scotland.

To get to Foula, our best plan, we were told, was to drive north over the hill to Scalloway, the ancient capital of Shetland, and seek our boatman,

Hans Smith. We found him among the sharp-prowed dinghies and fishing smacks, but as he was tied up, he said it would be best for us to telephone the post office on Foula to find out when the island boat would make its next crossing to the village of Walls in Vaila Sound. We did, found we had a day in hand, so off we drove.

Voe is the Shetland word for a sea-loch, and the north coast is so bitten into by them from east and west that, as you cross Northmavine, you need walk only a hundred yards to exchange the Atlantic for the North Sea. Ronas Hill is the dominant feature of all North Roe, rising as a granite hog-back 1,475 feet, and with a name the same as that of my wife it had to be climbed. Indeed Rhona was thinking it didn't have a top, until looming in the mist appeared a large summit cairn. At the same time, a black headland pierced by cliffs, and patterned with silvery lochs inland, lay below, and on the other side was the Island of Yell.

We stayed in the village of Walls that night to await the Foula boat due next day, and found we had a long wait, for it was eight o'clock on a misty wet evening before we were perched on the small deck, heading for the elusive island. 'Three hours on this tide,' said the younger of the two-man crew as the compass was laid on the deck, a bearing taken, and the sail hoisted. It was cold and gloomy as we slid into a little voe under a pall of cloud enveloping the hills.

Ashore, we bore our luggage to the headland above the landing place on Ham Voe, pitched our tent and snuggled into our sleeping bags, weary with travelling, but delighted to be here at last, and to be awakened at six by the wailing of skuas and the fluttering cries of whimbrel. From the open flaps of the tent we looked out on the sun carving a path on the ocean, but the clouds were still down on the hills behind us. Previously I had seen and heard only one great skua in my life. On Foula we were to experience the first of many dive-bombing runs from some of the 800 pairs of these large brown parasitic birds locally known as Bonxies.

Nearest to the landing place was the North Ness, and, as the island is only three and a half miles in length and about two miles in greatest breadth, we were just setting off on exploration when we saw we were being watched by a lady in homespun clothing standing by her cow, and it seemed to us she wanted to speak. But as we approached, she drew back, pulling her headscarf over her mouth. Her retreat, it transpired, was due to fear of disease germs we might have brought from the outside.

She indicated, however, we should go with her. It was to give us a present of eggs and milk at her nearby croft. As she went inside, out came her brother, and when I produced my camera, he regaled us with how he and his sister, Jeannie, with other islanders, had been actors in Michael Powell's classic film *Edge of the World*, shot on Foula in 1936 and starring John Laurie, Finlay Currie and Niall MacGinnis.

He could remember every detail of the actors, living in Nissen huts from

June till October, and all the things that had been staged: a race up to the cliffs, a sermon in the kirk, a funeral, fishing at sea, and at the end everybody evacuated, except one who commits suicide by leaping from the cliff-top rather than leave his beloved island. It was the Royal Scottish Geographical Society that had suggested Foula as an alternative to St Kilda; ideal, because it had a native population of great character which showed in their resolute faces.

When Jeannie reappeared, so did a dark-phased Arctic skua – smaller and more stream-lined than the Bonxie. At once, Jeannie rushed into the house and came out with a salt-herring which she threw to the waiting bird; but before it could snatch it, a second skua appeared and a short tug of war ensued. The dark bird, Jeannie told us, had been coming to the house since 1918, and over the years had brought a variety of mates. She was positive she was not mistaken about the identity of the original bird, and pointed out that the habit of coming to a house was not shared by any other skua on Foula.

Now we turned our attention to the North Ness, reefed by the sea and great rock stacks sculpted by waves, one, with a great arch torn out of it, named the 'Broch Stack'. As immediate foreground, a storm beach of great boulders smooth as billiard balls by being rolled against each other by battering seas. Black guillemots flying in from the sea with fish to their nests underground were being harried constantly by Arctic skuas in attempts to make them disgorge their catch. 'Tystie' is the Shetland name for these delightful little auks, with red legs and white flashes on the wings. Failing to deprive the tysties, the skuas turned their attention to the downy young of Arctic terns creeping about the bare ground.

The North Ness soars up as a rock ridge at its grassy end, forcing you upward on an exciting edge that leaps evermore dramatically to end with a 1,250-foot drop into the sea. Writers have described this cliff as second only to Conachar of St Kilda. I would place it first, before Conachar, for unyielding verticality. Eight years earlier I had descended the face of Conachar with Douglas Scott. I would not have dared to do so on this ledgeless face which is responsible for the terrible force of the 'Foula flans' – whirlwinds that can result when storm-force Atlantic winds strike it in such a way that they are deflected up and over, descending on the crofts in miniature tornado form, whirling haystacks out to sea, carrying off boats and tearing off any weak roof.

We shared the ridge with little Shetland sheep, whose wool provides the softest and warmest garments made in Britain. Tiny animals, they are said to be genetically close to the peat-sheep domesticated by Neolithic man. They are, however, being superseded by more commercial breeds. Their primitive relatives are the St Kilda sheep, still roaming on this western island.

Traversing the full length of Foula's summit ridge we came down to

South Biggings and what is called the 'Lady's Ness'. Here we met a delightful woman with a face like a rosy apple. She was a good half-mile from the nearest house and was feeding potatoes to some sheep, giving the food to them because she had been taking their fleece, she explained. She refused my offer of help to carry her bundle, but walked along with us, speaking about Foula with a voice as expressive as music.

I learned afterwards she was nearer to ninety than eighty, and found it hard to believe, her mind was so sharp. She spoke of what a wonderful place Foula had been when the biggings were full of children; when over 200 people lived here at the beginning of the century, and any croft vacant was eagerly snapped up. There was pasture for over a hundred cows.

'The young people have left. I don't know what is going to happen on Foula.' She knew in her heart that times had changed; that young people want money to buy all sorts of food and goods unheard of in the old days.

Four years after we were there, their boat *Island Lass* was lost. One year before that, Foula was cut off from the outside world by wild seas for seventy-eight days, and a relief aircraft that attempted to land was bogged until a heavy steel net could be landed to make a firm carpet for take-off.

Formerly it was cod fishing that was the mainstay of the Foula folk, and boats from the mainland called three times a year to take off the cured fish. There is no quantity of cod around Foula now, we were told in 1959, but the white fishing was excellent according to a visiting fisherman who called at our tent with some haddocks for our breakfast. He had caught twenty-five hundredweight during the night, and reckoned that thousands of pounds worth of fish were taken every year off the Foula coast by seine net boats, whereas the locals could cash in only if they were prepared to fish from mainland harbours, and would rarely get home.

But Foula has held on to its population remarkably. In 1959 when we were there it was forty-five. In a book *Foula – Island West of the Sun* by Sheila Gair, who has lived on the island for sixteen years and is married to a crofter, I found inspiration. Mother of three children she is a zoologist, and her book published in 1983 gives the population as thirty-seven, and she tells in lively writing of their determination to stay, enjoy their isolation and practise the old way of life for the satisfaction they get from it. She is glad it is not any nearer to the mainland.

Fetlar has been justly described as one of the fairest of the Shetland Isles, by reason of its good pasture over much of its five miles width and six and a half miles length. We went there for a special reason and saw it in the morning, looking out on the crofts of Houbie and Aith. Soon we were being welcomed, first by a friendly herd of tiny Shetland ponies, then by two good friends, George and Irene Waterson, officials of the Royal Society for the Protection of Birds, who were in charge of a twenty-four-hour-a-day watch on the very first pair of snowy owls to nest in Britain.

Our arrival was perfectly timed to give a hand shifting a hen-house, being used as an observation post, nearer to the birds, for use by Eric Hosking who was there to photograph the owls and half a dozen chicks of different sizes. I didn't expect Eric to remember me from the meeting at Ryvoan bothy in 1940 when he was photographing merlins and I was on my way down from the Cairngorms to join the Ayrshire Yeomanry, but he did, and after an exchange of news we celebrated by photographing each other.

Just three years before I met him in 1940, he had lost an eye to a tawny owl which clawed his face. He did better with a barn owl, caught by the camera with a vole in its beak, which became his most famous picture. Now after travelling in many lands he had come to Shetland for yet another owl, and again he caught it to perfection.

Between meeting me, and the end of the war in 1945, he produced two remarkable books, *Birds of the Day*, and *Birds of the Night*. Then in the 1950s he travelled the world photographing birds, visiting sanctuaries in Pakistan, India, Jordan, the Galapagos and the Falklands; his pictures appearing in over 800 books, covering the world from the Arctic to the Antarctic eventually. Even when he was not taking pictures, Eric enjoyed playing with cameras, though he felt technology was making bird photography too easy. He it was, though, who was first to apply the technique of birds breaking a beam which set off the flash that caught them in perfect focus, every feather sharp, like Eric's famous shot of a nightjar.

What he most regretted was that he had lost his head for heights, but he was not complaining, for even his small stature was useful in the cramped hides he had occupied, perched on pylons or on cliff faces after such birds as the Imperial Eagle in Spain or the Lammergeir. My memory of him is of an approachable man with a smiling face, skinning a rabbit to make a stew for his fellow bird-watchers in the simple bothy that had been put at their disposal in Fetlar. I recommend his neatly titled autobiographical book – *An Eye for a Bird*.

From his camera position I viewed the bird the way he saw it, the face almost cat-like, the bill looking like a nose in the round head. Eyes were silvery, and heavy lidded. Turning its head like a gun turret it stood immobile, its feathered claws gripping on rock. I'd learned that it could sit there for hours, doing nothing. I was in luck, when a small rabbit passed below it and disappeared over a slight crest.

At that, the white owl opened its wings and skimmed low, practically ski-ing over the crest, to reappear moments later with the rabbit and drop to ground, then stand covering it for five minutes, perhaps squeezing the life out of it, before flying with it to the nest. On its arrival, the browner female took off, flew around a bit, landed on the nest, picked up the remains of a small black rabbit, flew off a short distance, and dropped it.

The male wasn't having this. He pounced on the discarded prey and bore it back to the nest as if to caution, 'waste not, want not'.

In all, twenty young snowy owls were raised on Fetlar between 1967 and 1975, fourteen of them females. Sightings have been frequent in different parts of Scotland, but at the time of writing in 1994 there are no records of breeding success.

After Fetlar, I never saw Eric Hosking again. We had been in each other's company only that twice, in the Cairngorms and Shetland, yet I felt I had lost a true friend when I read of his death in 1991 at the age of eighty-one. It is probably true to say that in his sixty years as a bird photographer, no other person spent so much time behind the camera in cramped hides to get the pictures he was after – always putting the interest of his subjects first. He even spent his honeymoon in 1939 photographing golden eagles in Scotland. In his last years he felt modern technology was stripping bird photography of the craft and skill of earlier days. But he certainly never lagged behind and was always ahead of his competitors. He always reckoned that the owl which took an eye did him a good turn by helping him on to make a career.

18

Faroes
The Faraways

Shetland and the Island of Foula was actually a second-best choice for my
honeymoon with Rhona. We had hoped to get to the Faroes lying 200
miles north-west of our Northern Isles. We had been hoping to be taken
there by fishing trawler from Aberdeen – an offer by a friend with a part
share in the boat. However, as it was not available when we needed it, we
were glad to accept the lift in July 1961 when it was offered.

The vessel *Admiral Drake* was modern. We had comfortable berths, and
thirty-six hours out of Aberdeen the Mate was calling us up from below to
'smell the land', and look upon a monstrous wedge of cliff, clouds like
steam from a kettle, revealing huge terraces of rock and grass cleft by steep
gullies where waterfalls plunged over cliffs from ravines where beds of old
snow still lay. 'You'd be better to come with us to Iceland than climb
about these God-forsaken cliffs after birds,' said the Skipper at the wheel.

Tucked into a green oasis on a ledge above the Atlantic we could see
what looked like toy houses on the edge of tiny fields, terraced like
gardens, against the wild sweep of mountain-wall above. The gay colours
of the pink and white houses made a bright show indeed against such
bleakness. Then we found ourselves facing a milling throng of boats. The
boats were in pursuit of whales and trying to head off a bobbing school of
dolphin-like forms, triangular fins showing as they planed up and down.

What we were seeing was a 'grindarakstur', the driving of the whales by
anybody who could muster a boat. Under the leadership of a 'master' the
screen of boats was hoping to drive the whales down the fjord into
Klakksvig harbour. The whales were coming towards us, like car tyres
bobbing on the swell. A Faroese shouted that they had been hunting this
school of 'blackfish' for more than twenty-four hours, but could not turn
them. In fact they lost them that night, which was a blow to the
community, for these twenty-five-feet-long whales provide meat as tasty
as beef in a bare country which cannot support enough grazing animals.
(They are currently condemned for not observing the whaling ban.)

There was a stir of excitement when we pulled in to the head of the
fjord, since those armed with knives at the ready had expectations of the

whales arriving at any moment. The killing is said to be a real blood bath as the driven whales become stranded in shallow water, and their hunters fall upon them with clubs and knives, wading knee-deep in the crimson waters. The hunting is traditional, and regarded as good sport echoing back to more poverty-stricken times when the food was necessary.

Anyone will tell you that it was the big prices for fish during the war which brought prosperity to the Faeroese, who disregarded the German blockade and lost many lives en route to Aberdeen to bring fish for distribution to beleaguered Britain. With the profits, they had rebuilt the fishing fleet, and are not going to allow foreign trawlers to clean their home waters of fish, hard as it may be for British boats to be excluded from traditional fishing grounds. The view they take is that Britain lives ninety-eight per cent by means other than fishing. They live ninety-eight per cent by fishing.

In Klakksvig we now began making enquiries about how to get to Mykines, which is the remotest island of the group, often isolated by rough seas, so its people follow an ancient way of life that makes them largely independent of the outside world, as were our own St Kildans in their hey-day. So we took ship to Thorshavn, from where we were told a little ship called the *Ritan* would be making a special journey with cargo at five o'clock that evening. It was a stroke of luck, otherwise we would have been obliged to stay overnight on another island closer to Mykines.

The *Ritan* had still to load its cargo of timber when it nosed in to the quay, and to speed it on its way waiting passengers, including us, lent a hand on what was to be a rough journey on a cold evening, with clouds down on a steel grey sea, and with lots of pitch and toss in the grip of tide-races. When we hit the first one I was on deck and was getting drenched, but had no hope of getting down because I needed my two hands on the rail to avoid being swept overboard. After that we were invited into the wheelhouse.

Then after a bit I knew we must be getting close to land as the sea became crowded with swimming puffins, guillemots, razorbills and gliding fulmars. Soon speed was reduced as a black cliff loomed ahead, and blasts on the ship's horn were sounded. Now we were close enough to see a tiny opening below the cliff, the island harbour.

Soon, out of this mouth appeared a white skiff, powered by three pairs of oars, expertly wielded in the heavy swell to a position from which to throw us a rope. Thus secured, a human chain of crew and male passengers was formed to take aboard the cargo and those landing; then we were see-sawing into harbour where skiffs hung on ropes clear of the water and a crude staircase led steeply up to a sky-line sufficiently far off for us to be glad of help with our kit.

What a surprise, over this rocky tip, to see before us a green bowl of fertility where, glowing out of the creeping mist, were brightly painted houses ranged both sides of a gully with a fast-flowing stream in its depth! It reminded me of a Himalayan village. Where would be the best place to camp? We didn't have to, because the first man who spoke to us was a fellow Scot who knew me – Donald Baird from Kilmacolm – a twenty-six-year-old research zoologist who had attended one of my lectures, and as it happened, I had attended one of his.

Donald had come here in order to make a closer study of Leach's petrels than he had been able to do on North Rona and the Flannans, two of the most remote uninhabited islands in Scotland where these nocturnal birds nest. With the aid of a Nature Conservancy grant he had come here with his wife from the Hebridean island of Barra in April, just one week after his marriage, and this was their first home. So instead of pitching the tent we were guests for the night of Moira and Donald.

They were loving it here, and with Donald's help we were able to rent an empty house and get to know the islanders by personal introduction, so I was able to join the finest bird-catcher on the island and see how he used the famous 'fleyg', the twelve-foot pole with a net attached to snatch puffins out of the air high above the sea. These 'sea-parrots', nesting in burrows dug out from grassy ledges banding the great cliffs, have difficulties with the wind because of their short wings. Mykines wild-fowlers choose their stances on the cliffs where the birds returning from the sea are most likely to have trouble.

Eli Jacobsen, that day I was out with him, was in his element, perched above a sheer drop with his 'fleyg' held straight in front of him, the weight of three cricket bats. What a power and precision of eye and hand went into the drive of the net as he half-rose to his feet to intercept the flight of a wind-swept puffin. Whether using forward or back-hand movements, he caught fifty puffins in one hour, extricating birds from the net as well as getting them inside it.

He told me that in a good day for him, but not for the birds, he could take from 500 to 700, and in former times the main work of summer was to obtain enough birds to salt down for the winter. This, with dried fish and sun-dried mutton, was the mainstay of diet. But times have changed. Puffins are now exported to other islands whose populations have no time for bird-catching because they are crewmen on trawlers and make a lot of money. So selling puffins enabled the Mykines folk to buy Danish bacon or other imported goods.

Eli wanted me to see how other birds are caught, and that afternoon he lowered his heavy boat down the cliff to make a raid on a guillemot ledge accessible only by sea. Even getting through the narrow harbour, with heavy swell breaking on the skerries, called for skill; then we were leaping out of the heaving craft to climb 200 feet to where a narrow ledge rose obliquely and sensationally upward. As it was hardly more than a shelf across the rock face and, furthermore, was overlaid with deep and sticky guano, footing was none too secure.

I don't think Eli was too happy, but the guillemots when we reached the catching place were packed like little penguins row on row, sharp bills pointing and white shirt fronts out. The weapon this time was a long pole with a nylon noose on its end. The method was to reach out very slowly with the pole and drop the noose over an outstretched neck. The growling of the birds, and the crying of thousands of kittiwakes, affected catcher and watcher, and after a few birds had been bagged we made our way down.

What I was surprised to hear was that a fowler can go to any recognised catching place provided he gives half his catch to the owner of that piece of cliff, for here on Mykines the high ground and the cliffs are divided amongst the people in relationship to the amount of land they own in the cultivated area known as the Bour. Each season had its task, from lambing time when the kittiwakes lay their eggs, to catching time for puffins and guillemots, followed by the raiding of the gannet ledges for fat gugas before they leave the nest.

Mist and drizzle is what the Mykines people regard as Faeroese sunshine, so that men and women go out and make hay in it, clad in what is standard wear in lieu of a jacket, beautifully knitted woollen jerseys. Loads of peat are carried from the moors by head band, as in the Himalaya, sensible when everything has to be back-packed over steep, rough, or rocky ground.

But fishing prosperity from the Second World War years onwards had brought depopulation problems to this last bastion of an old way of life; until now, as on Foula, there is an imbalance of old to young. People are better off with Government pensions for the aged and high wages for the able-bodied at the Greenland fishing, but this itself threatens the way of life on an island which needs young people to stay at home for the continuance of the community.

The ideal compromise on Mykines used to be one where the young men went to sea for six months and spent the other six months at home. Then there were always enough men to go over the cliffs on ropes to collect kittiwakes' eggs in the spring, to work the peats, build houses, or haul loads from the jetty; while in autumn the greatest proof of manhood was to dangle over a cliff on the end of a 200-foot rope, in darkness, to catch the young gannets asleep on the airiest ledges on the Faeroes.

As it was, when we were there in 1961, the Mykines folk were delighted to have another pair of willing hands among them in the person of Donald Baird. Donald's field work took place on Mykines Holm – a separate island reached by crossing the Atlantic by high steel bridge. I will not forget the traverse of the Rogvukollur, where a hand-rail goes along the edge of a cliff and petrels flit round one's face like bats; mostly storm petrels giving way to Leach's petrels on gentler ground where their nesting burrows fringe an Arctic ternery. The terns are parasitic on the puffins which crowd this area, and pick up any small fish dropped by puffins en route to their burrows. Two o'clock in the morning was the peak hour for mist-netting petrels, when the air is filled with these delightful and most oceanic of birds. In my diary I wrote:

> Dawn was breaking as we came back over the ridge and through puffin-land where these birds were snoring below ground. The high tops were in mist and a ring of milky surf combed the foot of the black rocks plunging down on each side of the village. In their beds lay a people unique in Europe, and our hope was that they would continue to live here as a community, and not be forced to give up because the younger generation no longer wanted the old way of life.

Eli Jacobsen was not only the most outstanding bird-catcher on the island: in religious services he was also the Pastor, and at fifty-five years of age preached the value of community living in preference to leaving it to make big money on deep sea trawlers. He was a steadying force on the island, but sadly, he was killed not long after our visit, and the story I got from Donald Baird, in a letter, was that Eli had been on the cliffs trying to move sheep from a dangerous place, when the ledge that he was following high above the sea collapsed, and he fell to his death.

Tourists holiday-making in the Faeroes can now fly by helicopter to Mykines, where there is a hotel for those who want to stay for a few days. But they will not see the way of life that we saw. It is good to know, however, that the island is still being farmed in a sustainable way, and it is reassuring to know that some natives still want to live on isolated islands of noble scenery like Foula and the Faeroes where seas between can truly roar.

19

Corsica
The Scented Isle

It was the lure of islands that took Rhona and me, in 1962, to Corsica at Easter with our camping kit. From the crinkled sea we were suddenly swooping down over hills green with the spring. Then, as the wings of the ancient plane tilted, we had a television-screen view of a curve of bay panning to orchards of apple blossom, swinging up to mountain tops where threads of road climbed to dizzy villages. In that whirling moment I felt a surge of elation, for this was an island I had always longed to visit and I had the feeling we were not going to be disappointed.

We had left Glasgow airport at 8.20 am, flying in a Caravelle of Air France at 29,000 feet, arriving in Nice at mid-day. By contrast to the posh Caravelle, we were ushered into a real bone-shaker full of peasant Corsicans, and felt lucky to have obtained the connection, for we had been told in Glasgow that there was little likelihood of our finding an air service to Ajaccio in early April. So in one hour, instead of nineteen hours by sea, we were landing in the birthplace of Napoleon. At 7.45 next morning we were on a bus, climbing from the sea and mounting through thickets of dazzling blackthorn blossom, but losing the sunshine as we zig-zagged upwards into mist. I was feeling a bit squeamish with all the twists and turns.

Then the world began solidifying about 2,500 feet. Above us was blue sky; beyond the mouth of a gorge, sharp snow-peaks spiked the horizon, and the roadsides were hedged by three-foot-high white-blossoming heath. A short distance on, we dismounted at the mountain town of Corte. The hotel – one star – fixed us up with a room at once, so in the rich light of mid-afternoon we were walking up the Restonica Gorge, looking back on the houses piled one on top of another. Below us tumbled the river, its torrent as white as the blossom overhanging the terraced fields. Serin finches seemed to be everywhere, singing their wheezy jingles, while crag martins darted over our heads.

Our appetites whetted by what we had seen, we sorted out our camp kit and made plans to leave early in the morning, by hired taxi, to the limit of the driving road, at 3,000 feet, in a canyon booming with the sound of

212

water. This gorge forms a natural pass through the mountains by the Lac de Melo, but the road above our camping platform had been swept away by an avalanche whose cone of snow had blocked the river, and huge boulders lay above the place we would have to cross in order to climb Monte Rotondo, 8,400 feet.

After reconnaissance, and a pleasant day exploring the forest in company with ring ousels and alpine choughs, we were away early next morning enjoying the red flush of alpenglow against a green sky. Down we went to the snow-bridge, then walked on a grassy track zig-zagging up a pine-clad shoulder for 2,000 feet, until quite suddenly we were faced by an icy corrie where step-cutting began. Ahead of us the black tooth of our peak looked tantalisingly close, flanked by rows of pinnacles each side, but as rope length followed rope length, it never seemed to get nearer. Meantime an advancing sea of grey-black clouds was swallowing up the valleys, and flakes of snow began to fall.

I had no intention of turning back now, not with the best bit of the climb before us – a steep gully in the final crag. We were on top at 4 pm so the climb had taken eight hours, all of it full of interest. Among the splendid Corsican pines, 150 feet and 200 feet high, mistle thrushes had been singing, greater spotted woodpeckers were distributed almost to the snow-line, and I'd seen my first wheatears of 1962 just below the snow, among dwarf birch and alders.

Now there was no time to linger, but push down the steps we had cut in the icy snow until it was possible to glissade on our backsides on open slopes free of rocks, to cross the snow-bridge over the river at dusk, climb up to the tent and get the Primus on for welcome soup and tea. What a night of rain followed! Waterfalls becoming noisier, and now and again there was the crash of rock-falls. We feared we might be flooded out, camped on such thin soil, but the ground held firm and I suspect was the only dry spot in the Restonica Gorge when we lifted our camp in the morning and pushed down to Corte. In the village we were just in time to catch a bus to Bastia in the north.

We found friendly people here among the orchards and orange groves, but in the mist and rain I felt the southern coastal marshes on the east side of the mountain could be more rewarding. We boarded a bus and simply stayed on it until we came to Cateriggio where I signalled the driver to let us off. Here was a sluggish river and scrublands bordering the Mediterranean. As there was no place to stay, we kept on walking. It was no hardship, with corn buntings jangling, tortoises and lizards by the roadsides and, overhead, lesser kestrels, easily recognised by their unspotted reddish backs.

Then we came to Aleria, an aloof settlement of tall houses enclosing a single street, and asked an elderly lady if it would be possible to find a place to sleep. Instantly she despatched a small boy to take us to a house where we were given an upstairs room with white-washed walls, wash-basin and comfortable bed. From up there we commanded the marshlands, and I could hardly wait to get to them!

Everything was so unexpected on each side of a firm dyke edged by eucalyptus trees, but hemmed by wetland: staccato bursts from a melodious warbler; the flash of a pied bird that became a woodchat shrike, cinnamon head and neck showing vividly; ashy-headed wagtails; nightingales, blackcaps; spotted and pied flycatchers, and the sight of a tiny falcon flash past, mount skyward, and circle round. Through the glass I could see it was catching large insects with its feet, grabbing them without checking speed. The rufus trousers told it was a Hobby. It was feeding young in a nest high in a eucalyptus tree, and we could hear them squealing as they were fed.

The finest part of the Etang lay ahead, in open salt-marsh where we heard the ringing calls of greenshank. Near a trio of them were woodsandpipers and ruffs, one of them in breeding dress of black chest ornamentation. There were Kentish plovers, black winged stilts and hosts of duck – garganey, pintail, shoveller, mallard and wigeon. Suddenly there was an alarmed scatter of birds: the culprit, a marsh harrier skimming the reeds, its creamy head conspicuous. We saw three kinds of herons, grey, purple and night, by the Tavignano River where snow-white egrets strutted around some cattle.

The broad river was jumping with fish and swarming with swallows: there must have been thousands of them darting about. I had the suspicion that the sheer quantity of birds of so many kinds was due to the bad weather of the last three days driving them down, when otherwise they would have passed on. I felt reasonably satisfied that this was so when we visited the marsh next morning, in sunshine and superb visibility, and there were few birds.

For compensation we now had a view over the sunlit village to the snow peaks. We walked far that day in woodlands looking for the unique Corsican nuthatch. We failed, but we did get a flight of six brilliant golden orioles before breaking through to the Mediterranean sand to splash along in our bare feet for a couple of miles. It was Good Friday, and we found it hard to believe that only a few days before we had been camped in an alpine gorge where icicles hung from the trees.

Corsica was a place to come back to, and seven years later, in the month of May, Len Lovat and I camped below the Punta di Ferro in the range known as the Aiguilles di Bavella, and every day for a week looked out from our tent at 4,000 feet on the red ball of the sun rising above the Mediterranean.

Generally we were awake by 4.30 am and away as soon as possible so as to avoid being fried on the granite. The mornings were so beautiful, wandering through alpine meadows and gullies spiked with Corsican

214

pines, to rocky places that could be described as hanging gardens. Also, without guide-books, there was the joy of exploration, finding our own ways. This was rock-climbing enjoyment where our eyes for a route didn't always work out.

We had hired a Renault car, and after a week on this range drove north on the corkscrew roads for the highest peaks on the island, for mixed climbing on rock and snow. Palia Orba is the Matterhorn of Corsica and, restocked with food, we camped below it a few days later.

Pine trees, a roaring river, green-sward for our tent, no one but ourselves in the glen, Palia Orba before us, and we were away at six in the morning to storm the bastion. Instead of a mixed climb we were surprised, once we had negotiated two red-rock towers, to find its upper part very like the snow-plastered crags of Ben Nevis in April, when Scotland's highest summit is still in part-winter condition.

Soon we were hacking a way up the frozen snow, covering the rocks, and gradually, from cold blue shadow, we crept into warm sunshine and took to the clean rocks to reach the summit at mid-day. One peak in particular held our eyes, the famous Tafonato, a narrow pinnacled blade whose perpendicularity is pierced by a window through which we could see daylight.

We visited it two days later, after a technically hard rock climb on the Cinque Fratti, and a traverse of its five pinnacles. From up there we had the sight of two golden eagles being mobbed by an attacking force of squealing alpine choughs and a croaking raven.

Now for the Tafonato. Everything about it had a special aura, even the take-off point from the narrow col – a veritable neck of snow cornice between red pinnacles. The beginning was, in fact, a bergshrund – a miniature crevasse formed by the snow-ice shrinking away from the rock wall. We had one anxious moment here when a boulder whizzed past us from above.

We waited, listening, then feeling that this was just a one-off rock-fall, we stepped across the gap between snow tongue and rock, moved up unroped, and were soon whooping with delight, so sound and bristling with holds was the steep rock.

We went straight for the great hole gashing the upper mountain and arrival on its sill was an exciting moment, looking down on a new valley, vertically, below. What a situation, on a rock peak so thin that from the window to the summit we wound right round the mountain, finishing on a superb wall that was airy rock climbing at its best, near vertical, and with small perfectly shaped holds for toes and hands!

There was an unexpected moment of magic on the way down, when at the window, I heard an absent-minded whistle which I thought was from Len and he thought was from me. It was a glissando of four notes – whee-oowhee-ooo' – then the maker flew past in flash of lavender and crimson,

215

and like a butterfly landed near us, to be joined by two others – wall creepers, birds I had last seen in the Himalaya at around 7,000 feet in Nepal. What a delight they were to watch in this setting, dove grey on chest and back, wings red edged with black, white spotted on the primaries, short black tails and longish curved bills, and black throats. Constantly as they climbed they flocked their wings, as if to show their red flashes.

Our last climbs involved a bivouac high in a corrie of high crags and snow-fields. I slept little, because the night was too perfect, with the brightness of the stars and the Milky Way like lace. Also there was a half moon poised on the crest of a jagged ridge, and as it dropped, the pinnacles were edged in halo. With only a light sleeping bag, I was glad of my quilted jacket. We got the eggs on the boil at 4 am to be away at five.

Above us was the Punta Minuta, 8,800 feet, no more than four hours away, up rock ribs and frozen snow. From its summit we looked down on Calvi and across the glen to Paglia Orba and Tafonato, which gave a feeling of intimacy with this wild country where we were the only climbers.

In all, we climbed ten peaks and failed on one after attempts on two different days. We just could not find any route to the top. But that is what exploration in an unguide-book area is about. We were lucky with the weather, which broke down just after we got back to camp from our last climb.

We enjoyed our evening meal all the more amid the crash of thunder, lightning flashing and rain battering the canvas. It was still raining next morning as we packed our soaked tent, and with regret, motored to Bastia to hand in our hired car. We had a lot to remember: the sight of a lammergeyer, like a small aeroplane, on nine-foot wings, with narrow wedge tail – a vulture known as the 'bone breaker' to get at the marrow. Then there was the sight of a pair of golden eagles being mobbed by an attacking force of squealing alpine choughs and a croaking raven. As for alpine plants, I have never seen such a flowering, not even in the Dolomites.

20

Tales of a Grandfather

'Can you think of a nice unclimbed gully?' Bob Grieve queried as we discussed where we might go for the weekend. 'It's a daft notion, but since becoming a Grandpa, I've had a great notion to do a new route and call it Grandfather's Gully.'

The mountain that came immediately to my mind was Garbh Bheinn of Ardgour. But what I had in mind was not a gully but a buttress of that rocky hill. 'Let's go for that,' I said. 'It looks like being a scorcher and the rocks will be dry.'

'It's nineteen years since I was on that hill, and I've aye been meaning to go back.' So off we drove in Bob's Dormobile, travelling de luxe, with seats in the back that convert to bunks and a galley unit, sink, gas cooker, plate racks, food cupboards and a table to make you feel you are in a restaurant. 'A big change since the days when we knocked about the hills with nothing more than an old army blanket, a tea-can and an army pack,' said Bob, grinning, as we hummed northwards up the western shore of Loch Lomond for Glencoe and the Ballachulish ferry.

We can never pass through that glen without a stop, and who should be standing at the very spot where we would have stopped to pay homage, but Bob's best pal, Calum Finlayson, back that morning from Denmark, yet here he was in Glencoe heading for Appin. He had been over there, he told us, singing Gaelic songs with a team of artists from the Glasgow Police, and we chaffed him on his new appointment as Superintendent of the Southern Division.

Bob told me how they had first met. He was drumming up by a wee fire, making pancakes, when another youth came over a knoll. 'Smells good,' said the stranger. 'Try them,' said Bob, holding out one straight from the pan. Together they scoffed the lot, and set off. Walking or talking they have been companions ever since, never getting into a rut by living adventurously and 'getting on' in the more conventional sense to reach top jobs in their professions. 'A pair of softies!' I said, for he too was driving a bothy on wheels exactly like Bob's.

Then down we went in convoy to the ferry, and who should we meet

217

but Jock Nimlin, founder of the Ptarmigan Mountaineering Club, on his way to Kintail with a National Trust Adventure Camp party from an approved school. Jock was a crane driver on the Clyde shipyards until the spring of 1963 when he became Assistant Master of Works for the National Trust for Scotland.

Brown as a berry he looked, not so very different from my first memory of him when he led the Ptarmigan Club on one foray after another, crossing to Arran in a home-made canoe, or forcing sensational rock routes on the Cobbler.

Our ways parted once we had left the ferry, since we were crossing the Corran Strait into Ardgour, a quieter world of narrow roads and Hebridean peace. By a shingly beach overlooking across the water to Ben Nevis we drew up in the car, raised the ventilator hood and got the supper cooking. Yes it was comfortable, with window space to give you the feeling you were out in the open, on one side the moon turning silver, and on the other, the soft pink of a cloudless sky.

'This reminds me of the Alps,' said Bob as we walked up Glen Iubhair next morning, 'the sun's so hot so early.' We had a fair way to go, but at last the twin buttresses hove into view. You can never judge rocks until you get your feet on them. 'Oh boy!' muttered Bob, more to himself than to me, when he saw the lovely textured rock, steep and bristling with holds. 'Will you do me the honour of letting me lead it?'

There was only one answer to that! He tied on the rope and swung up, neatly and confidently, hands low, feet always close together as he made use of every excrescence. Soon he had put a hundred feet between us, had found a belay and was bidding me to come on. It was the kind of pure balance climbing that I like, and from Bob's position there were two routes: straight up by an overhang, or an evasion left on less intimidating rock.

He chose the overhang, carefully testing holds and warning me of a loose block. The climbing was hard, as was another overhang higher up, but after 350 feet we could claim that Grandfather's Buttress was a worthy route, leading to another, harder than the first, which we named Grand-daughter's Buttress. From this climb we were able to continue on rock all the way to the summit of Beinn Bheag, 2,275 feet. The heat had taken some of the puff out of us, and as there was nothing in the way of distant views, due to haze, we had only one thought, to get down into the corrie, find a deep pool and dive into it. Ah, that was bliss! Tip-toeing out along the waterfall, then plopping into the deep pot to emerge and sun ourselves on the grassy bank.

It was already five o'clock, but we didn't want to spoil the day by rushing. There was time to find nests of sandpiper and oyster catcher, to cook a meal, drink a glass of beer, and enjoy the drive through banks of June flowers to Corran Ferry.

Shortly after that, I went to Glen More Lodge in the Cairngorms to record a BBC radio programme with Glasgow children who were being given a fortnight or a month of outdoor education in a splendid setting of pine forest, loch and mountains. To most of them the Highlands came as a revelation, an open door to a life of adventure. They were full of it, telling me of their rock climbs, their great treks over the hills carrying camping kit, the deer, the snow buntings they had seen, and how they had been forced by mist to steer by compass to find their way back down.

I liked the impression a boy gave me: 'The whole countryside looks as if it had been picked up and dropped again, and sort of all scattered over the place, boulders strewn, obviously relics, the glaciers and such-like.' Another boy said: 'Most of the time down here you've got someone to help you if you're in difficulties, but up there you're all on your own and you've to use your skill and judgement.' I enjoyed hearing this respect for the hills, and I was impressed by the width of training given, and by the free and easy atmosphere.

Rhona and I, over the years, held an annual outing for school children, and that year when we went to Ben Venue in the Trossachs, it was voted the best yet. 'Why do you like it more than Ben Ledi or Ben Lomond?' I asked young veteran climber, Diane Rankin. 'Because it's steeper,' she lisped, words of a born mountaineer. It certainly was steep, by the face above Loch Katrine where hands had to be used in places, and great were the slides on the way down. What youngsters like is action, plenty of it, so the job of whipping them in has to be well done. In many village outings over the years, to most of the high hills forming the Highland Boundary fault, we have had not one accident. It is not the scenery children remember; it is the fun they had, playing at a waterfall, or the great place where they had their picnic.

Weather is a factor too. Better to cancel when it involves children than take a risk of their getting into trouble. In fact, just after our outing to Ben Venue a neighbour suggested to Rhona and me that we join him in his yacht for a sail on Loch Lomond, land on the island of Inchcailloch and sleep out under the stars. However, we were so late in getting to the island I suggested sleeping on board, tight fit as it would be for three on his small deck.

Because of the sweltering humidity, the unusual heat which was almost tropical, and the fact that the midges were desperate, I felt it would be a mistake to go ashore. As it was impossible to get a full leg stretch, the night seemed very long. I must have dozed, for suddenly I was awake, listening to a strange rustling – strange because there was no breath of wind. Then my sleepy head grasped its meaning as the rustling got louder. 'Rain,' I yelled. 'Get the tarpaulin over.' We were just in time, as an absolute deluge struck, rattling and bouncing on the stretched sheet.

What I remember with most pleasure was the sail home, silently gliding in the grey of the morning in cool air.

Before the weather forecasts were anything like as good as they are now, thanks to satellite pictures, I used to get long-distance telephone-calls from English climbers asking me about snow and ice conditions. If I said they were cast iron for crampons and ice-axe, they would head north for Glencoe or Ben Nevis.

When Alf Gregory, my film partner in Morocco, phoned me from Blackpool asking about conditions, I told him I had never seen them better: low temperatures with hardly any wind, and spoke of a marvellous time I'd had ski-ing down from the top of Ben Lomond on as fine a crisp winter day as I had ever seen. I told him that on Deeside, Adam Watson had skied eight miles across his local hills on hard-packed snow, and had described the conditions as Canadian, minimum temperature 7 degrees F, and the maximum of 14, the lowest he could recollect.

I urged Alf to bring his skis as well as his climbing kit. What did happen however was that by the time Alf left Blackpool on 14th February 1968, the snow had spread south, disorganising railway lines everywhere and creating chaos on the roads. At Shap, Alf and his pal Jack were told the road was getting to be impassable and our visitors arrived exhausted with driving and ready for bed. Theirs was the only car that got through.

In our house events began moving about midnight, when the wind shifted to north-west and we were finding it difficult to sleep, as the whistle of the wind in the chimney became a shriek that didn't die away because one gust followed another.

I slept at last, to be jerked awake by loud cracks and repeated falls of stuff down the chimney which I took to be soot. There was no electricity in the morning, and Alf refrained from any sarcastic remarks when I took him his breakfast, cooked on the Primus stove. Since his stormy days on Everest's South Col he can sleep anywhere. Neither he nor Jack seemed to have noticed anything abnormal about the night.

Rhona, however, was noticing that village folk who normally pass our house at day-break were stopping and looking up at our roof. Stepping outside we saw why. Our chimney, and its stonework, was precariously balanced, having been pulled by a power pole which itself was being supported by the electric cable attached to our chimney head. As for our roof-ridge, it had been stripped of lead and many slates.

But not until we climbed Duncryne Hill did we realise just what a pounding its trees had taken, bowled over, snapped off or waving amputated limbs ready for severing. Holly, rowan, oak, ash and beech had been torn up by the roots, while other trees has acted as sledge hammers for those beside them. Owl, buzzard, spotted flycatcher, woodpecker, tree creeper and many another bird would have to locate new nesting places.

In the village we learned that all roads out were blocked; that train services were cancelled; that Glasgow was as battered as Clydebank in the blitz, millions of pounds of damage having been done. Hundreds of chimney heads and roofs were torn off, causing death and injury and rendering hundreds homeless. One who was in a multi-storey block that night told me it was terrifying, and that furniture and chairs were actually moving in the swaying building.

The height of the storm was around four in the morning with gusts of over 100 mph when the wind-measuring machine on Lowther Hill in Lanarkshire was blown down. But the industrial belt in the Clyde-Forth valley was worst hit because of the funnelling effect of the wind that enabled the gusts to deliver a stronger punch, blowing down a 500-ton dockside crane as well as two 370-foot electricity pylons at Erskine which fell into the Clyde.

Without light and heat, vacuum cleaner, television and radio, you realise how much you depend on these marvellous conveniences for cooking and cleaning and for entertainment. I had always wondered why our cottage was called 'Fir Tree'. Now I learned that it was because there had been a big fir wood opposite which was blown down in 1926, as were the larches which used to crown the top of Duncryne Hill.

The year 1892 saw the greatest freeze of Loch Lomond that anyone could remember, repeated in 1963 when Douglas Scott and I skated from Drymen Bridge down the frozen River Endrick and across Balmaha Bay. Then, when the loch froze over completely, Alex MacFarlane, who normally made his postal delivery to Inchmurrin island by boat, walked from Balmaha over the ice with his head through the rungs of a ladder, so that if he went through he would be supported. That was a wonderful winter. Rhona made the most of it because the school toilets were frozen resulting in children being sent home early and she had a lot of time off.

So we enjoyed the windless sunny days and the very hard night frosts. A highlight that February was an ascent of Ben Lomond on ski with my old friend Douglas Scott, while Rhona and some of her Ladies' Scottish Climbing Club friends broke a snow-trail on foot. Conditions were perfect, the loch glass calm, and on the mountain dry powder snow on a hard base.

Our run down was pure bliss, feelings of being disembodied so smoothly the skis turned by simply changing the weight from one to the other, and continued all the way down the west face to the loch shore at Rowardennan.

21

Island of May-Be

Until that bad weather in Corsica which caused us to abandon the cloud-covered mountains for the marshes of Aleria, I had seen only one fall of migrating birds forced down by storm, and it was on the Isle of May in the Firth of Forth situated at the open mouth of the estuary and renowned since 1907, in spring and autumn, as a place where mighty rushes of birds could occur.

The island is a pancake of grass and rock, one and a half miles long and half a mile wide, once the home of missionaries and monks, and occupied only by lighthouse keepers in November 1954 – a time with a risk attached to it of being storm-stayed. In fact the weather was too good: sunny days of marvellous visibility and nights of brilliant moon, ideal conditions for migrating birds, but bad for the ornithologist.

A boat was supposed to be coming from Anstruther to take us back to the mainland on the 9th, but on the 8th the wind shifted east with rain, and backed south-west, and in the morning we looked out on a raging sea with binoculars in the faint hope of seeing a boat. Then quite suddenly we began spotting birds at wave-top level beating against the wind, sometimes lost in the trough of the waves. At the same time we were seeing blackbirds scuffling about near us where earlier there had been nothing.

Hurrying to open the bird traps we were excited by the variety we were seeing: starlings, fieldfares, redwings, woodcock, snipe, bramblings, and a mysterious finch like a crossbill, but rusty coloured with a black tail, ash-grey back, and with a pale wing-bar, the breast with a cinnamon tinge. We jotted down its description, then concentrated on catching tired birds, weighing, measuring and ringing them.

How glad we were that our boat could not reach us that day when, by lamplight, we went through the Observatory species books and found our bird fitted perfectly the description of a pine grosbeak, never before recorded as far as we knew. We resolved to search for it first thing in the morning, and incredibly the bird came to the trap and hopped in. Thus we held in our hands *Pinicola Enucleator*, a bird of the northern forests of Finland and the Soviet Union, that must have been caught up in the same weather system that brought the birds we had been ringing from Scandinavia.

Since the previous autumn we noted that some 1,400 birds of various kinds had been ringed by approximately one hundred observers, and it was interesting to see the results of other years: of a starling ringed on the May recovered two years later in Norway, of meadow pipits from France, of pied wagtails from Cardiff, of a wood warbler from Algiers, or song thrushes from Spain and Portugal, redwings from the Frisian Islands, a wheatear from Sweden, robins from Norway and Portugal, sandwich terns from the Gold Coast and Liberia, lesser blackbacked gulls from Morocco and Lisbon.

One looks at birds differently when one can visualise their journeys over desert and seas or mountain ranges, marvelling how their stories have been unravelled by ornithologists. It was two local ladies from Fife, Miss E.V. Baxter and Miss L.J. Rintoul, living near Largo, who were first to discover the riches of the Isle of May when they went there in September 1907 and stayed with the lighthouse keepers for fourteen days, getting several first records for the Forth.

That was the beginning of a series of spring and autumn visits lasting until 1933, recording the movements of migrating birds for as long as six weeks at a time. They posed a new and revolutionary proposition, now widely accepted in the world of ornithology, though disregarded by experts of that time. It was that wind-drift and not choice is the factor that causes birds to cast up on coasts and islands – relating bird movements to the weather environment.

I got to know these ladies in 1938 when they were joint-Presidents of the Scottish Ornithologists' Club, when that club had fewer than forty members, who used to meet alternately in Edinburgh and Glasgow. That is how I got to know George Waterston, already mentioned in connection with the snowy owls on Fetlar. George was the go-getter of a band of Edinburgh schoolboys who carried on the work of the Fife ladies, by unlocking some funds from those in authority and setting up the first co-operatively managed bird migration study centre in Britain when they were given a hut on the May, and later the disused Low Lighthouse.

Over the years I had got to know these pioneering schoolboys, and made a particular friend of George Waterson's cousin, Pat Sandeman, through sharing a common interest in golden eagles. But I had never been to the Isle of May with him, and in 1989, when my wife and I had booked for a crossing, I phoned him inviting him to come along, adding that if he could face the early morning rise we would pick him up in Bridge of Allan and drive him to Anstruther harbour.

Everything was in our favour that mid-summer day: sunshine, only a slight swell on the sea, and it was great to see the island grow ever closer. Soon, boatman Andy Hughes was slowing his launch, *QE2*, under the western cliffs so that passengers could enjoy the crowded bird ledges above, while below us birds were fluttering and diving to get out of our bow wave: puffins, guillemots, razorbills, shags, kittiwakes.

Next we had a frolic of porpoises, then rounding the south-west side of the island heads of bobbing Atlantic seals, glassy eyes examining us, and soon we were slipping into the Kirk Haven and tying up at its far end. Now we scrambled over the yellow lichened rocks to St Adrian's Chapel, once a place of pilgrimage visited by Kings and Queens of Scotland. James IV came many times to the May, not always to pray, but to shoot birds. Other pilgrims came for miraculous cures.

In the year 1837 a boat, the *St Johns*, carried sixty-five souls of all ages in July on an annual excursion from Cellardyke, near Anstruther, to the Isle of May on a summer day with white waves booming, oarsmen pulling in to Kirk Haven jetty, 'when a surge takes hold of the boat, lifts it, and pins it on a rock skerry. All is confusion and terror; the air is rent with the shrieks of women and children . . . the boat rolls from the skerry and sinks like a stone in deep water. Heroes plunge to the rescue . . . Yet after all the gallant deeds were done, thirteen sank to arise no more.'

Who was to blame for the tragedy? Skipper John Sutherland was charged with culpable homicide, but acquitted since no fisherman could say he had done anything wrong. With that tragedy ended what used to be a greatly anticipated annual excursion.

Moving up past the Chapel, Pat rememberd that there used to be a village here, for in his searches in the past he had found a commemoration stone in a hollow which read 'Here lyes John Wishart who died in March 1730, aged 45'. Said Pat, 'He may have been a fisherman, or a smuggler, or concerned with using lights to lure ships to their doom, for this was the first landfall for ships coming into the Forth.'

Climbing west from here, and seeing rabbits, descended from those farmed by the monks in 1329, we tried to visualise the scene when this area had had plots of grain and vegetables, grazing sheep and a few milk cows that had helped the holy community to survive.

Almost abruptly the grass comes to an end on the edge of a cliff, and we were level with two rock stacks known as the Angel and the Pilgrim. Just beyond was the neat curve of Pilgrim's Haven, with its stone-lined well of water, good to drink except when contaminated by salt spume borne on a beating wind.

Moving inland to sit with our backs against the rocks among bladder campion in white flower, we got out the tea flasks and sandwiches for a picnic, glad to be on what could almost have been a South Sea island with its warmth and colour. It set us thinking of artist Keith Brockie who spent the four seasons of the year here, painting and sketching the scenery and wild life of the May and from it producing his richly creative book *One Man's Island*.

The Isle of May has as many place names as a suburb: Prior's Walk, Monk's Brae, Black Heugh – a ravine impounded by a dam to make a loch at whose far end is the engine house. Leave the loch and you are on Fluke Street and facing a climb up Palpitation Brae to the massive Tower, whose light is 240 feet above the sea, with accommodation for three families.

Just east of these modern buildings is the remnant of the very first Scottish lighthouse, its right-hand corner worn away by swinging pans of coal to set ablaze and its flame acting as a light for all ships coming out of the Firths of Forth and Tay. On a stormy night it could consume as much as three tons, and was in use for 150 years.

It was while taking a direct route down to the bird observatory that we were accosted by summer warden Steve Holloway to turn us back.

He held out his hand when he saw me, since we were old acquaintances. He had come to warn us that we were on the brink of an important study area for puffins, and that walking over the ground could cause the collapse of some nesting burrows. Evidence of the researchers was indicated by the amount of food for the young below ground, but they would soon be leaving for the open sea.

As I was introducing him to Pat the air suddenly filled with flighting puffins. 'You are lucky,' said Steve. 'That rarely happens except at sunset.' I asked if he had an approximate figure for their numbers. He reckoned that 18,500 burrows were occupied, with perhaps two or three thousand non-breeders. The puffins dive so quickly into their burrows we think it's a safety measure against predatory gulls.'

Counting seabirds is an exhausting job, demanding hours of concentration and working to a system, so we appreciated what lay behind Steve's figures for other birds. Guillemots – 8,500 to 9,000 pairs, kittiwakes 7,500 nests, herring gulls 1,600 nests, shags 1,700 pairs, eider ducks 680 nests, fulmars 200 nests. Terns were not doing so well as of yore – only 215 arctics and 65 common.

When we began to talk about migration, Steve's eyes opened wide when Pat told him of how his gang from Edinburgh Academy had been playing football against the lighthouse keepers in the autumn of 1933 when the goalie noticed an odd bird. It was identified as a red-spotted blue throat, and was the first of six seen before the game ended. During the previous night of drizzle and south-east wind, birds had fluttered round the lighthouse beam until dawn. It was to be Pat's first experience of a rush of migrants.

This gang of boys had named themselves the Inverleith Field Club, because it was in George Waterston's home in Inverleith Terrace that they determined they would band together for a weekend at each of the four seasons, New Year, spring, summer and autumn, birding by day and having sing-songs at night. The more serious survivors formed a private group and named it the Midlothian Ornithological Club, to which it was an honour to belong.

Alas there are no lightkeepers on the May now. Their three-and-a-half centuries of service, dating back to 1636, has come to an end. In 1989 the Tower light became fully automatic, and ownership has passed from the Northern Lighthouse Board to the body that was the Nature Conservancy Council, but is now Scottish National Heritage. Visitors, however, are not unwelcome as long as they stick to prescribed paths. Naturally we preferred the old freedom to do our own thing and act responsibly.

The eleven log books filled since the Observatory opened in 1934 tell many dramatic tales not only about birds but about shipwrecks. Thirty-nine ships have come to grief on the rocks of the May, half of them ending up as total wrecks; yet in only two cases was there loss of life. Near the Kirk Haven two were drowned and two saved in 1889; and on the North Ness, in fog, two drowned and four were saved. During our visit Greenpeace conservation warriors were carrying out an exercise with rubber boats and skin-diving gear.

On hearing that I had been to the Isle of May, Mrs Jean Baird wrote telling me she was born on the island in 1903, when it housed seven lightkeepers, one of them her father William Crowe. 'I left it aged six months when my father was transferred to Girdleness Lighthouse near Aberdeen. From there we went to the Point of Ayre in the Isle of Man whence in November 1909 we were sent to Muckle Flugga in Shetland – a journey which took nine days from start to finish, as far north as you could go. We were there for almost ten years as the Great War broke out and we were asked to stay. While at the Flugga my father sent regular notes on bird migration to a periodical called *The Scottish Naturalist* and in appreciation received a beautiful bird book with an inscription and the signatures of Evelyn V. Baxter and Leonora Jeffery Rintoul, the two Fife ladies you mentioned.'

I responded to that interesting letter by suggesting we might do a broadcast together talking about then and now. We spoke on the telephone but her modesty prevented her from doing it.

22

Snatching the Sleeve of Today

> Since happiness is most often met by those
> who have learned to live in every moment of
> the present, none has such prodigal opportunities
> of attaining that art as the traveller.
>
> Tom Longstaff, *This is my Voyage*

This great explorer was to enlarge on this in a letter he sent to us that we were lucky to receive on our way back to Ranikhet; lucky because we would have missed it but for being delayed for another day owing to torrential rain. His words of wisdom stayed in my mind in my future journeyings. One of his paragraphs read:

> There is no more lovely country in all Himachal. You have seen the best – and now will understand what I mean by 'living in the present'; just forget all before-and-after and soak the moment into you so that it will never come out. Just travel is the thing. Number your red letter days by camps not by summits (no time there).
>
> Ask the Dhotials to get you green-maise heads on your way back through Kumaon: also wild-honey with plenty of grubs in it. Regard the butter flies. I hope you will see the millet red round the villages of the middle Hills and hear the francolins (black partridges) calling. But boil all milk or water there. You should try 'goor', solid loaves of molasses.
>
> You had good climbs in the Rishi. You will have completed ascents east of Malari. Perhaps you have forced the Girthi Gorges and had a glimpse of cis-Himalayan Tibet with whistling marmots. Enjoy and for always, as you can through concentration.
>
> Y'rs,
>
> Tom Longstaff

This book is 'an autobiography of sorts' because it leaves out much that can be read in a dozen other books of mine, not to mention my monthly contributions to the *Scots Magazine* which began in 1956 and still continue in 1994. Apart from this long record of my doings, there are the dozens of travelogues for Scottish Television covering virtually the whole country north of Berwick-on-Tweed. Then there was the television interview with Magnus Magnusson, *Tom Weir at Seventy*. Now *Weir's World* comes out in my eightieth year, a disorientated mixture, entangling past and present which, to my surprise, the publisher said 'worked'. I consider it to be the hardest thing I have ever tried to write.

Before submitting the manuscript to the publisher I offered it to my candid friend W.H. Murray who criticised it thus:

> The general impression I have is one of amazement at all you have managed to pack into your life. In a book of life one can turn the pages, back as well as forward; the ingredients are so many, not set down in chronological order that it's like a well-stirred brew. I think your marriage should come in a lot earlier, and that you should ask yourself what are the important things you have learned from your life, but maybe that is coming in your last chapter. I wish you all good fortune and sales.
>
> Yours,
Bill Murray

I began this autobiography with a letter from John McNair, the railwayman I met near the top of Ben Ime, which led to his inviting me to meet him at Achnashellach with camping kit. Once there, we would cross the Coulin Pass into Glen Torridon, put the tent down at Loch Clair, climb Liathach, Beinn Eighe, Beinn Alligin, Slioch, Beinn Liath Mor and Sgorr Mhor, then cross back over the pass for a last camp before catching the train home.

Talk about learning to live every moment in the present! I had never seen such mountains, or been with a more stimulating companion who could tell me so much. I could not get the peak of Liathach out of my head. It released in me the desire to write, to try and describe the magic of these wonderful Torridon mountains. In Glasgow's Mitchell Library I searched the bound volumes of the *Scottish Mountaineering Club Journal* for photographs and articles about Torridon, and came across this poem:

LIATHACH

Glover, the High-Priest of Liathach
   Thus did decide and decree,
That each one must fall down and worship,
   Whatever his rank or degree;
When first his eye falls on that mountain
   His knee he must bend and adore,
And then with due awe he must scale It,

Its shrines and temples explore.
Is the sun shining bright on Its summit
Or the mist gently veiling Its crest?
Are the storms raging over Its ledges?
Is a snow mantle garbing Its breast?
Then sing ye the hymn of that mountain,
And chant ye Its psalm, and depart,
But never while life may be in you,
Let Its worship die out of your heart.
                                        J.S.M. Jack

Strange things happen. Seventeen years later, when my first book was published I had a letter from this very George Glover. It said:

My wife and I consider your *Highland Days* to be easily the best of the numerous Highland books which are all on our shelves, as you will see here – if you come and look us up when passing. We would send a car to meet you at Carlisle.

We wish you all the best for 1951
                                Yours sincerely,
                                    George T. Glover

When I replied to him from 41 Adamswell Street, Springburn, he noted that I lived near where he had lodged 'in dear old Vulcan Street when I was serving my time in Hyde Park Locomotive Works'. That was before I was born for I discovered that by 1912 Glover was Chief Mechanical Engineer to the Great Northern Railway of Ireland, and returned to this post after enlisting in the 1914–18 war as Colonel in charge of French Railways.

It was a happy coincidence when, by invitation, I was with him when he celebrated his eighty-third birthday in his Brampton home, and with him too on that day was his friend Willie Ling, boon companion in fifty-five years of mountaineering. It was stirring to hear them talk together with the enthusiasm of young men about their mutual passion – mountains. Instead of candles on his birthday cake, George Glover had eighty-three sugar ball-bearings.

I am so glad I got to know these two modest men whose experience ranged from Mont Blanc range to the Caucasus and Lofotens, both of them pioneers of Scottish alpinism, true men, as Mummery put it: 'who loved to be where no human being had been before, who delight in gripping rocks that have never felt the touch of human fingers; or hewing a way up ice-filled gullies whose grim shadows have been sacred to the mists and avalanches since "Earth rose out of chaos"'.

Glover was the first to go. His 'In Memoriam' notice was written by

Ling for The Scottish Mountaineering Journal. But Ling never saw it in print. He died of a seizure in the house of a climbing friend in Stirling. They were to travel together to attend the Scottish Mountaineering Club New Year get-together. It would have been his 106th Club Meet. He had not been ill. In September 1953 he had climbed Beinn Eighe in Glen Torridon when he was eighty. From 1919 to 1922 he was President of the SMC. George Tertius Glover was President from 1928 to 1930, and I had the considerable honour of occupying this same post from 1984 to 1986.

I have two great reminders of Glover and Ling: the first is a photograph of them I took on the last occasion I saw them together. A framed copy of it hangs in the SMC Cottage in Glen Torridon, named 'The Ling Hut'. Step outside and you look upon Liathach: 'rising sheer from river bed to the sky, grey courses of masonry tier on tier, and pinnacles splintered on high.'

The other keepsake is Glover's complete set of *Scottish Mountaineering Club Journal* going back to Volume I in 1890, when much had still to be discovered of the true nature of the Scottish hills for alpinism.

These early journals reflect a sense of wonder in the explorers and the philosophy that it is not so much what you do but what you see that matters. Only this week I had the pleasure of listening to the author of *Arabian Sands* and *The Marsh Arabs*, Wilfred Thesiger, talking to David Attenborough on television. The remarkable eighty-four-year-old was talking about his early life as revealed in his autobiography *A Life of My Choice*.

He no longer wishes to travel to see new places. If he goes, it is to stay, as he did with the Marsh Arabs of Iraq for seven years, and before that living with the Bedouins on camel journeys across the Empty Quarter of Arabia. He made it clear he has no wish to travel now, but to live in a mud hut with the Masai with little in the way of possessions.

He hated when remote places became easily accessible to tourism for its destroying effect on native culture. Brought up in Ethiopia, when it was risky to travel, he accepted that he might be castrated while exploring where no white man had been before, this being a sign of manhood in young warriors, who knifed first and asked questions afterwards. He discovered with the Bedouin, 'the greater the hardship the finer the man'. He did not travel in order to write. The war saw him in North Africa fighting with the SAS behind the enemy lines, destroying many Germans, which troubled his conscience not one whit. When he said, 'Silence has been completely driven from our world,' I knew what he meant.

In the heart of this nomad there must be great sadness at what Saddam Hussein is doing to the Marsh Arabs. Bent on their destruction, Hussein is not only bombing them by air but draining the wetlands on which this unique tribe depend. Pictures of this affront to human decency are flashed on television from satellites circling the earth.

Oil instead of being a blessing has been a curse. It has put power into the hands of men like Hussein who for revenge against the allies polluted the Gulf with oil and set it alight, killing its wildlife.

It is frightening, too, to contemplate that in fifty years' time the world population is expected to double unless the human animal is willing to practise birth control in order to save our planet. Apart from food it is said there will not be enough water to go round. Another school of thought is that an increase of population would be good for trade and never mind the environment.

It is my belief that television which can be so wholesome in portraying the diversity of our wonderful world, its wild-life and scenery and its educational value, undoes much of its good by showing so much sex and violence, resulting in copycat behaviour, even among children.

Horace, the Roman poet wrote: 'Snatch the sleeve of today and trust as little as you may in tomorrow. No lot is happy on all sides.' How true. Without unhappiness we would not know we were happy. When my friend, Bob Grieve, was honoured with an eightieth birthday celebration three years ago, he was asked the question, 'Would you say you were happy?' He answered: 'I am not happy but I am content. I have contained myself to that which I know I can do.' He had run his race, had reached his summit.

As for health, a vital factor for a free-lance adventurer, I've been lucky. I think I've used up my nine lives, but have been carried off a mountain only once in over sixty years of climbing, and it was 1990 before I had my first surgical operation. If you have a dog you will know how easy it is to tell when it is unwell. Even the word 'walk' won't evoke a brightening of the eye and a rush to the door. Instead, it looks weary, hangs its head and follows reluctantly as if it doesn't want to disappoint you.

I felt like such a dog as summer approached. A terrible lethargy, an unquenchable thirst for water, and a sudden loss of weight forced me to visit the doctor who referred me to a specialist. After two visits to this renal expert, I had a phone-call telling me that a bed was available in Ward 7 at Glasgow's Western Infirmary. Old-fashioned the open ward was, with twenty occupied beds, and soon I got to know the most mobile as they passed down to the toilets. I quickly became used to seeing men being wheeled away on trolleys, giving a wave as they passed, and being wheeled back to their beds unconscious. I remember nothing about my own operation and was surprised to wake up three hours later as from a deep sleep.

At the back of my mind was the suspicion of cancer, for I had lost a stone in a matter of six weeks. Relief after five days of tests, I was allowed home for the weekend before the operation, scheduled for Monday morning. Saturday I spent with my wife in the garden, then a leisurely walk down to the Loch Lomond shore and on to the marshes, brilliant with flowers. The most charming sight was a goosander, with a tiny chick on her back, and seven others diving and learning to feed. Since I had been away, shallow pools had become pink with persicaria, and white flowers of water crowfoot floated at the edge.

Sunday morning I went off with two climbing pals for a drive to Crieff; then from Loch Turret, boots on, we took the ridge to King Kenneth's Hill, and at 2,535 feet, in a wonderfully fresh breeze, traversed two other peaklets, with superb views over the fertile fields of Strathearn to the Fife Lowlands, and north-west peaks extending from Ben More to Ben Lawers. I enjoyed the jog downhill too, and was back in the hospital by 8 pm. A good job, too, for I was hardly settled before there was a smiling nurse at my side, apologising for the bad news that shortly she would be giving me an injection into the rectum as cleaning out preparation for tomorrow's operation. Ten minutes later I was having it.

Of that enough said! It didn't undo the good feeling left by being on the hills that day, so I was content to lie on top of the bed, have a read and get below the sheets when the lights were dimmed and quiet descended.

What I would emphasise about the operation is the consideration shown, and the moral support I got, before the anaesthetic took effect. I remember the nurse who held my hand, saying softly: 'Just relax, relax.' The rest is blank until I awoke a few hours later back in the ward, feeling ready for supper, and thoroughly enjoying what came on the tray. Before he went home Mr O'Dwyer, the surgeon, went round the patients he had operated on that day. When I told him there was no bleeding, he said if there were no after effects I could go home next morning. There were none and my request to go was granted.

There were two reasons why I wanted out. One was that I had agreed to record a BBC Radio Appeal on behalf of multiple sclerosis in Scotland, where the highest incidence of the disease in the world occurs, and money is needed for research. It had already been billed in the *Radio Times*, and as I have had a long association with sufferers by giving a local group a slide-show every year, I didn't want to disappoint them. The other reason was that I had a date with visiting Americans at Ross Priory, the Staff Club of Strathclyde University only a mile from where I live, and after an evening slide-show on the wild-life and scenery of Loch Lomond, would climb Duncryne Hill overlooking our village and explain the geography and geological history at the meeting place where the Highlands and Lowlands meet. Once accomplished, we now went on a bus for Inversnaid and a rocky path to scramble down to Rob Roy's Cave. They loved it, especially when apprehension during the clinging descent to the cave gave them a sense of danger and achievement.

It was an atmospheric day. Thunder clouds had been building up, and the sunny world of glittering loch and colourful hillsides became sombre and threatening as we wound along the single-track road on the bus. Then down came the rain, Indian monsoon style, and the windscreen wipers could hardly cope. The most senior of our group were three eighty-three-year-olds, young in mind if not in body. They had loved their day.

Next to health comes friendship, which enlarges life. I was thinking of that a few days later when I was being driven to Rannoch Moor by Ian McNicol, with Bill Donaldson, and another good comrade, glad to see me back on the hills. From Ba Bridge on the old military road, now part of the long-distance path, we took to the moor, following the river into the great cirque of Corrie Ba and entering a different world, peat hags where roots of Caledonian pines, like bones of dinosaurs, were eroding from the peat, and blue flowers of butterwort and milkwort contrasted with the yellows of trefoil and hawkbit, the pink of lousewort, and the green tassels of alpine ladies' mantle.

Distantly I could hear the reeling of dunlin. Near-hand a golden plover fluted, followed immediately by the staccato too-too-too of greenshank. We ate our pieces by a beer-brown river, beside us bog-cotton gleaming white in the sun. Then suddenly there was a barking of angry ravens, and we saw what looked like a huge bomber being attacked by two Spitfires – a golden eagle, fairly low above us, being made to change course by the darting attacks of the territorial ravens.

Our objective was a rocky little summit projecting into the corrie with a fine command of the near ridges seamed with deep gullies holding snow in summer; a striking mountain scene in contrast to the level moor stretching in a watery maze to where the West Highland Railway crosses the moor at Rannoch Station, fifteen miles or so from where we sat. We had seen the silhouettes of red deer looking down on us as we climbed. Not until we were seated on the granite slabs of the top, when I was glassing with binoculars the snow-gullies, did I realise that what appeared to be huge boulders were actually red deer lying down on the snow, cooling off to combat the fierce heat of the sun.

Then I noticed movement on the boulder-fields between the gullies, and saw that the whole face was spattered with slow-moving deer unhurriedly climbing to make a crossing on the only easy opening between two rock waterfall pitches. Without binoculars the deer would have been hard to pick out against screes and rocks.

'This is the best bit of the day,' said Bill Donaldson, naked to the waist to add another layer of brown to his skin. Reluctantly we left the top and picked our way down to the river for the amble back to the military road and, by the lochans, to reach the A82 where we had parked the car. We had tea from the flask and, in the golden light of the western sun, headed south by Glen Falloch down the length of Loch Lomond.

Four days after our Rannoch Moor outing, I called, by arrangement, on Pat Sandeman, and his wife Mary. He mentioned that this date in May had special significance for him, for it was exactly fifty years since he and the survivors of his unit, the 57th Medium Regiment, Royal Artillery, escaped

233

by rowing boat from the Dunkirk beaches. Like most of the 335,000 officers and men, the chances of evacuation seemed slight, as all the vessels lying off-shore waiting to evacuate them were under constant attack.

One of Pat's most vivid memories of waiting their turn to get away was of the three senior Generals, Gort, Alexander and Alanbrooke standing chatting, seemingly unaware of the continuous flak and dive-bombers. It took twelve hours to row the 160 men of Pat's unit to the naval destroyer which took them off, and it was 4th June 1940 before 299 British warships and 420 other vessels completed the evacuation.

On 22nd June 1940, France accepted terms for an Armistice and Britain stood alone. Churchill said in a speech to the nation on BBC:

> Hitler knows he will have to break us on this island or lose the war. Let us therefore brace ourselves to our duties and so bear ourselves that if the British Empire and its Commonwealth last for a thousand years, men will still say: 'This was their finest hour'.

Back in England, Pat's regiment was sent to guard a stretch of the Devon coastline, and it was there that the black cloud of war was to have a silver lining. In an orchard Pat met a lass called Mary, whom he was to marry one year later, and live happily ever afterwards. At the time of his marriage, I was manning the Dover beaches in the thick of the war zone and having a grand-stand view of thrilling aerial dogfights. With twelve years of soldiering between us we feel ourselves lucky to be alive and to have lived to enjoy and appreciate life as never before.

Tell a Norwegian that you come from Scotland and he would likely say: 'Ah, your country is like ours.' It is, geographically, but there the resemblance ends. Norway depends upon herself. She stands and falls by her own efforts, and this is the mainspring of her vitality. The period when Norwegians were dominated by Denmark is known as 'the four hundred year-night'. The Vikings, who discovered America 500 years before Columbus, and whose colonies stretched from the Isle of Man to Greenland, had reached their zenith in the thirteenth century. They went under when the aggressive spirit died. In states, as in people, there is no equilibrium. In energy and quality of output you are either on the way up, or on the way down. National consciousness in Norway awoke again with a free constitution in 1814. Norway founded an economy based upon the

234

peculiarities of an enormous coast hung with waterfalls and woods: developed fishing, invented the harpoon gun for whaling, built a great Merchant Navy, created pulp mills for the rafts of timber swirling down the rivers from the forests, and harnessed that same water for hydro-electricity more effectively than any other country in the world.

The Norwegians were re-discovering their identity, as we in Scotland were losing ours. They forged ahead, developing their far-flung country, while the Scots in droves emigrated rather than starve. Glasgow flourished, yes, until the slump came. Lack of opportunity in Scotland still drives many thousands of people a year from it. Scotland has no real identity any more; we must face the fact that we are a poor, remote offshoot of England, whose problems are small compared to the greater problems of crowded south Britain. In Norway, just after the war, I was amazed at what I saw in Narvik, Tromso, Lyngen Fjord and the Lofotens. Town and villages burnt to ashes by the Germans had been entirely re-built, and thumping up and down the fjords sailed a brand new fishing fleet, zig-zagging in and out of rock skerries to dump their catches at newly placed fish processing factories.

The Germans took their revenge on this isolated part of the world to embarrass Norway, whose seat of Government, Oslo, lies nearly 1,000 miles away. In northern Norway you are within 1,700 miles of the North Pole. In winter it is continuously dark for two months. Life is harder than in the more densely populated part of the country, many hundreds of miles to the south, and depopulation goes on all along the top third of this long narrow country of fjords and islands, as it does in north Scotland.

But the Norwegians have proved the wisdom of a planned economy. They realised that without it they would lose so many people to the south that they would have an unbalance of population unless they made it possible to achieve a full life in the north. The result was 'The Development Plan for North Norway'. The wisdom of this plan is worth going into, especially as Norway, with a small population of just three and a half million scattered over 1,100 miles, could have let the north languish and die the slow death of Scotland's own remote communities.

The best brains in the country, and the best local knowledge, have been used to tackle a problem area where men have always had to work harder to earn less than other Norwegians. I saw enough in 1951 to form a clear idea in six weeks of how the northern population lived. In summer the men were at home cutting peats and harvesting the hay, then off they went to catch whales until the autumn herring shoals appeared. Richest of all was the cod fishing in spring, I was told, but seasonal unemployment between times robbed them of much of the profit. The middle-aged were content to stick it out. They had homes and shares in boats. But the young were leaving in thousands to seek their fortunes in urban areas where they could find easier work and higher incomes.

In 1963 I found a healthier and more prosperous Norway when my wife and I drove from Bergen north over the Arctic Circle to Bodo, and took ship to Rost in the Lofotens. It was, however, interesting to hear fishermen of this island complaining about grants being given to build big boats at the expense of small ones. The Norwegian is independent, and prefers to be a self-supporting unit rather than a member of a team, but the whole future of fishing is in big boats, as we know very well in Aberdeen and Peterhead where already our fleet of modern trawlers, built for middle waters, is inadequate to meet a change in the fishing situation, compelling us to seek more distant grounds.

I found houses all over the Norwegian Islands lit by electricity when previously they had oil lamps. The whole atmosphere was of urban life, busier than before. The fishing season had been excellent, I was told and was still going strong with a coming and going of boats at all times of day and night. It was marvellous to behold a thriving settlement of fisher-folk in Rost on what is little more than a collection of Arctic rock skerries linked to each other by concrete causeways, each skerry with its own warehouse, fish-drying frames and gay-coloured houses.

The prosperity and optimism of north Norway sprang from two things: a block grant of 225 million kroner (£11,250,000) with, behind it, expert teams acting in collaboration with local leaders who put this money to good use. Hundreds of enterprises were begun with the help of this fund, which attracted capital from private investors because of taxation relief obtainable under special regulations. Direct appropriations from the Treasury enabled power schemes and schools of various kinds for training in many technological branches.

A Highland panel went to Norway in the 1960s and saw efficient decentralisation at work. As yet, we look to American businessmen rather than Scots or English to invest money in Scotland. The Scottish Council (Development and Industry) have done good work in persuading American companies to set up factories here because it paid them to do so. It puzzles me why we cannot find Scottish industrialists willing to take a plunge in their native land. Norway lives by industry, agriculture, shipping, fishing and more recently from North Sea oil. Like a vast Switzerland cut by deep-trenched sea-lochs, the agricultural land flows along steep valleys or bottom land, so farms tend to be small patchworks of cultivation lapping the forest. The slopes do not lend themselves to mechanisation, so most of the work is done by hand, or with horses. In July, when I was there, I saw the haymaking in full swing, scythes sweeping and families snatching up the swathes to hang them like washing on a line. The green hayricks turned to gold in a remarkably short time, and the scythe is the perfect tool for cutting the short grass, leaving a lawn-like smoothness behind it, even on the steepest slopes. But the feature of Norwegian farming I liked best is the life of the summer shielings, the 'saeters' as they are called. To these high pastures the womenfolk, and the children, go with their cattle and goats every summer, milking them twice a day, living in simple little chalets high in the alpine pastures. They may seem isolated, but they are not cut off. Far from it. They get visitors from neighbouring saeters, and however tortuous the road may be, milk lorries manage to reach them three times a week to collect the churns and whisk them down precipitous passes for distribution at the fjord head. Not until the autumn blaeberries have been gathered and made into jelly will the families start back again, with the herds, to the farms far below. Some of these saeters are hundreds of years old and have the character of something eternal about their meadows. I spoke to a government economist about this summer migration to the high pastures, and I found him sceptical about its advantages. He thought the people did it for a holiday rather than a necessity, and he reckoned that the tradition would die as old buildings collapsed and it became uneconomic to erect new ones. He may be right. Farming in Norway is likely to become more streamlined and scientific, just as a close organisation of the fishing industry has made a full-time occupation of what used to be a part-time one.

Oslo was chosen as the capital of Norway when the country regained its independence. But Bergen reflects a truer picture of a land of old wooden walls as well as artistic and modern buildings, where the sea makes a jig-saw of piers and jetties for the boats which have always been life and hope to a people who can claim several tons of shipping per head of population.

When we think of a Norwegian we have in our mind's eye a clear picture of an individual, a man who is master of his fate and captain of his soul. Can you say the same for us who live in what is perhaps the most varied small country in the world with a tremendous history of enterprise behind it, but is still governed by Westminster when we should have a Scottish Parliament? After all, think of the number of Scottish Prime Ministers within the last one hundred years or so – Gladstone, Rosebery, Balfour, Campbell-Bannerman, Bonar Law, Ramsay MacDonald, Harold Macmillan and Douglas-Home, not to mention others of Scottish extraction who have made it to the top in the Dominions and former colonies.

In his perceptive *History of the Scottish People, 1500–1830*, T.C. Smout poses a rhetorical question for social historians to answer. How can we account for the unprecedented cultural achievements in the century after 1740?

Among those of genius stature, he lists the philosophers, David Hume and Adam Smith; our national bard Robert Burns; Joseph Black, chemist and Professor of medicine; inventor and civil engineer James Watt; architect Robert Adam; James Hutton, father of modern geology, author of the theory of the earth; Thomas Telford, Caledonian Canal builder and Colossus of roads.

Walter Scott is also on the list: *Waverley*, his first novel, published in 1814, is a tale about the 1745 Jacobite Rising, culled from true stories told to him first-hand by soldiers who had been out with the Prince. It was the first historical novel ever written, and it inspired Tolstoy to write *War and Peace*.

A book that inspired me was *The Scenery of Scotland* by Sir Archibald Geikie, Director of the Geological Survey in Scotland, and Director General of the United Kingdom in 1881. In 1892, after being guest at the Scottish Mountaineering Club dinner, he gave a dissertation on Scottish mountains, reprinted in the Club journal in 1896. He said:

> Let anyone with an ordinary share of the observing faculty sail round the west coast of Scotland and take note of the successive mountain groups which pass before him and he will acknowledge that the voyage of a couple of hundred miles has been almost as instructive to him as if he had scoured over half the globe . . . Nowhere in Europe does colour come more notably forward in landscape than in the west of Scotland.

Once Ardnamurchan has been left behind, Geikie's excitement heightens with the sight of Rum, Eigg and the ragged edge of the Cuillin:

> the most jagged peaks in Europe until you reach the Lofoten Isles of Norway.

Then he goes on to other unique peaks, those of Applecross and Torridon:

> bizarre yet fascinating . . . suggesting gigantic exaggerations of human architecture . . .

It was Geikie who sent Dr Ben Peach and Dr John Horne to the north-west Highlands in 1883 and it was they who made what has been called 'the most spectacular discovery of all time in British geology'.

In simple terms, a gigantic wave of rock, called moine schist, had been thrust westwards over the Lewisian gneiss and Torridonian sandstone on a hundred-mile line between Sleat in south Skye and Loch Erribol in Sutherland. There is a memorial stone to these two men on a knoll above Loch Assynt.

Having had the good fortune to have spent decades travelling the Borders, Highlands and Islands at all heights and seasons, I am in the position, I think, to make comparisons with other countries. The only thing I am disappointed in is that we don't run our own affairs as does

Norway. We have the resources, and history shows we have the people. England has its own problems for its fifty million or so to contend with. With only five million Scots we can manage ours, and I think the same goes for Wales. I hope I shall live long enough to see it happen, and another age of enlightenment dawn.

Index

241